PUSHKIN

PUSHKIN

Selected Verse

With introduction and prose translations
by John Fennell

BRISTOL CLASSICAL PRESS

First published in 1964 by
Penguin Books Ltd

This edition first published in 1991 by
Bristol Classical Press
an imprint of
Gerald Duckworth & Co. Ltd
The Old Piano Factory
48 Hoxton Square, London N1 6PB

Reprinted 1995

A catalogue record for this book is available
from the British Library

ISBN 1-85399-173-2

Available in USA and Canada from:
Focus Information Group
PO Box 369
Newburyport
MA 01950

Printed in Great Britain by
Booksprint, Bristol

To my wife

CONTENTS

vii

CONTENTS

INTRODUCTION

ALEXANDR SERGEYEVICH PUSHKIN was born on 26 May 1799. On his father's side he could claim aristocratic descent: his ancestors were of untitled boyar stock, and, although they never shone in any particular sphere of public life, at least the family had more claim to distinction than much of the upstart nobility of the eighteenth century, as Pushkin pointed out with justifiable pride and humorous contempt in *My Genealogy*. On his mother's side he was the great-great-grandson of an Abyssinian 'prince', whose son Abram was allegedly shipped as a hostage to Constantinople and thence delivered to the court of Peter the Great in 1706. Pushkin's father, a retired army officer with a dilettante's taste for literature who had little to live for but the pleasures of society, and his silly, capricious, hedonistic mother, were by their very mode of life incapable of taking more than a nominal interest in their children's upbringing. But the young Pushkin thrived on this absence of parental care. His early education was entrusted to a series of *émigré* French tutors; he was sensibly allowed to devour his gallomanic father's large library of seventeenth- and eighteenth-century French literature; and at an early age he was able to listen to the conversation of many of the leading Russian literati who met at the Pushkin house, attracted no doubt by the hospitality of Pushkin's father and by the vivacity of his uncle Vasily, himself something of a poet with a gift for facile, frothy verse. At the same time he received a thorough grounding in the succulent language and the earthy traditions of his own country at the hands of his eminently sensible maternal grandmother (herself, oddly enough, a Pushkin by birth) and of his splendid nanny, whom he remembered in his later poetry with deep affection and whose influence he gratefully acknowledged.

In 1811 he won a place in the Lyceum of Tsarskoye Selo, just outside St Petersburg, an academy founded in that year by Alexander I to prepare gifted children from cultured and noble families for senior governmental and military posts. The studies were liberal, the teaching was on the whole good, and most of the pupils were intelligent. Pushkin during his six years at the school distinguished himself by his brilliance, his memory, his laziness, and towards the end by his dissolute and uninhibited behaviour. Literary activities were encouraged in Tsarskoye Selo, and Pushkin acquired the reputation of the school's outstanding poet. His output of poetry during his school years was large, but most of his poems were imitative and based on French or contemporary

Russian models. Full of immature bombast, worldly wisdom, and sophistication, they included highly conventional love-poems, erotic epicurean lyrics, odes, scurrilous epigrams; only occasionally in the simpler unsophisticated poems (e.g. *To my Sister*, or *The Cossack*) are there glimpses of the taste and technique which were later to be peculiarly Pushkin's own. Yet such was his renown that he was even elected to the short-lived Arzamas society (founded 1815, disbanded 1818), a group of writers including Zhukovsky, Batyushkov, and Vyazemsky whose aim was to promote new ideas in literature, to support the literary reforms initiated by Karamzin, and to combat and parody the activities of Admiral Shishkov and his 'Slavonic' party, the 'Society of Lovers of the Russian Word'. Shishkov was a theoretician who bitterly opposed all neologisms and borrowings from the West, and sought to establish the supremacy of Old Church Slavonic as the foundation of the Russian literary language and to defend the old literary traditions of the Middle Ages. From such stagnant conservatism the Arzamas society did much to preserve Russian literature.

On leaving the Lyceum in 1817 Pushkin was given a minor and purely nominal post in the Foreign Office in St Petersburg. Almost all the next three years were spent in the capital, where he embarked upon a life of dissipation. Yet in the midst of debauchery and drunkenness he kept up his literary acquaintances and continued to write abundantly. Many of the poems of this period reflect his *train de vie* (e.g. *To Olga Masson*), and there is often little to distinguish them from his school verse, except for a surer touch and an increased elegance. He produced erotic elegies, witty epigrams, satires, and one long epic, *Ruslan and Lyudmila*. But apart from occasional gems of simplicity (such as *The Water-Nymph*), his writing during this period was little more than an exercise in turning out polished verse.

Among his literary and social acquaintances of this period were many who were directly connected with the pre-Decembrist secret political societies. I. I. Pushchin, one of his closest friends from the Lyceum, was a member of the first secret society, the Union of Salvation. So too was Nikolai Turgenev, whose family Pushkin frequented during the years 1817–20. Pushkin himself became a member of the 'Green Lamp' – a literary society which may have been a branch of the second pre-Decembrist secret society, the Union of Welfare – whose members, as well as indulging in what appear to have been bacchanalian orgies of extreme licence, discussed 'liberal', freethinking literature and forbidden political topics. At the same time Pushkin wrote a number of poems and epigrams against the political and social conditions of the age or against prominent persons. His ode *Freedom* (1817), with the lines:

> Tremble, O tyrants of the world,
> And you . . . O fallen slaves, arise!

could be, and was, construed as a call to revolution. *The Village*
(1819) – which in its bitterness of tone foreshadows Lermontov's
Death of a Poet (1837) and Nekrasov's sour *Home* (*Rodina*) (1846)
– contains an undisguised attack on the inhumanity of contemporary serfdom. Alexander I is held up to ridicule in *Noël* (1818)
and *You and I* (1820); Arakcheyev, the favourite of Alexander and
Minister of War, is scorned in the celebrated epigram *Against
Arakcheyev*. But for all his revolutionary connexions and his
'liberal' poetry, Pushkin was never a member of any of the secret
societies. Perhaps distrusting his garrulity and what they considered to be his lack of character, his friends carefully kept the
existence of all conspiratorial activity a secret from him. He
contributed, however, in no small way to their cause by his inflam-
matory verse. Not only were his so-called 'revolutionary' poems
'known to everybody', but 'at that time there was not a single
literate ensign in the army who did not know them by heart', so a
contemporary of Pushkin tells us. Indeed, according to the evidence of one of the conspirators: ' It was from his poetry that at least
nine out of ten (if not ninety-nine out of a hundred) of the young
people of that time got their first idea . . . of the extreme application of the principle "the end justifies the means", i.e. of *extreme
revolutionary measures*.' Pushkin's political poems, which were
passed from hand to hand in manuscript, were not unnoticed by
the authorities. In May 1820 he was sent off to Yekaterinoslav in the
south. Only the intercession of influential friends saved him from
banishment or imprisonment.

His 'southern exile' started propitiously with a trip to the
Caucasus in the company of the cultured and attractive Rayevsky
family. The idyll did not last long. In September 1820 he left for
Kishinev, the capital of Bessarabia, whither his chief in Yekaterinoslav, the kindly General Inzov, had been posted. Kishinev was a
town inhabited by a mixed cosmopolitan population, in which the
absence of cultural amenities was barely compensated by a per-
vading spirit of forced gaiety and unbridled vice. Into this spirit
Pushkin entered with characteristic gusto. But the two and a half
years which he spent there were relatively fruitful from a creative
point of view, if only because they enabled him to work off a
certain amount of Romantic, pseudo-Byronic steam. Still haunted
by his memories of the Caucasus and influenced by his reading of
Byron, he completed his ebullient Byronic poem *The Prisoner of*

the Caucasus, drafted earlier in the Crimea. In Kishinev he also wrote the equally Byronic *Fountain of Bakhchisarai*, exotic, gorgeous, chaotic in its poetic disarray and stuffed with Romantic clichés. It was only in the more civilized city of Odessa, where Pushkin spent the last year of his 'southern exile' (July 1823 – July 1824), that he began to shed most of the trappings of Byronism. Here he wrote nearly all his first truly 'Pushkinian' long poem, *The Gipsies*, in which he retained only certain structural devices reminiscent of Byron's Eastern poems and introduced two features new to Russian literature: a concrete descriptive style shorn of all vague embellishments, and a problem (indeed two problems) the solution of which is left to the reader. Instead of the traditionally Romantic situations of his two earlier 'Southern poems', with their somewhat unrealistic Byronic protagonists, we have a simple tale, which is built around two questions: What is freedom? And what is fate?, and in which the hero, a typically Byronic shunner of civilization, is shown up in his true light as a despicable egoist. In Odessa, too, Pushkin began his novel in verse, *Yevgeny Onegin*, the early stanzas of which show the influence of the Byron of *Don Juan* and no longer the Byron of *The Corsair* or *The Giaour*. When he left Odessa in July 1824, transferred to his parents' estate at Mikhaylovskoye in north-west Russia, thanks to the determination of the intolerable and intolerant governor-general Vorontsov to be rid of him, Pushkin had finally broken with a false Romanticism which had never suited his classical spirit. Perhaps the best illustration of his creative evolution during these years is shown allegorically in *Onegin's Journey* (see p. 205), where he describes the 'wildernesses, the pearly crests of waves, and the sound of the sea, and rocks piled high, and the "ideal" portrait of a proud maiden, and nameless sufferings . . . the high-flown reveries' of his 'spring' and the subsequent watering-down of his 'poetic goblet'.

He spent two years in Mikhaylovskoye (August 1824 – September 1826) under police surveillance – years of tedium and of longing to escape. But they were creative years: his lyrical poetry began to show a new terseness of style and objectivity of manner, of which only glimpses can be caught in his earlier works; he began to experiment in new genres, new modes of expression – in the idiom of popular folk-poetry (see *The Bridegroom*, *To my Nanny*, *Winter Evening*), and, as a result of his enthusiastic reading of Shakespeare (probably in the French translation of Pierre Letourneur), in historical drama (see *Boris Godunov*). And at the same time he continued work on *Yevgeny Onegin* and rounded off *The Gipsies*.

It was probably during these years in Mikhaylovskoye that his liberal enthusiasm and his spirit of protest began to wane. The manifest lack of confidence in him shown by the conspirators (it was only in January 1825 that Pushchin disclosed to him the existence of the secret societies), his increasing awareness of his aristocratic origins (Ryleyev, one of the leaders of the revolt, took him to task in 1825 for 'boasting of his five-hundred-year-old nobility'), the realization that the approach of many of the Decembrists to questions of aesthetics and literature was fundamentally different from his own, and the eventual failure of the uprising (14 December 1825), all served to dim his revolutionary ardour. True, he is alleged to have told Nicholas I that he would have been in the ranks of the rebels had he been in St Petersburg on the day of the uprising; true, he wrote two further poems (*Epistle to Siberia* and *Arion*) which can only be interpreted as sympathetic to the Decembrists and their cause. But just as the fiery Romantic poetry of his youth had simmered down, so had his progressive liberalism moderated. Poetry and the freedom to write poetry were perhaps of more importance to him. After the failure of the rebellion there was no alternative but to compromise and to conform. As he wrote in a letter to Zhukovsky (March 1826): 'I do not intend foolishly to oppose the generally accepted order.'

In September 1826 he was at last summoned to Moscow. The new Tsar, Nicholas I, received him, freed him from his 'disgrace', and announced that henceforth he would be his censor. Pushkin was now free to go where he wished, except St Petersburg. One may well ask why Nicholas showed such unexpected clemency towards Pushkin, on the eve of one of the harshest periods of reactionary rule in pre-revolutionary Russian history. Perhaps it was because, as one of Pushkin's biographers has remarked, 'the authorities preferred to have Pushkin on their side, for exile, they realized, would not prevent him from writing seditious poetry'. Perhaps Nicholas was won over by the eloquence of Pushkin's influential friends Zhukovsky and Karamzin. Whatever the reasons, Pushkin appears to have been entirely taken in, at first at any rate, by the 'magnanimity' of the Tsar. 'In hope of glory and virtue I look to the future without fear,' he wrote in a sycophantic poem (*Stansy*, 1826) in which he set before the Tsar the model of Peter the Great; just over a year later he was still able to write in his poem *To my Friends* (1828): 'No, I am no flatterer when I sing free praise of the Tsar.'

His freedom was illusory, however, for he was placed under the close surveillance of the secret police, whose chief, Benckendorff, acted as intermediary between him and the Tsar. Furthermore, he was informed that all his writings must be submitted to the Tsar for approval. For nearly three years he led a life of renewed dissipation and restless wandering between Moscow and St Petersburg, which he was graciously allowed to visit 'on family business'. He drank, gambled, made love; he undermined his health. He wrote very little compared to when he was in 'exile', the only major work of the period being the heroic epic poem *Poltava*, written in a few days in October 1828 during a sudden burst of creative energy. He felt an urgent need for change, and in vain sought permission to travel abroad. In May 1829 he did the next best thing and set off for Transcaucasia to accompany the army, which was fighting the Turks.

His journey lasted four months. He was attached to the army as a civilian and saw some action. But although the change was refreshing, he soon became disillusioned, and by the end of September he was back in Moscow. After a winter in St Petersburg, during which he engaged in journalism, running the *Literary Gazette* with his friend Delvig, he returned to Moscow in the spring and proposed to and was accepted by the beautiful, but naïve and empty, Natalia Goncharov, whose acquaintance he had first made in 1828. Pleased with his proposed marriage, his parents gave him part of their estate at Boldino, in the district of Nizhny Novgorod. At the end of August 1830 he went there to look over his new property, but an outbreak of cholera prevented him from returning and he spent three remarkably productive months there. Not only did he finish the first draft of the last chapter of *Yevgeny Onegin*, but also he wrote the delightful 'bourgeois' epic, *The Little House in Kolomna*, and his so-called 'little tragedies' in blank verse – terse, psychological studies of the passions of man (see *Mozart and Salieri*) – as well as a number of memorable short lyrical poems. In Boldino he also wrote his first experimental works in prose fiction – the five short stories entitled *The Tales of Belkin*. Before the year was over he was back in Moscow. In February 1831 he was married.

Pushkin's marriage brought him little lasting happiness, deprived him of much of the time and energy he needed for writing, and caused him incessant worry. His wife was coquettish, vain, extravagant, and entirely uninterested in the intellectual pursuits of her husband. Yet the first period of their married life appears to have been reasonably happy. They spent the late spring and summer of 1831 in a house rented in Tsarskoye Selo, where Pushkin had been at school. In spite of financial anxieties and constant attention to his wife, Pushkin managed to achieve a certain mental stability, and it was here that he wrote the first of his long folk poems – *Tsar Saltan*, a fairytale epic of startling simplicity and directness of manner.

The two years following the 'honeymoon' of Tsarskoye Selo were difficult and relatively uncreative years for Pushkin. His wife, between bearing two children (Maria in May 1832, Alexandr in July 1833), lived in a whirl of social gaiety in St Petersburg, while Pushkin moved restlessly between the capital and Moscow, where he was granted permission to work in the archives and thus satisfy his newly-aroused interest in eighteenth-century Russian history. In August 1833 he was allowed to travel to Kazan and the Ural districts, the scenes of the great Pugachev rebellion which so intrigued him. On his way back to St Petersburg he again stopped at Boldino, and again the solitude and the peace of his estate enabled him to write prolifically. The six weeks he spent there (October–November 1833) were his last period of concentrated uninterrupted work. He finished off his prose history of the Pugachev rebellion; he wrote two more folk poems, *The Dead Princess* and *The Tale of the Fisherman and the Fish*; and he produced the first draft of his epic poem *The Bronze Horseman* (see p. 233), which, with its contrapuntal handling of styles, its subtle posing of unanswered questions, its daring imagery, and its striking thematic contrasts, is regarded by many critics as the supreme poetic achievement of Pushkin.

The last three years of Pushkin's life were for him years of disillusionment and intellectual loneliness. He was deeply offended by the Tsar, who at the end of 1833 gave him the ludicrous appointment of 'gentleman of the chamber' – an appointment usually reserved for youths – in order to oblige him and his wife to attend court functions. He was enraged by the stupid meddling of officialdom in his private life – to his disgust he discovered that his correspondence was being read by postal officials in Moscow. He was jealous of the many admirers whom his wife attracted. He was angry at and hurt by the growing indifference of the public to his poetry. He was tormented by debts and the petty worries of providing for a family. In vain he asked to be relieved of his post and to be allowed to settle in the country; he begged for extended leave, and was refused. True, he was given permission to start his own quarterly journal, *The Contemporary*, but it met with small success and brought him insufficient money to pay his debts. Compared with earlier years, he wrote remarkably little: two prose works, *The Queen of Spades* – the greatest of all his short stories – and his novel of the age of Catherine II, *The Captain's Daughter*; one major verse work, *The Golden Cockerel*, the only poem written during his third and final stay at Boldino (Autumn 1834); and a few short poems, including the prophetic rhetorical *I have erected a Monument*.

Pushkin's misery was increased by the fact that an arrogant young officer in the Horse Guards, d'Anthès, the adopted son of the odious Dutch ambassador in St Petersburg, was overtly courting his wife, and by the scandalous rumours which a hostile society was only too ready to spread. Eventually, when he could stand it no longer, Pushkin challenged d'Anthès to a duel. He was shot in the stomach on 27 January 1837 and died two days later.

*

It has long been an accepted practice amongst most critics to call Pushkin the greatest of all Russian poets, and to lavish extravagant, if hackneyed, eulogy on his poetry. Few critics can talk of Pushkin's art or describe his greatness without using such phrases as ' classical restraint', 'universality of spirit', 'harmony between style and content', 'humanity of outlook', and so on. Now, all these tags may be applicable to some or all of Pushkin's poetry; but at the same time they are often singularly unhelpful to the reader – especially to the non-Russian reader – who is trying to understand the essence of Pushkin's greatness as a poet. But can this 'greatness' be explained in a satisfactory way? Must the commonplaces of literary criticism be used? His 'greatness', after all, is not a constant: it depends on the interpretation of the individual reader, and this in its turn depends to a large extent on the impression which the poetry makes on him. It is a thankless and, I think, a hopeless task to try to communicate anything so subjective as one's own feelings on the poetry of a given poet in a few pages of introduction. Perhaps, then, it would be better here to eschew such a task, to limit oneself to an appreciation of something slightly more tangible, and simply to try to find out what Pushkin was aiming at, what he considered to be the role and function of the poet, and where his originality as a poet lay. This approach will not of course give us the answer to the question: why was Pushkin a great poet? But perhaps it will help the reader in some small way to discern points of departure for his own appreciation of Pushkin; it may even take him a step further and enable him to share in the joy and the anguish, the calm and the restlessness of Pushkin's own creative process, to 'feel rapture in harmony and to shed tears of joy at the creation of [his] fantasy' (see *Elegy*, p. 61) – for this surely must be one of the main aims of reading poetry, namely to attempt to experience something of the intensity of the poet's own emotional and intellectual experience.

In order to begin to understand Pushkin's poetical aims or to appreciate his originality, it is necessary first of all to consider his creative range. Of all Russian poets in the nineteenth century Pushkin was the most universal in scope. He made use of, and adapted to suit his own purposes, virtually every existing literary genre known to the Russians and practised by them at the beginning of the nineteenth century; he even introduced entirely new forms and new subject-matter into Russian literature. It must not be imagined that he merely accepted the traditional forms and adhered to the rules of literary convention which had been laid down by the legislators of the eighteenth century (Lomonosov and Sumarokov) and which were observed to a certain extent even by the early Romantics (Karamzin and his followers). The classical division of poetry into established genres, each with its own shape, style, and metre, was repugnant to Pushkin; the canons of eighteenth-century poetics which obliged the writer to distinguish sharply in shape and content between, say, the epic and the ode, the satire and the epigram, were too rigid for his flexible, creative mind. By the time he reached full maturity as a poet (in other words, by the middle twenties of the nineteenth century) he had established an independence of form and content which would have shocked his predecessors. Whereas his school poems tend to be highly conventional and to abide by the classical laws governing form and content, his mature works show a remarkable freedom and independence, a refusal to be bound by rules. The framework of the genre is no longer rigid; the poetic form no longer of necessity dictates or is dictated by the nature of the subject-matter.

There were few fields of poetry in which he did not experiment. His favourite genre – or at any rate the genre in which he ventured most frequently – was the *poema*, the long narrative poem. Here his range was large: the mock-heroic (*Ruslan and Lyudmila*), the Byronic-Romantic (*The Prisoner of the Caucasus, The Fountain of Bakhchisarai*), the heroic-epic (*Poltava*), the comic-anecdotal (*Count Nulin, The Little House in Kolomna*), the fairy-tale (*Tsar Saltan, The Sleeping Princess, The Golden Cockerel*, and others), and the purely narrative (*The Gipsies, The Bronze Horseman*).

An extension of the narrative poem was the so-called 'novel in verse'. 'I am now writing not a novel, but a novel in verse – the devil of a difference! Something like *Don Juan*' he wrote in a letter of 1823. It was the beginning of *Yevgeny Onegin*. This 'free novel', as he also called it, consisted of eight chapters, or cantos, each of some fifty fourteen-line stanzas, as well as *Fragments from Onegin's Journey*, originally planned by Pushkin as Chapter VIII.

It is not merely a 'novel in verse': in other words, it is not just a story based on the development of the relationship of the characters to one another and to their background; it is a vehicle for much of Pushkin's experimentation – for expression of his theories of art, for the demonstration of new techniques, for parody, for folk-lore, for literary criticism, for esoteric literary and linguistic polemics, for psychological analysis, and for a portrayal of a whole social milieu. It is a kind of literary encyclopedia which Pushkin used to discuss not only his own poetic development (see p. xii above), but also contemporary literary movements in Russia and in Western Europe (Sentimentalism, Romanticism) and, above all, literary forms (the ode, the elegy, 'album poetry', the classical epic poem, etc.). In its deliberate mixture of styles and forms it fits into no genre known to Russian literature of the eighteenth and early nineteenth centuries. It was a complete innovation. Although the novel in verse was never successfully adopted by any subsequent major Russian writer, *Yevgeny Onegin* none the less indirectly influenced virtually every aspect of nineteenth-century Russian literature, from the lyrical poem to the novel.

Yevgeny Onegin was conceived, at first at any rate, as a reaction against the lifeless pseudo-classicism of the eighteenth century, as an attempt to burst the shackles of convention and to free literature, to give it new directions in which it might develop. This, too, was undoubtedly one of the main aims of Pushkin in writing his historical drama, *Boris Godunov*. Discontented with the lamentable state of Russian drama at the time – during the eighteenth and early nineteenth centuries Russian drama was largely imitative of the West, tied up with the conventions of the French classicists, and (except for a few comedies of some talent) utterly unrealistic – he was determined to write a 'truly Romantic tragedy' (i.e. untrammelled by classical rules), based on the dramatic concepts of 'our father, Shakespeare'. It was an enormous and hazardous experiment, intended to revolutionize the Russian theatre. As a play it was not a success, owing to Pushkin's deliberate and seemingly capricious neglect of stagecraft; nor did it influence the Russian theatre, except indirectly. But it was a glorious and successful experiment in language, in character portrayal, and in historical realism.

His other ventures into drama, the so-called 'Little Tragedies', are likewise experimental, but in a very different way. Here Pushkin is not concerned so much with tragic conflict or with the dramatic development of character, and certainly not with historical realism or stylistic experimentation; he is intent on illustrating the tragedy of human 'passions' in some form or other, in investigating the inner workings of the mind of man obsessed by over-powering emotion. *Mozart and Salieri*, for instance, is an essay in envy, as *The Covetous Knight* is in miserliness. As one critic has rightly pointed out, the intense and highly concentrated psychological analysis of the 'Little Tragedies' is 'the grain from which springs up the work of Dostoyevsky'.

But the true extent of Pushkin's poetic range is best to be seen in his short poems. This selection alone, which represents but a small proportion of all Pushkin's lyrical poetry, illustrates the extraordinary compass not only of his poetic thought but also of his style and manner. Here the subject-matter ranges from the banal to the magnificent; from frivolous erotic love (*To Olga Masson*, p. 4) to majestic political pronouncements (*To the Slanderers of Russia*, p. 69), from the cosy mundaneness of life in the country (*It is winter*, p. 50, cf. *The Confession*, p. 30) to the rugged splendour of wild nature (*The Avalanche*, p. 54), from humour (*My Genealogy*, p. 64, *From a Letter to Wolf*, p. 12) to philosophical meditation (*To the Poet*, p. 59, *Fruitless gift, chance gift*, p. 40). Nothing seems to have been deemed unworthy of his poetry, no emotion or experience was considered fit only for 'base prose'. The style ranges from the simplicity of the modern vernacular (see *The Drowned Man*, p. 42) to the majesty of archaic, biblical speech (see *Desert Fathers*, p. 74). Virtually every possible poetic form is used – from the ballad to the epigram, from the elegy to the epistle. If any further evidence of the catholicity of Pushkin's poetical tastes and the breadth of his experimental field were required, one would only have to consider his ability to assimilate and adapt not only the folk legends of Russia (see *The Drowned Man*), but also the literary idiom of other countries (see *Raven flies to Raven*, p. 46, *Before a noble Spanish woman*, p. 63, *Once upon a time there lived a poor knight*, p. 47; cf. his adaptations of Old Church Slavonic, *In my blood the fire of desire burns*, p. 29, *Desert Fathers*, p. 74).

Pushkin's originality, of course, does not rest merely on his universality, nor can we understand his aims and his conception of the function of the poet simply by listing the themes and genres of his poetry. I would like here to consider certain aspects of Pushkin's work which contribute towards his originality and which will perhaps help the reader to understand his views on some at any rate of the functions and purposes of poetry. Now Pushkin was not primarily a didactic poet. Tendentiousness and utilitarianism in poetry were anathema to him. The aim of poetry was poetry itself. For Pushkin the poet is literally inspired by the 'divine word'; he is 'beloved by Apollo', and poetry is the highest creative manifestation of the human spirit. This does not mean, however, that Pushkin was not interested in the contact between the poet and his reader. Indeed, Pushkin was the first Russian writer to make considerable intellectual demands on his reader. In his mature long works he is not content merely with telling a story just for the sake of narrative (the only pure 'narrative for narrative's sake' is to be found in his fairytales and in some of his prose). He is determined that the reader shall cooperate, shall make an effort to interpret the symbolism of the characters or the plot, and above all shall seek a solution to the particular problem posed. An example will help. In *The Gipsies* the narrative is simple: Aleko, tired of civilization, joins a gipsy band and lives a life of 'freedom' with Zemfira, who bears him a child. When he finds that she is unfaithful to him, he kills her and her lover. Her father rebukes him for his pride and egoism, and bids him leave the gipsies. The gipsy encampment moves off, leaving Aleko quite alone in the steppes. Now Aleko has received the ultimate punishment – his ideals are shattered, he is completely abandoned, he has nowhere to turn. Why was he punished? Not, of course, for the murder – the murder merely serves as the story's dénouement. Pushkin characteristically refuses to give a direct answer. But indirectly he tells us that Aleko was punished for refusing to acknowledge the power of Fate – in other words for living only for himself – and for confounding true freedom with purely physical freedom: and true freedom, or happiness, for Pushkin and indeed for many subsequent Russian thinkers, consisted in self-mastery, in control over one's 'passions'. The reader, however, is left not only to decide for himself what the problem of the story is, but also to find the answer to it. And only by an intellectual effort of co-operation with the author can he derive true satisfaction from the work.

Much the same applies to *Yevgeny Onegin*. In many ways the story is similar; it ends with the hero punished by rejection – and again the punishment, one feels, is the ultimate punishment. There is nothing left for Yevgeny to do after Tatyana's final speech; spiritually he is stripped bare by the only truly noble character in the book. But his sin? Pushkin no longer provides the helpful clues which simplified the reader's task in *The Gipsies*; one is left to puzzle out the problem for oneself. Yet this time the problem is enriched by Pushkin's treatment of it; for whereas Aleko, Zemfira, and the Old Man are little more than algebraical symbols in an equation, in *Yevgeny Onegin* both the main characters are live human beings.

In *The Bronze Horseman* still more is left to the imagination and cooperation of the reader. Here we are presented with three symbols: the majestic figure of Peter the Great, the founder of St Petersburg, the conqueror of the elements, the ruthless autocrat; Yevgeny, the miserable, downtrodden clerk, insignificant, depersonalized, and doomed to suffer; and the river Neva, inexorably flooding the City and shattering in its wake everything except the bronze statue. Is the theme man's defencelessness before the powers of Fate? Is it the clash between the ruthlessness of power and man's claim to happiness? Is it the conflict between man and Fate, or man and nature? Or is it the eternal problem of the State versus the individual: can the ends – the ultimate happiness of the majority – justify the means, the suffering of even one individual, in the name of progress? Pushkin refuses to commit himself. Only the reader can and must discover for himself that answer which will satisfy him. Pushkin refuses to be didactic. He only permits his reader to extract from the work whatever lesson he is capable of extracting.

However much the universality of Pushkin's taste and his original approach to subject-matter may have contributed to and enriched Russian literature, they are of small importance beside his stylistic and linguistic reforms. From his predecessors he inherited a poetic language that was, broadly speaking, either bombastic, solemnly lofty, and closely allied to the dead, unproductive Old Church Slavonic, or artificially modelled on French and German patterns and abounding in barbarisms and clichés. The vernacular of the people had never been seriously considered a fit vehicle for poetry. Consequently the poetic language of the early nineteenth century tended to be akin to the language of the Church or the language of the refined gallomanic salon. Clumsy periphrasis, outworn classical conceits, archaic vocabulary and morphology, unwieldy syntax, and above all drab clichés expressing the whole gamut of artificial, borrowed emotions – all abounded in the poetic language which Pushkin found at his disposal.

It was only by careful pruning and rejecting and by the introduction of new elements hitherto considered unsuitable for poetry that Pushkin managed to evolve his own, peculiarly Pushkinian, poetic medium. He eliminated the unnecessary epithets and adverbs, the abstract ideas and all the vaguer parts of speech, which in the poetry of so many of his predecessors and contemporaries were mere padding. He economized in words, reduced similes and metaphors to a minimum, simplified the syntax, and brought the language of poetry close to that of everyday speech, having no scruples in using what were often considered by his contemporaries to be vulgarisms. By this means he achieved the ideal medium for purely visual description. It was painting of the Flemish school introduced into poetry, realistic, unemotional, and yet by virtue of its very simplicity immensely moving and effective. Take, for example, the stanza from *Onegin's Journey* (see p. 206) describing a country scene. The syntax is simplicity itself – no intellectual effort is needed on the part of the reader, who is able to derive immediate enjoyment from the picture. There is nothing abstract here – only things we can see and sounds we can hear. It is the very essence of Pushkin's poetry. And such passages are not isolated. *Yevgeny Onegin* alone abounds in them: landscapes, townscapes, action (e.g. the final preparations for the duel, pp. 185–6, Tatyana's dream, p. 169, Tatyana's dash into the garden to meet Onegin, p. 157), conversations between Tatyana and her nanny – all are couched in this same idiom, all are impregnated with Pushkin's realism. The same applies to the wonderful descriptive passages of *The Gipsies* (see the opening lines of the poem, p. 77), to most of Pushkin's folk poetry (see especially *The Drowned Man, The Water-Nymph,* and *The Golden Cockerel*) and to much of his lyrical poetry as well.

It must not of course be imagined that all Pushkin's poetry was written in this vein, or that his ultimate aim was to confine himself to the concrete, realistic-descriptive technique. The field of application was too limited for him. The technique could not satisfactorily be used, for example, for the description of complex emotions, for psychological upheavals, nor was it always suitable for lofty subjects (e.g. *The Avalanche,* p. 54, *To the Slanderers of Russia,* p. 69). It follows, then, that Pushkin was obliged to retain many of the traditional poetic mannerisms of the age, but these he refined and polished to suit his own particular style. And he knew how to manipulate the various linguistic and stylistic elements at his disposal with astonishing skill and tact. It was not just a question of using archaisms to express lofty sentiments, abstract Romantic clichés to convey emotions, or popular speech to describe the more prosaic things in life. Indeed, we often find Pushkin deliberately using an Old Church Slavonic word or expression, not to impart a flavour of archaism to the content, but to embellish a phrase, simply because it happened to be the *mot juste* or the perfect expression in that particular context, or because it happened to afford Pushkin aesthetic pleasure. Likewise, in a passage written predominantly in the so-called 'Flemish' vein we may suddenly come across a word or an expression which is deliberately vague and romantic and evocative of another emotional mood altogether. Or again in the middle of a passage of sustained Romantic abstraction we may be jerked out of our complacent enjoyment of the mellifluous verbiage by an unexpected vulgarism, brought down from the heights by an earthy phrase. Such juxtapositions do not jar; they are part of the very fabric of Pushkin's poetic system, part of his incessant experimentation with style.

It is, of course, in the longer works that Pushkin's manipulation of style is most evident; the lyrical poems, by their very nature and limitations, tend to be homogeneous as far as manner is concerned. We know what to expect. But the longer works are often used by Pushkin for stylistic experiment – in particular for the interweaving and blending of stylistic patterns. Already in *The Gipsies* we can see the deliberate application of two distinct techniques, which are used for different purposes: for physical description, conversation, and action the language is brittle, terse, and realistic; there is a refreshing absence of clichés, emotional epithets, and archaisms; when epithets are used they are rich and accurate (see, for instance, the description of Aleko and the gipsies entertaining the public), each containing 'an abyss of space', to use Gogol's term. On the other hand, the passages describing the background and psychological make-up of the artificial hero are written in the purely Romantic vein. In *Yevgeny Onegin* there are subtle gradations of style to convey the poet's attitude to the events or characters described, from the absurd (and parodied) Romantic jargon used for the description of Lensky and Olga (see, for instance, Chapter 4, Stanzas XVII, XX–XXII) to the crystalline simplicity of Tatyana's dream.

But the greatest example of Pushkin's ability to handle his style is undoubtedly to be found in *The Bronze Horseman*. Here the richness of content is matched by the richness of stylistic devices. Three distinct, contrasting streams run through the poem, sometimes separately, sometimes merging together. For the descriptions of Peter the Great, the miraculous birth of the city, the great eulogy of Peter, the balcony scene, the statue, and particularly the latter's pursuit of Yevgeny, Pushkin uses the lofty manner reminiscent of the odes of the eighteenth and early nineteenth centuries. Such passages abound in archaisms, bombastic phraseology, and ringing euphony, all devices dear to the numerous court poets who had glorified St Petersburg, its founder, and his successors since the early eighteenth century. In complete contrast to the lofty style, we find the prosaic intonations of the passages describing the lowly hero, his occupations, his movements, his thoughts. The language is stripped of adornment and greatly simplified; enjambements proliferate, breaking the poetic flow and reducing the verse almost to the rhythm of prose; there are vulgarisms, everyday words and expressions, conversational turns of phrase;

indeed, the prosaic nature of the language is in complete harmony with the prosaic nature of the hero's character.

The third manner avoids the extremes of the other two. It is used to describe nature, the elements, the river, the city, and the flood. More personal and intimate than the depersonalized lofty style, and more lyrical than the prosaic intonations of the Yevgeny passages, this third manner is often reminiscent of the descriptive technique used by Pushkin in *Yevgeny Onegin*. But in some ways it is more mature, more adventurous, more harmonious. Many features characteristic of Pushkin's richest poetry are to be found here – the subtle and tactful use of euphonic devices, the tendency to string together large numbers of nouns or verbs, the simplicity of vocabulary and syntax, the complete eschewance of hackneyed phraseology and insipid clichés, and the daring though restrained use of imagery ('The Neva tossed like a sick man in his restless bed'). Perhaps it is here, in these exquisite passages which provide the background for the clash of the two protagonists, that we can see most clearly the direction in which Pushkin was moving at the end of his life, that we can glimpse the ultimate poetic technique which he was perfecting, and that we can understand the true extent of his contribution to Russian literature.

*

Forty years after Pushkin's death, Dostoyevsky wrote: 'Everything we have comes from Pushkin.' This is no exaggeration. Pushkin's literary legacy is so vast and varied that it would be hard to point to any one contemporary or subsequent Russian writer whose work was not affected by him in one way or another. Even his early, 'Byronic' writings had a widespread, if only temporary, influence on the literature of the day (Ryleyev and Bestuzhev placed *The Fountain of Bakhchisarai* and *A Prisoner of the Caucasus* on a higher artistic level than the first chapter of *Yevgeny Onegin*) – Baratynsky's epic poem *Eda*, for instance, and Lermontov's Caucasian tales (*Hadji-Abrek, Ismail-bey*) have their origins in *A Prisoner of the Caucasus*, while what is commonly accepted as one of Lermontov's greatest works, *Mtsyri*, can be traced back through his own early poetry (*Boyarin Orsha* and *The Confession*) to Kozlov's highly Byronic *The Monk* (*Chernets*), which in its turn bears the imprint of Pushkin's 'Southern poems'. *Yevgeny Onegin* has been described as the egg from which all the plots of Turgenev's novels were hatched; Onegin and Tatyana are the forerunners of a whole series of heroes and heroines in Russian fiction. *The Little House in Kolomna*, with its tale of simple people in simple surroundings told in a down-to-earth manner, has many close parallels in

Russian literature, including Turgenev's *Parasha*, which was strongly influenced by *Yevgeny Onegin* and *Count Nulin* as well, Lermontov's *Sashka* and *A Fairytale for Children* (both unfinished), and Fet's *Talisman* and *The Dream*. *The Bronze Horseman*, with its remarkable fusion of realism and fantasy and its grim, ominous townscapes, anticipates Gogol's St Petersburg stories, the early Dostoyevsky, and Andrey Bely's novel *Petersburg*. Much of Pushkin's folk verse led directly to the vigorous popular poetry of Nekrasov; even the latter's rhetorical invective can be traced back to Pushkin (compare *Home* with Pushkin's *The Village*), while the formal link between his *Poet and Citizen* and Pushkin's *Conversation between Bookseller and Poet* is obvious (cf. Lermontov's *Journalist, Reader, and Writer*).

These are not isolated instances of Pushkin's influence on his contemporaries and successors; they are merely examples chosen to illustrate the extraordinary extent of his poetic legacy. Indeed it would be surprising if his influence were less extensive; for Pushkin virtually recreated Russian literature, sweeping away the past as it were, and forming a base on which future generations of writers could build. As one of the leading Soviet Pushkinists has said: 'After Pushkin there was no longer any need to turn to the traditions of the eighteenth century; the work of Pushkin *replaced* preceding literature.'

*

Lastly a word on the selection. With the exception of *Yevgeny Onegin* and *Boris Godunov* (of which I have had regretfully to confine myself to extracts, owing to the demands of space), only complete poems have been included. This meant limiting my selection of the long poems to four only. These, however, can be considered fairly representative of Pushkin's main poetic genres. As for the short lyrical poems, these were chosen purely according to the pleasure which they happen to afford me. I realize, of course, that many lovers of Pushkin will be annoyed or upset by the omission of this or that particular poem; I only hope that they will forgive me for selecting the poems in this book on so arbitrary a basis. In order to save space, none of the poems in the *Penguin Book of Russian Verse* has been included in this collection.

The Russian text is taken from the most recent Soviet edition of Pushkin's works – *A. S. Pushkin: Sobraniye sochinenii* (*Gosudarstvennoye izdatelstvo khudozhestvennoi literatury*, Moscow, 1959–62).

КАЗАК

Раз, полунощной порою,
  Сквозь туман и мрак,
Ехал тихо над рекою
  Удалой казак.

Черна шапка набекрени,
  Весь жупан в пыли.
Пистолеты при колене,
  Сабля до земли.

Верный конь, узды не чуя,
  Шагом выступал;
Гриву долгую волнуя,
  Углублялся вдаль.

Вот пред ним две-три избушки,
  Выломан забор;
Здесь – дорога к деревушке,
  Там – в дремучий бор.

«Не найду в лесу девицы, –
  Думал хват Денис, –
Уж красавицы в светлицы
  На ночь убрались».

THE COSSACK

ONCE at midnight a dashing Cossack quietly rode above the river through mist and darkness.

His black hat was at an angle, his *zhupan* [Cossack coat] was covered in dust. Pistols were by his knees; his sabre reached to the ground.

His true steed, not feeling the bridle, moved at walking pace; with long mane billowing, it went off far into the distance.

Now before him there are two or three little huts, a broken fence; here is the road to the little village, there the one to the dense pine-forest.

'I shall not find a maiden in the forest,' thought the dashing Denis. 'The pretty young girls have already departed to their upstairs chambers for the night.'

Шевельнул донец уздою,
    Шпорой прикольнул,
И помчался конь стрелою,
    К избам завернул.

В облаках луна сребрила
    Дальни небеса;
Под окном сидит уныла
    Девица-краса.

Храбрый видит красну деву;
    Сердце бьется в нем,
Конь тихонько к леву, к леву –
    Вот уж под окном.

«Ночь становится темнее,
    Скрылася луна.
Выдь, коханочка, скорее,
    Напои коня».

«Нет! к мужчине молодому
    Страшно подойти,
Страшно выйти мне из дому
    Коню дать воды».

The Don Cossack twitched the bridle and pricked the horse with his spur, and the horse galloped off like an arrow and turned off towards the huts.

In the clouds the moon was silvering the distant heavens; beneath her window a fair maid sat despondently.

The brave fellow espies the fair maid; his heart beats; gently his horse moves to the left, to the left – and now he's right beneath her window.

'The night is becoming darker, the moon has hidden. Come out, beloved, quickly, come water my horse.'

'No, I am frightened to come close to a young man. I am frightened to leave the house and give water to your horse.'

«Ах! небось, девица красна,
　　С милым подружись!»
«Ночь красавицам опасна».
　　«Радость, не страшись!

Верь, коханочка, пустое;
　　Ложный страх отбрось!
Тратишь время золотое;
　　Милая, небось!

Сядь на борзого, с тобою
　　В дальний еду край;
Будешь счастлива со мною:
　　С другом всюду рай».

Что же девица? Склонилась,
　　Победила страх,
Робко ехать согласилась.
　　Счастлив стал казак.

Поскакали, полетели.
　　Дружку друг любил;
Был ей верен две недели,
　　В третью изменил.

'Ah, do not be afraid, fair maiden, be friendly with your beloved!' 'The night is dangerous for fair maidens.' 'My joy, be not frightened!

'Believe me, beloved, it is nothing; cast aside false fear! You are wasting golden time; my dearest, do not be afraid!

'Mount my swift horse, with you I shall go to a distant land; you will be happy with me: with your loved one, everywhere is paradise.'

What did the girl do? She submitted, she conquered her fear, and shyly agreed to go. The Cossack was happy.

They galloped off, they flew off. They loved each other. He was true to her for two weeks; in the third he was unfaithful.

[1814]

O. МАССОН

Ольга, крестница Киприды,
Ольга, чудо красоты,
Как же ласки и обиды
Расточать привыкла ты!
Поцелуем сладострастья
Ты, тревожа сердце в нас,
Соблазнительного счастья
Назначаешь тайный час.
Мы с горячкою любовной
Прибегаем в час условный,
В дверь стучим – но в сотый раз
Слышим твой коварный шепот,
И служанки сонный ропот,
И насмешливый отказ.

Ради резвого разврата,
Приапических затей,
Ради неги, ради злата,
Ради прелести твоей,
Ольга, жрица наслажденья,
Внемли наш влюбленный плач –
Ночь восторгов, ночь забвенья
Нам наверное назначь.

TO OLGA MASSON

OLGA, goddaughter of Cypris [Aphrodite], Olga, miracle of beauty, how accustomed you are to lavish caresses and insults! Disturbing our heart, you fix the secret hour of seductive happiness with a kiss of voluptuousness. With amorous fever we run up at the appointed hour and knock at the door – but for the hundredth time we hear your cunning whispering, and your maid's sleepy grumbling, and your mocking refusal.

For the sake of sportive dissipation and priapic follies, for the sake of sensual pleasures, for the sake of gold, for the sake of your charms, Olga, priestess of enjoyment, hearken to our amorous plaint – appoint for us without fail a night of rapture, a night of oblivion.   [1819]

РУСАЛКА

Над озером, в глухих дубровах,
Спасался некогда монах,
Всегда в занятиях суровых,
В посте, молитве и трудах.
Уже лопаткою смиренной
Себе могилу старец рыл —
И лишь о смерти вожделенной
Святых угодников молил.

Однажды летом у порогу
Поникшей хижины своей
Анахорет молился Богу.
Дубравы делались черней;
Туман над озером дымился,
И красный месяц в облаках
Тихонько по небу катился.
На воды стал глядеть монах.

Глядит, невольно страха полный;
Не может сам себя понять . . .
И видит: закипели волны
И присмирели вдруг опять . . .

THE WATER-NYMPH

Once, above a lake, in dense woods, a monk sought salvation, ever
engrossed in austere practices, in fasting, prayer, and toil. Already
with humble spade the old man was digging himself a grave – and
he prayed to the holy saints only to grant him longed-for death.

Once in the summer, at the entrance to his sagging hut, the
anchorite was praying to God. The woods became blacker; mist
steamed over the lake, and the crimson moon, covered in clouds,
slowly rolled across the sky. The monk began to look at the
waters.

He looks, filled with involuntary fear; he cannot understand
himself . . . And he sees the waters boil and suddenly grow calm

5

И вдруг . . . легка, как тень ночная,
Бела, как ранний снег холмов,
Выходит женщина нагая
И молча села у брегов.

Глядит на старого монаха
И чешет влажные власы.
Святой монах дрожит со страха
И смотрит на ее красы.
Она манит его рукою,
Кивает быстро головой . . .
И вдруг – падучею звездою –
Под сонной скрылася волной.

Всю ночь не спал старик угрюмый
И не молился целый день –
Перед собой с невольной думой
Все видел чудной девы тень.
Дубравы вновь оделись тьмою;
Пошла по облакам луна,
И снова дева над водою
Сидит, прелестна и бледна.

again . . . And suddenly, light as a shadow of the night, white as
early snow upon the hills, a naked woman emerges and sits in
silence by the shore.

She gazes at the old monk and combs her damp hair. The holy
monk trembles with fear and looks at her charms. She beckons him
with her hand, nods her head quickly . . . and suddenly, like a
falling star, she disappeared beneath the sleepy wave.

All night the gloomy old man could not sleep, and he did not
pray all day – with thoughts which he could not suppress, he saw
before him all the time the shade of the wondrous maiden. Again
the woods were clothed in darkness, the moon set off among the
clouds; and again the maiden sits above the water, beautiful and
pale.

Глядит, кивает головою,
Целует издали шутя,
Играет, плещется волною,
Хохочет, плачет, как дитя,
Зовет монаха, нежно стонет . . .
«Монах, монах! Ко мне, ко мне! . . . »
И вдруг в волнах прозрачных тонет;
И все в глубокой тишине.

На третий день отшельник страстный
Близ очарованных брегов
Сидел и девы ждал прекрасной,
А тень ложилась средь дубров . . .
Заря прогнала тьму ночную:
Монаха не нашли нигде,
И только бороду седую
Мальчишки видели в воде.

К МОЕЙ ЧЕРНИЛЬНИЦЕ

Подруга думы праздной,
Чернильница моя;

She gazes, nods her head, mockingly blows kisses from afar, plays, splashes in the wave, laughs, weeps, just like a child, calls the monk, groans tenderly . . . 'O monk, O monk! Come to me, come to me!' And suddenly she sinks in the transparent waves, and all is in deep silence.

On the third day the hermit, torn by passion, was sitting near the enchanted shore and waiting for the beautiful maiden, while shadows fell within the woods . . . Dawn dispelled the dark of night: the monk was nowhere to be found, and only his grey beard was seen in the water by some boys.

[1819]

TO MY INKWELL
My inkwell, friend of idle thought! I have adorned my variegated

7

Мой век разнообразный
Тобой украсил я.
Как часто друг веселья
С тобою забывал
Условный час похмелья
И праздничный бокал;
Под сенью хаты скромной,
В часы печали томной
Была ты предо мной
С лампадой и мечтой.
В минуты вдохновенья
К тебе я прибегал
И музу призывал
На пир воображенья.
Прозрачный, легкий дым
Носился над тобою,
И с трепетом живым
В нем быстрой чередою
. . . .

Сокровища мои
На дне твоем таятся.
Тебя я посвятил
Занятиям досуга
И с ленью примирил:
Она твоя подруга.
С тобой успех узнал

life with you. How often I, the friend of merriment, forgot with
you the appointed hour of drunken revelry and the festive goblet;
in the shelter of a humble hut, in the hours of grievous sorrow,
you were always in front of me, together with my lamp and my
dream. In minutes of inspiration I turned to you and I called my
muse to a feast of imagination. Light, transparent smoke swirled
over you, and with lively trepidation, in it in swift succession . . .
[*A page of Pushkin's exercise book was torn out here.*]
My treasures are hidden at your bottom. I have consecrated you
to the occupations of my leisure and I reconciled you with Idleness:

Отшельник неизвестный . . .
Заветный твой кристалл
Хранит огонь небесный;
И под вечер, когда
Перо по книжке бродит,
Без вялого труда
Оно в тебе находит
Концы моих стихов
И верность выраженья;
То звуков или слов
Нежданное стеченье,
То едкой шутки соль,
То правды слог суровый,
То странность рифмы новой,
Неслыханной дотоль.
С глупцов сорвав одежду,
Я весело клеймил
Зоила и невежду
Пятном твоих чернил. . . .
Но их не разводил
Ни тайной злости пеной,
Ни ядом клеветы.
И сердца простоты
Ни лестью, ни изменой
Не замарала ты.

she is your friend. With you the unknown hermit knew success . . . Your sacred crystal preserves a heavenly fire; and towards evening, as my pen wanders over the book, without sluggish toil it finds in you the ends of my verses and truth of expression; now an unexpected confluence of sounds or words, now the salt of a pungent joke, now the harsh style of Justice, now the strangeness of a new rhyme, unheard-of hitherto. Tearing off the clothes of fools, I merrily branded Zoilus an ignoramus with the stain of your ink . . . But I did not water down your ink either with the scum of secret spite or with the venom of slander. And you did not sully simplicity of heart with either flattery or unfaithfulness.

Но здесь на лоне лени,
Я слышу нежны пени
Заботливых друзей. . . .
Ужели их забуду,
Друзей души моей,
И им неверен буду?
Оставь, оставь порой
Привычные затеи,
И дактил, и хореи
Для прозы почтовой.
Минуты хладной скуки,
Сердечной пустоты,
Уныние разлуки,
Всегдашние мечты,
Мои надежды, чувства
Без лести, без искусства
Бумаге передай . . .
Болтливостью небрежной,
И ветреной, и нежной
Их сердце утешай . . .

Беспечный сын природы,
Пока златые годы
В забвенье трачу я,
Со мною неразлучно

But here, in the lap of idleness, I hear the gentle reproaches of solicitous friends . . . Surely I shall not forget them, the friends of my soul, and be unfaithful to them? Abandon now and then, abandon your customary fancies, your dactyls and your trochees, for the prose of letter-writing. Without flattery or art commit to paper the minutes of chill tedium, of emptiness of heart, the melancholy of parting, my everlasting dreams, my hopes, my feelings . . . Gladden their hearts with carefree chatter, both playful and tender . . .

While I, the carefree son of nature, waste my golden years in

Живи благополучно,
Наперсница моя.

Когда же берег ада
Навек меня возьмет,
Когда навек уснет
Перо, моя отрада,
И ты, в углу пустом
Осиротев, остынешь
И навсегда покинешь
Поэта тихий дом . . .
Чадаев, друг мой милый,
Тебя возьмет, унылый;
Последний будь привет
Любимцу прежних лет.
Иссохшая, пустая,
Меж двух его картин
Останься век немая,
Укрась его камин.
Взыскательного света
Очей не привлекай,
Но верного поэта
Друзьям напоминай.

oblivion, live with me inseparably, prosperously, my confidant . . .

But when the shore of hell takes me for ever, when my pen – my joy – falls asleep for ever, and when you, orphaned in your empty corner, grow cold and leave forever the quiet house of the poet . . . Chaadayev, my dear melancholy friend, will take you. Be the last greeting to my dearest friend of former years. Dried up and empty, remain for ever dumb between his two pictures, adorn his mantelpiece. Do not attract the eyes of the exacting world, but remind friends of a true poet.

[1821]

УЗНИК

Сижу за решеткой в темнице сырой.
Вскормленный в неволе орел молодой,
Мой грустный товарищ, махая крылом,
Кровавую пищу клюет под окном,

Клюет, и бросает, и смотрит в окно,
Как будто со мною задумал одно.
Зовет меня взглядом и криком своим
И вымолвить хочет: «Давай улетим!

Мы вольные птицы; пора, брат, пора!
Туда, где за тучей белеет гора,
Туда, где синеют морские края,
Туда, где гуляем лишь ветер . . . да я! . . . »

ИЗ ПИСЬМА К ВУЛЬФУ

Здравствуй, Вульф, приятель мой!
Приезжай сюда зимой,
Да Языкова поэта
Затащи ко мне с собой

THE PRISONER

I sit behind bars in a damp prison. My sad companion, a young eagle reared in captivity, flaps its wings and pecks at its bloody food beneath my window.

It pecks, then stops, and looks in through the window as though it shared the same thought as I. It calls me with its look and its cries and would say: 'Let us fly away!

'We are free birds; it is time, my brother, it is time! Thither, where the mountain shines white beyond the cloud, thither, where the expanses of sea are blue, thither, where only the wind roams – and I!'

[1822]

FROM A LETTER TO WOLF*

HAIL, Wolf, my friend! Come here in the winter and make the poet Yazykov come with you to me, so that now and then we can

* A friend and neighbour of Pushkin.

Погулять верхом порой,
Пострелять из пистолета.
Лайон, мой курчавый брат
(Не михайловский приказчик),
Привезет нам, право, клад . . .
Что ? – бутылок полный ящик.
Запируем уж, молчи!
Чудо – жизнь анахорета!
В Троегорском до ночи,
А в Михайловском до света;
Дни любви посвящены,
Ночью царствуют стаканы,
Мы же – то смертельно пьяны,
То мертвецки влюблены.

К МОРЮ

Прощай, свободная стихия!
В последний раз передо мной
Ты катишь волны голубые
И блещешь гордою красой.

take a ride on horseback or do a bit of pistol-shooting. Lion [i.e. Lev Pushkin], my curly-headed brother (not the steward at Mikhaylovskoye [the estate of Pushkin's mother]), will truly bring us a treasure . . . What ? Why, a case full of bottles. We'll have a splendid feast . . . Quiet, no objections! What a wonderful thing is the life of a hermit! In Trigorskoye [the neighbouring estate] till night and in Mikhaylovskoye till dawn; the days are devoted to love, at night the goblets reign, while we are now fatally drunk, now dead in love.

[1824]

TO THE SEA

FAREWELL, free element! For the last time you roll your blue waves before me and shimmer in your proud beauty.

13

Как друга ропот заунывный,
Как зов его в прощальный час,
Твой грустный шум, твой шум призыв-
    ный
Услышал я в последний раз.

Моей души предел желанный!
Как часто по брегам твоим
Бродил я тихий и туманный,
Заветным умыслом томим!

Как я любил твои отзывы,
Глухие звуки, бездны глас,
И тишину в вечерний час,
И своенравные порывы!

Смиренный парус рыбарей,
Твоею прихотью хранимый,
Скользит отважно средь зыбей:
Но ты взыграл, неодолимый,
И стая тонет кораблей.

Не удалось навек оставить
Мне скучный, неподвижный брег,

Like the doleful murmur of a friend, like his call at the hour of parting, I have heard for the last time your sad sound, the sound of your call.

O longed-for region of my soul! How often have I wandered on your banks, quiet and gloomy, tormented by some cherished scheme!

How I loved your echoes, the dull sounds, the voice of the abyss, and the calm at evening-time, and the capricious blasts!

The fisherman's humble sail, protected by some whim of yours, glides bravely midst the waves: but suddenly you, the indomitable one, are aroused, and a whole shoal of ships sinks.

I did not succeed in quitting for ever your dull immobile shore,

Тебя восторгами поздравить
И по хребтам твоим направить
Мой поэтический побег!

Ты ждал, ты звал . . . я был окован;
Вотще рвалась душа моя:
Могучей страстью очарован,
У берегов остался я . . .

О чем жалеть? Куда бы ныне
Я путь беспечный устремил?
Один предмет в твоей пустыне
Мою бы душу поразил.

Одна скала, гробница славы . . .
Там погружались в хладный сон
Воспоминанья величавы:
Там угасал Наполеон.

Там он почил среди мучений.
И вслед за ним, как бури шум,
Другой от нас умчался гений,
Другой властитель наших дум.

nor in greeting you with rapture, nor in directing my poetic flight along the crests of your waves!

You waited, you called me . . . I was shackled; in vain my soul strove to free itself: bewitched by powerful passion, I stayed upon your shores . . .

What is there to regret? Whither shall I now direct my carefree steps? One object alone in all your wilderness would strike my soul.

One cliff, the sepulchre of glory [i.e. St Helena] . . . There majestic memories subsided into chill sleep: there Napoleon's flame died out.

There, midst torments, he fell into eternal sleep. And following him, like the noise of the storm, another genius fled away from us, another ruler of our thoughts [Byron].

Исчез, оплаканный свободой,
Оставя миру свой венец.
Шуми, взволнуйся непогодой:
Он был, о море, твой певец.

Твой образ был на нем означен,
Он духом создан был твоим:
Как ты, могущ, глубок и мрачен,
Как ты, ничем неукротим.

Мир опустел . . . Теперь куда же
Меня б ты вынес, океан?
Судьба земли повсюду та же:
Где капля блага, там на страже
Уж просвещенье иль тиран.

Прощай же, море! Не забуду
Твоей торжественной красы
И долго, долго слышать буду
Твой гул в вечерние часы.

В леса, в пустыни молчаливы
Перенесу, тобою полн,
Твои скалы, твои заливы,
И блеск, и тень, и говор волн.

He disappeared, lamented by freedom, leaving his garland to the world . . . Resound and rage, stirred up by storm! O sea, he was your bard.

Your image was stamped upon him, he was created by your spirit: like you, he was powerful, deep, and gloomy; like you, nothing could daunt him.

The world has grown empty . . . Where would you now carry me away to, O ocean? Earth's lot is everywhere the same: wherever there is a drop of goodness, there enlightenment or a tyrant is on guard.

Farewell, then, O sea! I shall not forget your triumphant beauty, and long, long shall I hear your thunder in the evening hours.

Full of your memories, I shall carry into the forests and the silent wildernesses your crags, your creeks, and the glitter and the shadow and the murmur of your waves.   [1824]

ФОНТАНУ БАХЧИСАРАЙСКОГО ДВОРЦА

Фонтан любви, фонтан живой!
Принес я в дар тебе две розы.
Люблю немолчный говор твой
И поэтические слезы.

Твоя серебряная пыль
Меня кропит росою хладной:
Ах, лейся, лейся, ключ отрадный!
Журчи, журчи свою мне быль . . .

Фонтан любви, фонтан печальный!
И я твой мрамор вопрошал:
Хвалу стране прочел я дальной;
Но о Марии ты молчал . . .

Светило бледное гарема!
И здесь ужель забвенно ты?
Или Мария и Зарема
Одни счастливые мечты?

TO THE FOUNTAIN OF THE PALACE OF BAKHCHI SARAI

FOUNTAIN of love! Fountain full of life! I have brought you two roses as a gift. I love your never-silent murmur and your poetic tears.

Your silver dust sprinkles me with chill dew: Ah, pour on, pour on, O joyous spring! Babbling, rippling, tell me your tale . . .

Fountain of love, fountain of sorrow! I too questioned your marble: on it I read praise for a distant land; but about Maria [Maria and Zarema: the heroines of Pushkin's poem, *Bakhchisaraysky Fontan*] you were silent . . .

O pale star of the harem! Can it be that even here you are already forgotten? Or were Maria and Zarema mere happy dreams?

Иль только сон воображенья
В пустынной мгле нарисовал
Свои минутные виденья,
Души неясный идеал?

Полу-милорд, полу-купец,
Полу-мудрец, полу-невежда,
Полу-подлец, но есть надежда,
Что будет полным наконец.

Храни меня, мой талисман,
Храни меня во дни гоненья,
Во дни раскаянья, волненья:
Ты в день печали был мне дан.

Or was it only the dream of my imagination, which in the waste darkness depicted its fleeting visions, the vague ideal of my soul?

[1824]

HALF-MILORD, half-merchant, half-sage, half-ignoramus; half-scoundrel – but there is hope that one day he will be a whole one.

[1824]

[*The subject of this epigram was Count M. S. Vorontsov, Pushkin's chief in Odessa. He was brought up in England* ('half-milord') *and had financial interests in Odessa* ('half-merchant').]

PRESERVE me, O my talisman, preserve me in days of persecution, in days of repentance and anxiety: in a day of grief you were given to me.

Когда подымет океан
Вокруг меня валы ревучи,
Когда грозою грянут тучи, –
Храни меня, мой талисман.

В уединенье чуждых стран,
На лоне скучного покоя,
В тревоге пламенного боя
Храни меня, мой талисман.

Священный сладостный обман,
Души волшебное свѐтило . . .
Оно сокрылось, изменило . . .
Храни меня мой талисман.

Пускай же ввек сердечных ран
Не растравит воспоминанье.
Прощай, надежда; спи, желанье;
Храни меня, мой талисман.

When the ocean raises its roaring waves around me, when the thunder-clouds burst in a storm – preserve me, O my talisman.

In the seclusion of foreign lands, in the lap of tedious calm, in the alarm of fiery battle, preserve me, O my talisman.

Sacred, sweet deceit, magic star of my soul . . . It has hidden itself, it has ceased to exist . . . Preserve me, O my talisman.

Let not recollection ever irritate the wounds of my heart. Farewell, hope; sleep, desire; preserve me, O my talisman.

[1825]

ЖЕНИХ

Три дня купеческая дочь
    Наташа пропадала;
Она на двор на третью ночь
    Без памяти вбежала.
С вопросами отец и мать
К Наташе стали приступать.
    Наташа их не слышит,
    Дрожит и еле дышит.

Тужила мать, тужил отец,
    И долго приступали,
И отступились наконец,
    А тайны не узнали.
Наташа стала, как была,
Опять румяна, весела,
    Опять пошла с сестрами
    Сидеть за воротами.

Раз у тесовых у ворот,
    С подружками своими,
Сидела девица — и вот

THE BRIDEGROOM

For three days Natasha, the merchant's daughter, was missing. On the third night she ran into the house in wild distraction. Her mother and father began to ply Natasha with questions. Natasha does not hear them; she trembles and barely breathes.

Her mother grieved, her father grieved, and long they plied her with their questions, and at last they gave it up, not having learned her secret. Natasha's cheeks regained their rosy hue, and she became cheerful as before, and again she went with her sisters to sit outside the gate.

Once at the shingle-gate the girl sat with her friends – and lo,

Промчалась перед ними
Лихая тройка с молодцом.
Конями, крытыми ковром,
    В санях он стоя правит,
    И гонит всех, и давит.

Он, поровнявшись, поглядел,
    Наташа поглядела,
Он вихрем мимо пролетел,
    Наташа помертвела.
Стремглав домой она бежит.
«Он! он! узнала! – говорит, –
Он, точно он! держите,
    Друзья мои, спасите!»

Печально слушает семья,
    Качая головою;
Отец ей: «Милая моя,
    Откройся предо мною.
Обидел кто тебя, скажи,
Хоть только след нам укажи».
    Наташа плачет снова.
    И более ни слова.

a swift troika with a fine young man rushed by before them. Standing in the sleigh, he drives the rug-covered horses, scatters everyone, and knocks the bystanders down.

Drawing level, he gazed – and Natasha gazed. He flew by them like the wind. Natasha froze. Headlong she runs home. 'It's he! It's he! I recognized him!' she says. 'It's he, it's he indeed! Stop him, my friends, save me!'

Sadly her family listens, shaking their heads; her father says to her: 'My dear one, reveal all to me. If someone has offended you, tell us, show us but a trace.' Natasha again weeps. And no word more is spoken.

Наутро сваха к ним на двор
    Нежданная приходит.
Наташу хвалит, разговор
    С отцом ее заводит:
«У вас товар, у нас купец;
Собою парень молодец,
    И статный, и проворный,
    Не вздорный, не зазорный.

Богат, умен, ни перед кем
    Не кланяется в пояс,
А как боярин между тем
    Живет, не беспокоясь;
А подарит невесте вдруг
И лисью шубу, и жемчуг,
    И перстни золотые,
    И платья парчевые.

Катаясь, видел он вчера
    Ее за воротами;
Не по рукам ли, да с двора,
    Да в церковь с образами?»
Она сидит за пирогом,
Да речь ведет обиняком,
    А бедная невеста
    Себе не видит места.

In the morning, unexpected, a matchmaker comes to their house. She praises Natasha, and starts a conversation with her father: 'You have the goods, we have a buyer; the lad's a fine young fellow, well-built and nimble, not cantankerous, nor disreputable.

'Rich, clever, he bows low to none; yet he lives like a boyar without a care in the world; suddenly he may give his bride a fox-fur coat, a pearl, gold rings, brocaded dresses.

'Yesterday, while driving round the town, he saw her by the gate; shall we not strike hands, and go straight from the house to the church and take the ikons [to bless the couple] with us?' She sits and eats the pie that's put before her, and her talk is all hints and roundabout phrases, while the poor girl fidgets uneasily.

«Согласен, – говорит отец; –
    Ступай благополучно,
Моя Наташа, под венец:
    Одной в светелке скучно.
Не век девице вековать,
Не всё косатке распевать,
    Пора гнездо устроить,
    Чтоб детушек покоить».

Наташа к стенке уперлась
    И слово молвить хочет –
Вдруг зарыдала, затряслась,
    И плачет и хохочет.
В смятенье сваха к ней бежит,
Водой студеною поит
    И льет остаток чаши
    На голову Наташи.

Крушится, охает семья.
    Опомнилась Наташа.
И говорит: «Послушна я,
    Святая воля ваша.

'I agree,' the father says. 'Go in happiness to the altar, my Natasha; it is dull to sit alone in the upper room. You should not while away your life unmarried, a swallow should not spend all its time singing – it is time to build a nest in order to nurture children.'

Natasha leaned against the wall and was about to speak – suddenly she began to sob and shudder and weep and roar with laughter. In confusion the matchmaker runs up to her, gives her cold water to drink, and pours the rest of the beaker on Natasha's head.

In great distress the family moans. Then Natasha came to and said: 'I will obey you, your will is sacred. Call my betrothed to the

Зовите жениха на пир,
Пеките хлебы на весь мир,
    На славу мед варите,
    Да суд на пир зовите».

«Изволь, Наташа, ангел мой!
    Готов тебе в забаву
Я жизнь отдать!» – И пир горой;
    Пекут, варят на славу.
Вот гости честные нашли,
За стол невесту повели;
    Поют подружки, плачут,
    А вот и сани скачут.

Вот и жених – и все за стол.
    Звенят, гремят стаканы,
Заздравный ковш кругом пошел;
    Все шумно, гости пьяны.

Жених

«А что же, милые друзья,
Невеста красная мо́я

feast, bake loaves for the whole world, prepare a matchless brew of
mead, call the law to the feast.'
    'For sure, Natasha, my angel! For your delight I am ready to
sacrifice my life!' And a sumptuous feast is prepared; prodigiously
they bake and cook. Now the worthy guests have come in their
numbers, and the bride has been brought to the table; the brides-
maids sing and weep – then, behind galloping horses, a sledge
arrives.
    It is the bridegroom – and all sit down to table. The glasses ring
and clatter, the toasting-cup goes round, all is noisy, the guests are
drunk.
THE BRIDEGROOM: 'Tell me, dear friends, why is my fair bride

Не пьет, не ест, не служит:
О чем невеста тужит?»

Невеста жениху в ответ:
«Откроюсь наудачу.
Душе моей покоя нет,
И день и ночь я плачу:
Недобрый сон меня крушит».
Отец ей: «Что ж твой сон гласит?
Скажи нам, что такое,
Дитя мое родное?»

«Мне снилось, – говорит она, –
Зашла я в лес дремучий,
И было поздно; чуть луна
Светила из-за тучи;
С тропинки сбилась я: в глуши
Не слышно было ни души,
И сосны лишь да ели
Вершинами шумели.

И вдруг, как будто наяву,
Изба передо мною.
Я к ней, стучу – молчат. Зову –
Ответа нет; с мольбою

not drinking, not eating, not serving? What is my bride grieving for?'

The bride answers the bridegroom: 'I will tell all, as best I can. My soul knows no rest, and day and night I weep: an evil dream oppresses me.' Her father says to her: 'Well, what is your dream about then? Tell us what it is, my dearest child.'

'I dreamed', she says, 'that I went deep into a dense forest, and it was late; the moon was faintly shining from behind a cloud; I strayed from the path: in the depths of the forest not a soul was to be heard and only the tops of the pines and firs rustled.

'And suddenly, as though I was awake, a hut appeared before me. I go up to it. I knock – silence. I call out – no answer. With a

Дверь отворила я. Вхожу –
В избе свеча горит; гляжу –
Везде сребро да злато,
Все светло и богато».

Жених

«А чем же худ, скажи, твой сон?
Знать, жить тебе богато».

Невеста

«Постой, сударь, не кончен он.
На серебро, на злато,
На сукна, коврики, парчу,
На новгородскую камчу
Я молча любовалась
И диву дивовалась.

Вдруг слышу крик и конский топ . . .
Подъехали к крылечку.
Я поскорее дверью хлоп
И спряталась за печку.
Вот слышу много голосов . . .
Взошли двенадцать молодцов,

prayer on my lips, I opened the door. I go in – in the hut a candle is burning. I look – everywhere is silver and gold, all is bright and sumptuous.'

THE BRIDEGROOM: 'What is so bad about your dream, say? Clearly yours will be a life of riches.'

THE BRIDE: 'Stay, sir; it is not finished yet. In silence I feasted my eyes upon the silver, upon the gold, upon the cloths, the rugs, the brocades, the silks from Novgorod, and lost myself in wonder.

'Suddenly I hear a shout and the clatter of horses' hoofs . . . Someone has driven up to the porch. Quickly I slammed the door and hid behind the stove. Now I hear many voices . . . Twelve

И с ними голубица
Красавица девица.

Взошли толпой, не поклонясь,
    Икон не замечая;
За стол садятся, не молясь
    И шапок не снимая.
На первом месте брат большой,
По праву руку брат меньшой,
    По леву голубица
    Красавица девица.

Крик, хохот, песни, шум и звон,
    Разгульное похмелье . . .»

Жених

«А чем же худ, скажи, твой сон?
    Вещает он веселье».

Невеста

«Постой, сударь, не кончен он.
Идет похмелье, гром и звон,
    Пир весело бушует,
    Лишь девица горюет.

young men have come in, and with them a pure and beauteous maiden.

'They came in, in a crowd, without bowing, without noticing the ikons; they sit down at the table without praying or taking off their hats. At the head sits the eldest brother, on his right hand the youngest brother, on his left the pure and beauteous maiden.

'Shouts, laughter, song, din and clangour, sounds of drunken revelry . . .'

THE BRIDEGROOM: 'Say, what is so bad about your dream? It augurs merriment.'

THE BRIDE: 'Stay sir; it is not finished. The drunken revelry, uproar, and clangour continue, the feast waxes riotously gay, and only the maiden grieves.

Сидит, молчит, ни ест, ни пьет
И током слезы точит,
А старший брат свой нож берет,
Присвистывая точит;
Глядит на девицу-красу,
И вдруг хватает за косу,
Злодей девицу губит,
Ей праву руку рубит».

«Ну это, – говорит жених, –
Прямая небылица!
Но не тужи, твой сон не лих,
Поверь, душа-девица».
Она глядит ему в лицо.
«А это с чьей руки кольцо?»
Вдруг молвила невеста,
И все привстали с места.

Кольцо катится и звенит,
Жених дрожит бледнея;
Смутились гости. – Суд гласит:
«Держи, вязать злодея!»
Злодей окован, обличен,
И скоро смертию казнен.
Прославилась Наташа!
И вся тут песня наша.

'She sits in silence, eats not, drinks not; and sheds tears in torrents, while the eldest brother takes his knife and, whistling, sharpens it; he looks at the fair maiden and, suddenly seizing her by the plait, the villain kills the maiden and cuts off her right hand.'

'Why,' says the bridegroom, 'this is downright nonsense! But grieve not; your dream is not evil, believe me, my beloved.' She looks him in the face. 'And from whose hand does this ring come?' the bride said suddenly, and all began to rise from their seats.

With a clatter the ring falls and rolls along the ground. The bridegroom blanches and trembles; the guests fall into confusion. The law announces: 'Stop the villain, bind him!' The villain is fettered, convicted, and quickly put to death. Natasha became famous! And this is the end of our song.   [1825]

В крови горит огонь желанья,
Душа тобой уязвлена,
Лобзай меня: твои лобзанья
Мне слаще мирра и вина.
Склонись ко мне главою нежной,
И да почию безмятежный,
Пока дохнет веселый день
И двигнется ночная тень.

Под небом голубым страны своей родной
Она томилась, увядала . . .
Увяла наконец, и верно надо мной
Младая тень уже летала;
Но недоступная черта меж нами есть.
Напрасно чувство возбуждал я:
Из равнодушных уст я слышал смерти весть,
И равнодушно ей внимал я.
Так вот кого любил я пламенной душой
С таким тяжелым напряженьем,
С такою нежною, томительной тоской,
С таким безумством и мученьем!

[*A free rendering of the first two chapters of the Song of Solomon*]
IN my blood the fire of desire burns, my soul is wounded by you;
kiss me: your kisses are sweeter to me than myrrh and wine. Bend
your sweet head towards me and let me rest serenely until the
cheerful day breathes and the shadows of the night flee away.

[1825]

BENEATH the blue sky of her native land she languished, faded . . .
At last she withered away, and doubtless her young shade flitted
above my head; but there is a line beyond all understanding which
divides us. In vain I tried to arouse some feeling within me: from
indifferent lips I heard the news of her death, and with indifference
I listened to it. So this is she whom in my passionate soul I loved
with such painful intensity, with such tender, agonizing grief, with
such madness and such torment! Where now are the torments,

Где муки, где любовь? Увы! в душе моей
Для бедной, легковерной тени,
Для сладкой памяти невозвратимых дней
Не нахожу ни слез, ни пени.

ПРИЗНАНИЕ

Я вас люблю, – хоть я бешусь,
Хоть это труд и стыд напрасный,
И в этой глупости несчастной
У ваших ног я признаюсь!
Мне не к лицу и не по летам . . .
Пора, пора мне быть умней!
Но узнаю по всем приметам
Болезнь любви в душе моей:
Без вас мне скучно, – я зеваю;
При вас мне грустно, – я терплю;
И, мочи нет, сказать желаю,
Мой ангел, как я вас люблю!
Когда я слышу из гостиной
Ваш легкий шаг, иль платья шум,

where now is the love? Alas! for that poor all-too-trustful shade, for that sweet memory of irrevocable days I cannot find within my soul either tears or reproach.

[1826]

THE CONFESSION

I LOVE you – even though it enrages me, even though it means useless toil and shame; and at your feet I confess my hapless folly! It becomes me not, nor does it befit my years . . . It is time, it is time to be wiser! And yet by all the symptoms I recognize love's disease within my soul: without you I am bored – I yawn; in your presence I am sad – I put up with it. And desperately I wish to say, my angel, how I love you! When from the drawing-room I hear your light tread, or the rustle of your dress, or your

Иль голос девственный, невинный,
Я вдруг теряю весь свой ум.
Вы улыбнетесь — мне отрада;
Вы отвернетесь — мне тоска;
За день мучения — награда
Мне ваша бледная рука.
Когда за пяльцами прилежно
Сидите вы, склонясь небрежно,
Глаза и кудри опустя, —
Я в умиленье, молча, нежно
Любуюсь вами, как дитя! . . .
Сказать ли вам мое несчастье,
Мою ревнивую печаль,
Когда гулять, порой в ненастье,
Вы собираетеся вдаль?
И ваши слезы в одиночку,
И речи в уголку вдвоем,
И путешествия в Опочку,
И фортепьяно вечерком? . . .
Алина! сжальтесь надо мною.
Не смею требовать любви.
Быть может, за грехи мои,
Мой ангел, я любви не стою!

girlish innocent voice, suddenly I lose my head entirely. You smile – it is a joy to me; you turn away – it is a grief to me; for a day of torment your pale hand is a recompense to me. When you sit, diligently at your embroidery, nonchalantly leaning over your frame, with lowered eyes and locks – then like a child, in sweet emotion, I silently gaze at you with tender joy! Am I to tell you of my unhappiness, of my jealous sorrow, when, sometimes even in rainy weather, you are just off for a long walk? And the tears you shed in solitude, and the talks together in the corner, and the journeys to Opochka, and the piano in the evening? Alina! Have pity on me! I do not dare to ask for love. Perhaps, my angel, because of my sins I am not worthy of love! But just pretend!

Но притворитесь! Этот взгляд
Всё может выразить так чудно!
Ах, обмануть меня не трудно!
Я сам обманываться рад!

НЯНЕ

Подруга дней моих суровых,
Голубка дряхлая моя!
Одна в глуши лесов сосновых
Давно, давно ты ждешь меня.
Ты под окном своей светлицы
Горюешь, будто на часах,
И медлят поминутно спицы
В твоих наморщенных руках.
Глядишь в забытые вороты
На черный отдаленный путь:
Тоска, предчувствия, заботы
Теснят твою всечасно грудь.
То чудится тебе . . .

This glance of yours can express everything so wondrously! Ah, it is not difficult to deceive me! for I am only too pleased to be deceived!

[1826]

TO MY NANNY

COMPANION of my bleak days, my dearest nanny, frail and old! Long, long have you awaited me, alone in the depths of the pine forests. Beneath the window of your upstairs room you grieve like a sentry on his watch, and with every minute your knitting needles move more slowly in your wrinkled hands. You gaze at the forgotten gate, at the black distant road: melancholy, forebodings, cares weigh down your breast with every passing hour. Now you seem to hear . . . [Unfinished]

[1826]

ЗИМНЯЯ ДОРОГА

Сквозь волнистые туманы
Пробирается луна,
На печальные поляны
Льет печально свет она.

По дороге зимней, скучной
Тройка борзая бежит,
Колокольчик однозвучный
Утомительно гремит.

Что-то слышится родное
В долгих песнях ямщика:
То разгулье удалое,
То сердечная тоска . . .

Ни огня, ни черной хаты,
Глушь и снег . . . Навстречу мне
Только версты полосаты
Попадаются одне . . .

Скучно, грустно . . . Завтра, Нина,
Завтра к милой возвратясь,
Я забудусь у камина,
Загляжусь не наглядясь.

WINTER ROAD

The moon threads through the undulating mists and sadly pours her light upon the sad glades.

Along the dreary winter road a swift troika flies; monotonously, wearisomely the little bell rings out.

Something close to the heart can be heard in the long-drawn-out songs of the coachman: now unbridled hilarity, now the sad longing of the heart . . .

Not a light to be seen, not a dark hut, nothing but desolation and snow . . . and all that meets me on my way are striped mileposts . . .

All is tedious, all is cheerless . . . Tomorrow, Nina, tomorrow, when I return to my beloved, I shall forget my sorrows by the hearth, stare in wonderment, never tiring.

Звучно стрелка часовая
Мерный круг свой совершит,
И, докучных удаляя,
Полночь нас не разлучит.

Грустно, Нина: путь мой скучен,
Дремля смолкнул мой ямщик,
Колокольчик однозвучен,
Отуманен лунный лик.

Во глубине сибирских руд
Храните гордое терпенье,
Не пропадет ваш скорбный труд
И дум высокое стремленье.

Несчастью верная сестра,
Надежда в мрачном подземелье
Разбудит бодрость и веселье,
Придет желанная пора:

Любовь и дружество до вас
Дойдут сквозь мрачные затворы,
Как в ваши каторжные норы
Доходит мой свободный глас.

Loudly the hour-hand will complete its measured circle, and midnight, removing all our irksome friends, shall not separate us.

I feel sad, Nina: my journey is dreary; slumbering, my coachman has fallen silent; the little bell rings monotonously; the face of the moon is misted over.

[1826]

In the depths of the Siberian mines preserve proud patience; your grievous toil and the high striving of your thoughts shall not be in vain.

Hope, true sister of misfortune, shall awaken vigour and cheerfulness in the subterranean gloom; the longed-for time will come:

Love and friendship shall reach you through gloomy bolts, just as my free voice reaches your prison burrow.

Оковы тяжкие падут,
Темницы рухнут – и свобода
Вас примет радостно у входа,
И братья меч вам отдадут.

СОЛОВЕЙ И РОЗА

В безмолвии садов, весной, во мгле ночей,
Поет над розою восточный соловей.
Но роза милая не чувствует, не внемлет,
И под влюбленный гимн колеблется и дрем-
     лет.
Не так ли ты поешь для хладной красоты?
Опомнись, о поэт, к чему стремишься ты?
Она не слушает, не чувствует поэта;
Глядишь – она цветет; взываешь – нет ответа.

The heavy shackles shall fall, the prisons shall crash down – and freedom shall receive you joyously at the entrance, and brothers shall give you back your swords.

[1827]

THE NIGHTINGALE AND THE ROSE

In the silence of the gardens, in spring, in the darkness of the night, the eastern nightingale sings above a rose. But the sweet rose does not feel and does not listen, and sways and slumbers while the nightingale sings its hymn of love. Is it not thus that you sing for some cold beauty? Bethink yourself, O poet: what are you striving towards? She does not listen to the poet, nor does she feel him. You look – she blooms; you call to her – there is no reply.

[1827]

АРИОН

Нас было много на челне;
Иные парус напрягали,
Другие дружно упирали
В глубь мощны веслы. В тишине
На руль склонясь, наш кормщик умный
В молчанье правил грузный челн;
А я – беспечной веры полн, –
Пловцам я пел . . . Вдруг лоно волн
Измял с налету вихорь шумный . . .
Погиб и кормщик и пловец! –
Лишь я, таинственный певец,
На берег выброшен грозою,
Я гимны прежние пою
И ризу влажную мою
Сушу на солнце под скалою.

АНГЕЛ

В дверях эдема ангел нежный
Главой поникшею сиял,
А демон мрачный и мятежный
Над адской бездною летал.

ARION

THERE were many of us in the bark; some of us were tightening the sail, others were plunging the powerful oars into the deep. Calmly leaning on the tiller, our clever helmsman steered the loaded bark in silence; and I – full of carefree faith – I sang to the sailors . . . Suddenly a boisterous gust swooped and rumpled the bosom of the waves . . . Both helmsman and sailor perished! Only I, the mysterious singer, hurled ashore by the storm, sing my former hymns and dry my damp garment in the sun at the foot of a rock.

[1827]

THE ANGEL

AT the gates of Eden stood a gentle angel, with bowed head shining, while a gloomy, restless demon flew over hell's abyss.

Дух отрицанья, дух сомненья
На духа чистого взирал
И жар невольный умиленья
Впервые смутно познавал.

«Прости, – он рек, – тебя я видел,
И ты недаром мне сиял:
Не всё я в небе ненавидел,
Не всё я в мире презирал».

Какая ночь! Мороз трескучий,
На небе ни единой тучи;
Как шитый полог, синий свод
Пестреет частыми звездами.
В домах все темно. У ворот
Затворы с тяжкими замками.
Везде покоится народ;
Утих и шум, и крик торговый;
Лишь только лает страж дворовый
Да цепью звонкою гремит.

The spirit of denial, the spirit of doubt gazed upon the pure spirit and for the first time obscurely felt the instinctive warmth of tenderness.

'Farewell,' he said. 'I have seen you, and not in vain have you shone upon me. Not everything have I hated in heaven, not everything have I despised in the world.'

[1827]

WHAT a night! The frost is brittle-hard and in the sky there is not a single cloud; like an embroidered canopy the deep-blue vault of heaven is densely spangled with stars. All is dark in the houses. On the gates the bolts with their heavy locks are shot. Everywhere the people are at rest; the noise and the shouting of the market-place have died down; only the guardian watchdog barks and rattles its ringing chains.

И вся Москва покойно спит,
Забыв волнение боязни.
А площадь в сумраке ночном
Стоит, полна вчерашней казни.
Мучений свежий след кругом:
Где труп, разрубленный с размаха,
Где столп, где вилы; там котлы,
Остывшей полные смолы;
Здесь опрокинутая плаха;
Торчат железные зубцы,
С костями груды пепла тлеют,
На кольях, скорчась, мертвецы
Оцепенелые чернеют . . .
Недавно кровь со всех сторон
Струею тощей снег багрила,
И подымался томный стон,
Но смерть коснулась к ним как сон,
Свою добычу захватила.
Кто там? Чей конь во весь опор
По грозной площади несется?
Чей свист, чей громкий разговор
Во мраке ночи раздается?
Кто сей? – Кромешник удалой.

And all Moscow sleeps peacefully, having forgotten the thrill of fear, while in the darkness of the night the square is still full of reminders of the executions of the day before. All around there are fresh traces of tortures: here a corpse, chopped in two at one fell swoop, here a pillar, here a fork; there cauldrons full of pitch which has now grown cold; here an overturned executioner's block; iron prongs stick out; heaps of ash and bones smoulder; twisted in agony, the corpses, stiffened, motionless, blacken on the stakes . . . Not long ago thin streams of blood were staining the snow crimson on all sides, and groans of anguish rose, but death touched its victims like sleep and seized its prey. Who's there? Whose horse gallops at full speed over the square of terror? Whose whistle, whose loud talk can be heard in the darkness of the night? Who is this? It is a bold *oprichnik* [member of Ivan the

Спешит, летит он на свиданье,
В его груди кипит желанье.
Он говорит : «Мой конь лихой,
Мой верный конь! лети стрелой!
Скорей, скорей! . . . » Но конь ретивый
Вдруг размахнул плетеной гривой
И стал. Во мгле между столпов
На перекладине дубовой
Качался труп. Ездок суровый
Под ним промчаться был готов,
Но борзый конь под плетью бьется,
Храпит, и фыркает, и рвется
Назад. «Куда? мой конь лихой!
Чего боишься? Что с тобой?
Не мы ли здесь вчера скакали,
Не мы ли яростно топтали,
Усердной местию горя,
Лихих изменников царя?
Не их ли кровию омыты
Твои булатные копыты!
Теперь ужель их не узнал?
Мой борзый конь, мой конь удалый,
Несись, лети! . . . » И конь усталый
В столбы . . . проскакал.

Terrible's bodyguard]. He hastens, flying to a tryst; desire seethes within his breast. He says: 'My swift steed, my true steed! Fly like an arrow! Quick, quick!' But his fiery steed suddenly shook its plaited mane and stood still. In the dark between two pillars on an oaken cross-beam swung a corpse. The stern horseman was prepared to gallop on beneath it, but the swift steed jibs beneath the whip, snorts, neighs, and rears. 'Whither, my swift steed? What do you fear? What is the matter with you? Did we not gallop here yesterday, did we not, burning with zealous vengeance, fiercely trample down the evil traitors of the Tsar? Is it not with their blood that your steel hoofs are washed? Can it be that you have not recognized them now? My swift steed, my dashing steed, rush on, fly on!' And the tired steed galloped on . . . through the pillars . . . (*Unfinished*)
[1827]

Дар напрасный, дар случайный,
Жизнь, зачем ты мне дана?
Иль зачем судьбою тайной
Ты на казнь осуждена?

Кто меня враждебной властью
Из ничтожества возвал,
Душу мне наполнил страстью,
Ум сомненьем взволновал?...

Цели нет передо мною:
Сердце пусто, празден ум,
И томит меня тоскою
Однозвучный жизни шум.

Кобылица молодая,
Честь кавказского таврá,
Что ты мчишься, удалая?
И тебе пришла пора;
Не косись пугливым оком,
Ног на воздух не мечи,
В поле гладком и широком
Своенравно не скачи.

FRUITLESS gift, chance gift, life, why were you given me? Or why were you condemned to death by secret fate?

Who summoned me with hostile power from nothingness, and filled my soul with passion and disturbed my mind with doubt?

There is no goal before me: my heart is empty, my mind is idle, and the monotonous sound of life oppresses me with melancholy.

[1828]

YOUNG mare, pride of the Caucasian brand, why do you gallop, swift and dashing? Now the time has come for you; look not askance with frightened eye, cast not your legs up in the air, run not capriciously about the smooth broad field. Wait; I will force

Погоди; тебя заставлю
И смириться подо мной:
В мерный круг твой бег направлю
Укороченной уздой.

Не пой, красавица, при мне
Ты песен Грузии печальной:
Напоминают мне оне
Другую жизнь и берег дальный.

Увы! напоминают мне
Твои жестокие напевы
И степь, и ночь – и при луне
Черты далекой, бедной девы.

Я призрак милый, роковой,
Тебя увидев, забываю;
Но ты поешь – и предо мной
Его я вновь воображаю.

Не пой, красавица, при мне
Ты песен Грузии печальной:
Напоминают мне оне
Другую жизнь и берег дальный.

you to calm down beneath me: I will direct your course in a
measured circle with shortened bridle.

[1828]

SING not before me, fair maiden, the songs of sad Georgia: they
remind me of another life and a distant shore.

Alas! your harsh melodies remind me of the steppe and the night
– and the features of a poor distant girl in the moonlight.

Seeing you, I forget that sweet fateful phantom; but when you
sing, I imagine it again before me.

Sing not before me, fair maiden, the songs of sad Georgia: they
remind me of another life and a distant shore.

[1828]

УТОПЛЕННИК

Прибежали в избу дети,
Второпях зовут отца:
«Тятя! тятя! наши сети
Притащили мертвеца».
«Врите, врите, бесенята, –
Заворчал на них отец; –
Ох, уж эти мне робята!
Будет вам ужо мертвец!

Суд наедет, отвечай-ка;
С ним я ввек не разберусь;
Делать нечего; хозяйка,
Дай кафтан: уж поплетусь . . .
Где ж мертвец?» – «Вон, тятя, э-вот!›
В самом деле, при реке,
Где разостлан мокрый невод,
Мертвый виден на песке.

Безобразно труп ужасный
Посинел и весь распух.

THE DROWNED MAN

THE children ran into the hut and hastily called their father: 'Father, father! Our nets have dragged up a dead man.' 'You're fibbing, you little devils,' their father growled at them. 'Oh, these children of mine! I'll give you a dead man, indeed!

'The law will descend on us – and I'll be the one to answer for it! I'll never be done with them. Well, can't be helped; wife, give me my *kaftan*: I suppose I'd better go . . . But where's the dead man?' 'There, father, just over there.' And, indeed, by the river's edge, where the damp net lay spread out, the dead man could be seen on the sand.

The dreadful corpse had turned a hideous blue and was all

Горемыка ли несчастный
Погубил свой грешный дух,
Рыболов ли взят волнами,
Али хмельный молодец,
Аль ограбленный ворами
Недогадливый купец?

Мужику какое дело?
Озираясь, он спешит;
Он потопленное тело
В воду за ноги тащит,
И от берега крутого
Оттолкнул его веслом,
И мертвец вниз поплыл снова
За могилой и крестом.

Долго мертвый меж волнами
Плыл качаясь, как живой;
Проводив его глазами,
Наш мужик пошел домой.
«Вы, щенки! за мной ступайте!
Будет вам по калачу,
Да смотрите ж, не болтайте,
А не то поколочу».

swollen. Was it some unhappy wretch who had destroyed his sinful spirit? Was it a fisherman caught by the waves? Or some drunken young fellow, or some slow-witted merchant robbed by thieves?

What does the *muzhik* care? Looking all around him, he hastens; he drags the drowned body by the legs into the water, and pushed it away from the steep bank with an oar, and the dead man floated off again downstream, in search of a grave, in search of a cross.

For long the dead man floated, swaying amidst the waves like a living person; having watched him float away, our *muzhik* set off home. 'Hey, you pups! Follow me! You'll get a bun each; but mind, no blabbing, otherwise you'll get a thrashing.'

В ночь погода зашумела,
Взволновалася река,
Уж лучина догорела
В дымной хате мужика,
Дети спят, хозяйка дремлет,
На полатях муж лежит,
Буря воет; вдруг он внемлет:
Кто-то там в окно стучит.

«Кто там?» – «Эй, впусти, хозяин!» –
«Ну, какая там беда?
Что ты ночью бродишь, Каин?
Черт занес тебя сюда;
Где возиться мне с тобою?
Дома тесно и темно».
И ленивою рукою
Подымает он окно.

Из-за туч луна катится –
Что же? голый перед ним:
С бороды вода струится,
Взор открыт и недвижим,

During the night the weather worsened and the wind whipped up the river; already the splinter has burned out in the *muzhik*'s smoky hut; the children are asleep, the wife slumbers; aloft on his bed of planks the husband lies. The storm howls. Suddenly he hears someone knocking at the window.

'Who's there?' 'Eh, let me in, master!' 'Well, what's the matter there? Why do you wander about at night, Cain? The devil's brought you here; why should I bother with you? Here inside it's crowded and dark.' And with lazy hand he raises the window.

The moon rolls from behind the clouds – what does he see? A naked figure stands before him: water streams from his beard,

Все в нем страшно онемело,
Опустились руки вниз,
И в распухнувшее тело
Раки черные впились.

И мужик окно захлопнул:
Гостя голого узнав,
Так и обмер: «Чтоб ты лопнул!»
Прошептал он, задрожав.
Страшно мысли в нем мешались,
Трясся ночь он напролет,
И до утра всё стучались
Под окном и у ворот.

Есть в народе слух ужасный:
Говорят, что каждый год
С той поры мужик несчастный
В день урочный гостя ждет;
Уж с утра погода злится,
Ночью буря настает,
И утопленник стучится
Под окном и у ворот.

his eyes are open and immobile; everything about him is fearfully lifeless – his hands hang down, and black crabs have dug into his swollen body.

And the *muzhik* slammed the window: when he recognized the naked visitor, he was struck with terror: 'A plague upon you!' he whispered, trembling. His thoughts became confused with terror; the whole night long he shuddered, and till the dawn the knocking went on beneath the window and at the gate.

There is a fearful tale among the people: it is said that since that time every year the wretched *muzhik* awaits his visitor on the appointed day; from morning on the weather rages; at night there comes a storm; and the drowned man knocks beneath the window and at the gate.

[1828]

Ворон к ворону летит,
Ворон ворону кричит:
Ворон! где б нам отобедать?
Как бы нам о том проведать?

Ворон ворону в ответ:
Знаю, будет нам обед;
В чистом поле под ракитой
Богатырь лежит убитый.

Кем убит и отчего,
Знает сокол лишь его,
Да кобылка вороная,
Да хозяйка молодая.

Сокол в рощу улетел,
На кобылку недруг сел,
А хозяйка ждет милóго,
Не убитого, живого.

RAVEN flies to raven, raven cries to raven: Raven, where are we
to have our dinner? How shall we find out about it?

Raven in reply to raven: I know we shall have our dinner; in the
open plain beneath a willow a *bogatyr* lies killed.

By whom he was killed, why he was killed – only his falcon
knows, and his black mare, and his young wife.

The falcon has flown off into the wood, the enemy has mounted
the mare, but the wife awaits her beloved, not killed, but alive.

[1828]

На холмах Грузии лежит ночная мгла;
  Шумит Арагва предо мною.
Мне грустно и легко; печаль моя светла;
  Печаль моя полна тобою,
Тобой, одной тобой . . . Унынья моего
  Ничто не мучит, не тревожит,
И сердце вновь горит и любит – оттого,
  Что не любить оно не может.

Жил на свете рыцарь бедный,
  Молчаливый и простой,
С виду сумрачный и бледный,
  Духом смелый и прямой.

Он имел одно виденье,
  Непостижное уму,
И глубоко впечатленье
  В сердце врезалось ему.

Путешествуя в Женеву,
  На дороге у креста
Видел он Марию Деву,
  Матерь Господа Христа.

NIGHT'S darkness lies upon the hills of Georgia; I hear the sound of the Aragva before me. I am sad and serene; my sorrow is bright; my sorrow is full of you, of you alone . . . Nothing disturbs or troubles my melancholy, and my heart again burns and loves – because it cannot help but love.

[1829]

ONCE upon a time there lived a poor knight, taciturn and simple, gloomy and pale of countenance, bold and true of spirit.

He had a single vision beyond all human understanding, and a deep impression was engraved upon his heart.

While travelling to Geneva, he saw by a roadside crucifix the Virgin Mary, Mother of the Lord Christ.

47

С той поры, сгорев душою,
Он на женщин не смотрел,
И до гроба ни с одною
Молвить слова не хотел.

С той поры стальной решетки
Он с лица не подымал
И себе на шею четки
Вместо шарфа привязал.

Несть мольбы Отцу, ни Сыну,
Ни Святому Духу ввек
Не случилось паладину,
Странный был он человек.

Проводил он целы ночи
Перед ликом Пресвятой,
Устремив к ней скорбны очи,
Тихо слезы лья рекой.

Полон верой и любовью,
Верен набожной мечте,
Ave, Mater Dei кровью
Написал он на щите.

From then on, his soul aflame, he did not look upon a woman, and he decided not to say a word to any woman till the grave.

From that time he did not raise the steel visor from his face, and he tied upon his neck a rosary in the place of a scarf.

Never once did the paladin pray to Father or to Son or to Holy Spirit; he was indeed a strange man.

He spent whole nights before the image of the Most Holy Mother, with mournful eyes fixed on her, silently shedding streams of tears.

Full of faith and love, true to his devout dream, he wrote *Ave, Mater Dei* in blood upon his shield.

Между тем как паладины
Ввстречу трепетным врагам
По равнинам Палестины
Мчались, именуя дам,

Lumen coelum, sancta Rosa!
Восклицал всех громче он,
И гнала его угроза
Мусульман со всех сторон.

Возвратясь в свой замок дальный,
Жил он строго заключен,
Все влюбленный, все печальный,
Без причастья умер он;

Между тем как он кончался,
Дух лукавый подоспел,
Душу рыцаря сбирался
Бес тащить уж в свой предел:

Он-де Богу не молился,
Он не ведал-де поста,
Не путем-де волочился
Он за матушкой Христа.

While the paladins galloped across the plains of Palestine to meet
their trembling enemies, calling out their ladies' names,

Louder than them all he shouted '*Lumen coelum, sancta Rosa!*',
and his menacing appearance scattered the Mussulmans on all
sides.

Returning to his distant castle, he lived in strict seclusion, still
enamoured, still sad; he died without the Sacrament.

Just as he lay dying, an evil spirit came to him; the demon
intended to drag the knight's soul into his own domain.

He had not prayed to God, so said the demon, he had not kept
the fasts; unduly had he courted the Mother of Christ.

Но Пречистая сердечно
Заступилась за него
И впустила в царство вечно
Паладина своего.

Зима. Что делать нам в деревне? Я встречаю
Слугу, несущего мне утром чашку чаю,
Вопросами: тепло ль? утихла ли метель?
Пороша есть иль нет? и можно ли постель
Покинуть для седла, иль лучше до обеда
Возиться с старыми журналами соседа?
Пороша. Мы встаем, и тотчас на коня,
И рысью по полю при первом свете дня;
Арапники в руках, собаки вслед за нами;
Глядим на бледный снег прилежными глазами;
Кружимся, рыскаем и поздней уж порой,
Двух зайцев протравив, являемся домой.
Куда как весело! Вот вечер: вьюга воет;
Свеча темно горит; стесняясь, сердце ноет;
По капле, медленно глотаю скуки яд.

But the Most Pure Mother devoutly interceded for him and admitted her paladin into the everlasting kingdom.

[1829]

It is winter. What shall we do in the country? I question the servant bringing me my cup of tea in the morning: is it warm? Has the snowstorm died down? Is there powder-snow upon the ground, or not? And can I leave my bed for the saddle, or would it be better to browse through my neighbour's old journals till dinner time? There is powder-snow. We get up and straightway mount our horses and trot through the fields at the first light of day, our crops in our hands, hounds following behind us; with attentive eyes we watch the pale snow; we circle, scour the land, and, at a late hour, having missed two hares, come home. How gay! Now it is evening: the blizzard howls; the candle burns dimly; the heart contracts and aches; drop by drop, I slowly swallow the

Читать хочу; глаза над буквами скользят,
А мысли далеко . . . Я книгу закрываю;
Беру перо, сижу; насильно вырываю
У музы дремлющей несвязные слова.
Ко звуку звук нейдет . . . Теряю все права
Над рифмой, над моей прислужницею стран-
    ной:
Стих вяло тянется, холодный и туманный.
Усталый, с лирою я прекращаю спор,
Иду в гостиную; там слышу разговор
О близких выборах, о сахарном заводе;
Хозяйка хмурится в подобие погоде,
Стальными спицами проворно шевеля,
Иль про червонного гадает короля.
Тоска! Так день за днем идет в уединенье!
Но если под вечер в печальное селенье,
Когда за шашками сижу я в уголке,
Приедет издали в кибитке иль возке
Нежданная семья: старушка, две девицы
(Две белокурые, две стройные сестрицы), –
Как оживляется глухая сторона!
Как жизнь, о Боже мой, становится полна!

poison of boredom. I try to read; my eyes slide over the letters, while my thoughts are far away . . . I shut the book; I take my pen and sit; forcibly I tear incoherent words from my slumbering muse. Sound does not match with sound. I lose all control over rhyme, over my strange handmaiden. Limply my verse drags on, cold and misty. Tired, I stop my struggle with my lyre and go into the drawing-room; there I hear a conversation about the impending elections, about the sugar-factory; the mistress of the house frowns just like the weather, nimbly plying her steel knitting-needles or telling fortunes by the king of hearts. Boredom! Thus, in seclusion, day follows day! But if towards the evening, when I sit in a corner playing draughts, some unexpected family – an old woman and two girls (two fair-haired, shapely sisters) – drives into our sad village in a carriage or a covered sledge, then how our dark part of the world is livened up! How life, my God, becomes full!

Сначала косвенно-внимательные взоры,
Потом слов несколько, потом и разговоры,
А там и дружный смех, и песни вечерком,
И вальсы резвые, и шепот за столом,
И взоры томные, и ветреные речи,
На узкой лестнице замедленные встречи;
И дева в сумерки выходит на крыльцо:
Открыты шея, грудь, и вьюга ей в лицо!
Но бури севера не вредны русской розе.
Как жарко поцелуй пылает на морозе!
Как дева русская свежа в пыли снегов!

Брожу ли я вдоль улиц шумных,
Вхожу ль во многолюдный храм,
Сижу ль меж юношей безумных,
Я предаюсь моим мечтам.

Я говорю: промчатся годы,
И сколько здесь ни видно нас,
Мы все сойдем под вечны своды –
И чей-нибудь уж близок час.

At first there are attentive side-glances, then a few words, then conversations too, then afterwards friendly laughter and songs in the evening and lively waltzes, and whispering at table, and languid glances and frivolous words, and lingering meetings on the narrow staircase; and at twilight the girl goes out on to the porch; her neck and bosom are uncovered, and the snowstorm blows into her face! But the storms of the north are not harmful to the Russian rose. How hotly burns a kiss in frosty weather! How fresh a Russian girl is in the powder of snow!

[1829]

When I wander along noisy streets, or enter a crowded church, or sit amongst hot-headed youths, I indulge in my daydreams.

I say to myself: the years will rush by, and however many of us may here be seen, we will all go down beneath the eternal vaults – and someone's hour is already close.

Гляжу ль на дуб уединенный,
Я мыслю: патриарх лесов
Переживет мой век забвенный,
Как пережил он век отцов.

Младенца ль милого ласкаю,
Уже я думаю: прости!
Тебе я место уступаю:
Мне время тлеть, тебе цвести.

День каждый, каждую годину
Привык я думой провождать,
Грядущей смерти годовщину
Меж их стараясь угадать.

И где мне смерть пошлет судьбина?
В бою ли, в странствии, в волнах?
Или соседняя долина
Мой примет охладелый прах?

И хоть бесчувственному телу
Равно повсюду истлевать,
Но ближе к милому пределу
Мне все б хотелось почивать.

When I gaze upon a solitary oak, I think: the patriarch of the forests will outlive my forgotten age, just as it outlived the age of my fathers.

When I caress a dear infant, I am already thinking: farewell! I yield my place to you: it is time for me to decay and for you to blossom.

I am accustomed to say farewell to each day, each year, with a thought, trying to guess which one among them will be the anniversary of my coming death.

And where will fate send me death? In battle, in my wanderings, among the waves? Or will the neighbouring valley receive my cold dust?

And although it is all one to the feelingless body wherever it may decay, I would still like to rest nearer to those places which I love.

И пусть у гробового входа
Младая будет жизнь играть,
И равнодушная природа
Красою вечною сиять.

ОБВАЛ

Дробясь о мрачные скалы,
Шумят и пенятся валы,
И надо мной кричат орлы,
    И ропщет бор,
И блещут средь волнистой мглы
    Вершины гор.

Оттоль сорвался раз обвал,
И с тяжким грохотом упал,
И всю теснину между скал
    Загородил,
И Терека могущий вал
    Остановил.

And at the entrance to the grave let young life play and let indifferent nature shine with everlasting beauty.

[1829]

THE AVALANCHE

SHATTERING against the gloomy crags, the waves roar and foam, and above me eagles cry and the pinewood murmurs, and the mountain peaks sparkle amidst the undulating mist.

Thence an avalanche once crashed down and fell with a thunderous roar, and blocked up the whole gorge between the crags and stopped the Terek's mighty wave.

Вдруг, истощась и присмирев,
О Терек, ты прервал свой рев;
Но задних волн упорный гнев
    Прошиб снега . . .
Ты затопил, освирепев,
    Свои брега.

И долго прорванный обвал
Неталой грудою лежал,
И Терек злой под ним бежал,
    И пылью вод
И шумной пеной орошал
    Ледяный свод.

И путь по нем широкий шел:
И конь скакал, и влекся вол,
И своего верблюда вел
    Степной купец,
Где ныне мчится лишь Эол,
    Небес жилец.

Suddenly, exhausted, you quietened down, O Terek, and stilled your roar; but the stubborn wrath of the waves behind broke through the snows . . . Bursting into fury, you flooded your banks.

And long the sundered avalanche lay in an unmelted heap, and the furious Terek flowed beneath it, and with its waters' dusty spray and noisy foam washed the icy vault.

And a wide path led over it: and along it a horse galloped, and an ox plodded, and a merchant of the steppes led his camel, where now only rushes Aeolus, the dweller in the heavens.

[1829]

МОНАСТЫРЬ НА КАЗБЕКЕ

Высоко над семьею гор,
Казбек, твой царственный шатер
Сияет вечными лучами.
Твой монастырь за облаками,
Как в небе реющий ковчег,
Парит, чуть видный, над горами.

Далекий, вожделенный брег!
Туда б, сказав прости ущелью,
Подняться к вольной вышине!
Туда б, в заоблачную келью,
В соседство Бога скрыться мне!...

Когда твои младые лета
Позорит шумная молва,
И ты по приговору света
На честь утратила права;

Один среди толпы холодной
Твои страданья я делю

THE MONASTERY ON MOUNT KAZBEK

HIGH above the family of mountains your royal tent, O Kazbek, shines with everlasting rays. Your monastery beyond the clouds, scarce visible, soars over the mountains like an ark hovering in the sky.

O distant, longed-for shore! Thither, having bid the ravine farewell, I would arise to the free boundless heights! Thither, to a cell beyond the clouds, to the close proximity of God, I would escape!

[1829]

WHEN noisy rumour defames your youthful years, and in the judgement of the world you have lost all right to honour,

Then I alone, amidst the unfeeling crowd, share your sufferings

И за тебя мольбой бесплодной
Кумир бесчувственный молю.

Но свет . . . Жестоких осуждений
Не изменяет он своих:
Он не карает заблуждений,
Но тайны требует для них.

Достойны равного презренья
Его тщеславная любовь
И лицемерные гоненья:
К забвенью сердце приготовь;

Не пей мучительной отравы;
Оставь блестящий, душный круг;
Оставь безумные забавы:
Тебе один остался друг.

Что в имени тебе моем?
Оно умрет, как шум печальный
Волны, плеснувшей в берег дальный,
Как звук ночной в лесу глухом.

and with fruitless prayer entreat the callous idol on your behalf.

But the world . . . the world does not revoke its harsh censure: it does not punish misdemeanours, but demands that they be secret.

Worthy of equal contempt are its vainglorious love and its hypocritical persecution: prepare your heart for oblivion;

Drink not the agonizing poison; quit your brilliant stifling circle; quit the senseless amusements: you have but one friend left.

[1829]

[*Written in answer to a request to inscribe his name in the album of the Polish beauty Karolina Sobańska.*]

WHAT need have you of my name? It will die, like the sad sound of a wave which has splashed on a distant shore, like the sounds of night in a dense forest.

Оно на памятном листке
Оставит мертвый след, подобный
Узору надписи надгробной
На непонятном языке.

Что в нем? Забытое давно
В волненьях новых и мятежных,
Твоей душе не даст оно
Воспоминаний чистых, нежных.

Но в день печали, в тишине,
Произнеси его тоскуя;
Скажи: есть память обо мне,
Есть в мире сердце, где живу я . . .

Когда в объятия мои
Твой стройный стан я заключаю
И речи нежные любви
Тебе с восторгом расточаю,
Безмолвна, от стесненных рук
Освобождая стан свой гибкой,
Ты отвечаешь, милый друг,
Мне недоверчивой улыбкой;

On the page of your album it will leave a dead mark, like the tracery of an epitaph in an unknown tongue.

What is there in my name? Long forgotten amidst new and stormy emotions, it will not give your soul pure, tender memories.

But on a day of sorrow, when all is peaceful, utter my name with melancholy. Just say: there is a memory of me, in the world there is a heart in which I live.

[1830]

WHEN I clasp your slender body in my embrace, and with rapture pour out tender words of love to you, silently you free your supple body from my encircling arms and, dear friend, answer me with a

Прилежно в памяти храня
Измен печальные преданья,
Ты без участья и вниманья
Уныло слушаешь меня . . .
Кляну коварные старанья
Преступной юности моей
И встреч условных ожиданья
В садах, в безмолвии ночей.
Кляну речей любовных шепот,
Стихов таинственный напев,
И ласки легковерных дев,
И слезы их, и поздний ропот.

ПОЭТУ

Поэт! не дорожи любовию народной.
Восторженных похвал пройдет минутный шум;
Услышишь суд глупца и смех толпы холодной,
Но ты останься тверд, спокоен и угрюм.

Ты царь: живи один. Дорогою свободной
Иди, куда влечет тебя свободный ум,

mistrustful smile; diligently harbouring in your memory sad recollections of infidelities, despondently you listen to me without interest or attention . . . I curse the sly endeavours of my wicked youth and the hours spent waiting for trysts in gardens in the silence of the night. I curse the whispered words of love, the mysterious melody of verses and the caresses of easily-persuadable young girls, and their tears and their belated plaints.

[1830]

TO THE POET

POET! Prize not the people's love. The brief noise of rapturous praise will pass; you will hear the judgement of the foolish man and the laughter of the insensitive crowd – but remain firm, calm, and sombre.

You are a tsar: live alone. Go along your free path, whither your

Усовершенствуя плоды любимых дум,
Не требуя наград за подвиг благородный.

Они в самом тебе. Ты сам свой высший суд;
Всех строже оценить умеешь ты свой труд.
Ты им доволен ли, взыскательный художник?

Доволен? Так пускай толпа его бранит
И плюет на алтарь, где твой огонь горит,
И в детской резвости колеблет твой треножник.

ЭЛЕГИЯ

Безумных лет угасшее веселье
Мне тяжело, как смутное похмелье.
Но, как вино – печаль минувших дней
В моей душе чем старе, тем сильней.
Мой путь уныл. Сулит мне труд и горе
Грядущего волнуемое море.

free mind calls you, perfecting the fruits of your cherished
thoughts, asking no rewards for your noble exploit.

Rewards are within yourself. You yourself are your highest
judge; you are able to appraise your work more strictly than anyone. Are you satisfied with it, exacting artist?

Are you satisfied? Then let the crowd abuse your work and spit
upon the altar where your fire burns and shake your tripod in their
childish gambols.

[1830]

ELEGY

THE burnt-out gaiety of my reckless years oppresses me like the
dull aftermath of drunkenness. But, like wine, the older is the
sorrow of bygone days within my soul, the stronger it becomes.
My path is joyless. The surging sea of the future foretokens toil
and sorrow for me.

Но не хочу, о други, умирать;
Я жить хочу, чтоб мыслить и страдать;
И ведаю, мне будут наслажденья
Меж горестей, забот и треволненья:
Порой опять гармонией упьюсь,
Над вымыслом слезами обольюсь,
И может быть — на мой закат печальный
Блеснет любовь улыбкою прощальной.

Глухой глухого звал к суду судьи глухого,
Глухой кричал: «Моя им сведена корова!» —
«Помилуй, — возопил глухой тому в ответ, —
Сей пустошью владел еще покойный дед».
    Судья решил: «Чтоб не было разврата,
Жените молодца, хоть девка виновата».

But, O my friends, I do not wish to die; I wish to live, in order to think and suffer. I know that I shall taste delights midst sorrows, cares, and tribulations: at times again I shall feel rapture in harmony, shed tears of joy at the creation of my fantasy, and perhaps at the sad sunset of my days love will flash a parting smile.

[1830]

A DEAF man summoned a deaf man to be judged by a deaf judge. The deaf man shouted: 'My cow has been stolen by him!' 'Indeed!' yelled the deaf man in reply. 'Why, my late grandfather already owned that waste plot.' The judge decided: 'So that there should be no impropriety, make the young man marry her, although the girl's to blame.'

[1830]

Я здесь, Инезилья,
Я здесь под окном.
Объята Севилья
И мраком и сном.

Исполнен отвагой,
Окутан плащом,
С гитарой и шпагой
Я здесь под окном.

Ты спишь ли? Гитарой
Тебя разбужу.
Проснется ли старый,
Мечом уложу.

Шелковые петли
К окошку привесь . . .
Что медлишь? . . . Уж нет ли
Соперника здесь? . . .

Я здесь, Инезилья,
Я здесь под окном.
Объята Севилья
И мраком и сном.

I AM here, Inesilla, I am here beneath your window. Seville is enveloped in darkness and sleep.

Filled with boldness, wrapped in my cloak, with my guitar and my sword, I am here beneath your window.

Are you asleep? I will wake you with my guitar. If the old man awakens, I will kill him with my sword.

Hang a silken loop to your window . . . Why do you tarry? There's surely not a rival here?

I am here, Inesilla, I am here beneath your window. Seville is enveloped in darkness and sleep.

[1830]

СТИХИ, СОЧИНЕННЫЕ НОЧЬЮ
ВО ВРЕМЯ БЕССОННИЦЫ

Мне не спится, нет огня;
Всюду мрак и сон докучный.
Ход часов лишь однозвучный
Раздается близ меня,
Парки бабье лепетанье,
Спящей ночи трепетанье,
Жизни мышья беготня . . .
Что тревожишь ты меня?
Что ты значишь, скучный шепот?
Укоризна, или ропот
Мной утраченного дня?
От меня чего ты хочешь?
Ты зовешь или пророчишь?
Я понять тебя хочу,
Смысла я в тебе ищу . . .

Пред испанкой благородной
Двое рыцарей стоят.
Оба смело и свободно
В очи прямо ей глядят.

LINES WRITTEN AT NIGHT DURING INSOMNIA

I CANNOT sleep, there is no light; all around is darkness and
irksome sleep. Only the monotonous ticking of the clock can be
heard near me, only the old wives' chatter of Fate, the trembling of
the sleeping night, the mouse-like scurrying of life . . . Why do
you disturb me? What do you mean, tedious whispers? Is it the
day that I have wasted reproaching me or murmuring? What do
you want from me? Are you calling me or are you prophesying? I
want to understand you, I seek a meaning in you . . .

[1830]

BEFORE a noble Spanish woman stand two knights. Both look her
straight in the eyes, boldly and freely. Both are radiant with beauty,

Блещут оба красотою,
Оба сердцем горячи,
Оба мощною рукою
Оперлися на мечи.

Жизни им она дороже
И, как слава, им мила;
Но один ей мил – кого же
Дева сердцем избрала?
«Кто, реши, любим тобою?» –
Оба деве говорят
И с надеждой молодою
В очи прямо ей глядят.

МОЯ РОДОСЛОВНАЯ

Смеясь жестоко над собратом,
Писаки русские толпой
Меня зовут аристократом.
Смотри, пожалуй, вздор какой!
Не офицер я, не асессор,
Я по кресту не дворянин,
Не академик, не профессор;
Я просто русский мещанин.

both are passionate of heart, both lean with powerful arms upon their swords.

To them she is dearer than life, and they love her as they love glory; but one she loves – Which one has the maiden chosen in her heart? 'Who is loved by you? Decide!' both say to the maiden; and with youthful hope they look her straight in the eyes.

[1830]

MY GENEALOGY

LAUGHING cruelly at their brother-writer, the Russian scribblers, in a throng, call me an aristocrat. Pray, look what nonsense! I am not an officer, I am not an assessor [a rank in the Civil Service]; nor am I a nobleman who owes his nobility to decorations; I am not an academician, nor am I a professor; I am simply a Russian bourgeois.

Понятна мне времен превратность,
Не прекословлю, право, ей:
У нас нова рожденьем знатность,
И чем новее, тем знатней.
Родов дряхлеющих обломок
(И по несчастью, не один),
Бояр старинных я потомок;
Я, братцы, мелкий мещанин.

Не торговал мой дед блинами,
Не ваксил царских сапогов,
Не пел с придворными дьячками,
В князья не прыгал из хохлов,
И не был беглым он солдатом
Австрийских пудреных дружин;
Так мне ли быть аристократом?
Я, слава Богу, мещанин.

I understand the vicissitude of times; indeed, I do not contradict
it: our aristocracy is new in lineage, and the newer the more
aristocratic. A fragment of degenerating stock (and not, alas, the
only one), I am the descendant of ancient boyars; I, my friends,
am a petty bourgeois.

My grandfather did not trade in pancakes [a reference to the
original profession of Prince A. D. Menshikov, Peter I's close
collaborator], nor did he polish the Tsar's boots [Count I. P.
Kutaysov, the valet of Paul I], nor did he sing with the court
choristers [Count A. G. Razumovsky, before becoming the Empress
Elizabeth's lover and then husband, was a court chorister], he did
not jump from Ukrainian peasant to prince [A. A. Bezborodko,
who was given the title of prince by Catherine II], nor was he a
runaway soldier of the powdered Austrian armies [the great-
grandfather of General P. A. Kleynmikhel]. Well then, am I to be
an aristocrat? I, thank God, am a bourgeois.

Мой предок Рача мышцей бранной
Святому Невскому служил;
Его потомство гнев венчанный,
Иван IV пощадил.
Водились Пушкины с царями;
Из них был славен не один,
Когда тягался с поляками
Нижегородский мещанин.

Смирив крамолу и коварство
И ярость бранных непогод,
Когда Романовых на царство
Звал в грамоте своей народ,
Мы к оной руку приложили,
Нас жаловал страдальца сын.
Бывало, нами дорожили;
Бывало . . . но – я мещанин.

Упрямства дух нам всем подгадил:
В родню свою неукротим,
С Петром мой пращур не поладил
И был за то повешен им.

My ancestor Racha served Saint [Alexandr] Nevsky with war-like arm; his descendants were spared by Wrath enthroned – Ivan IV [the Terrible]. Pushkins associated with Tsars; many a one amongst them won glory when the bourgeois from Nizhny Novgorod [Kuzma Minin, a butcher, who organized the army which drove the Poles from Moscow in 1612] measured swords with the Poles.

Having subdued dissension and perfidy and the fury of the storms of war, when the people called the Romanovs to the throne in their petition, we set our hand to it too, and the son of the martyr [Tsar Mikhail, whose father suffered under Boris Godunov] showed us his favour. There was a time when we were held in high esteem; there was a time . . . But – I am a bourgeois.

The spirit of stubbornness got us all into trouble: indomitable like the rest of his family, my ancestor did not hit it off with Peter, and was therefore hanged by him. [Fedor Pushkin, executed in

Его пример будь нам наукой:
Не любит споров властелин.
Счастлив князь Яков Долгорукой,
Умен покорный мещанин.

Мой дед, когда мятеж поднялся
Средь петергофского двора,
Как Миних, верен оставался
Паденью третьего Петра.
Попали в честь тогда Орловы,
А дед мой в крепость, в карантин,
И присмирел наш род суровый,
И я родился мещанин.

Под гербовой моей печатью
Я кипу грамот схоронил
И не якшаюсь с новой знатью,
И крови спесь угомонил.
Я грамотей и стихотворец,
Я Пушкин просто, не Мусин,
Я не богач, не царедворец,
Я сам большой: я мещанин.

1697.] Let his example be a lesson to us: sovereigns are not fond of arguments. Happy was Prince Yakov Dolgoruky [a friend and collaborator of Peter I], clever – the submissive bourgeois.

When rebellion arose in the court of Peterhof, my grandfather, like Minikh, remained true to Peter III in his fall [both L. A. Pushkin and Field-marshal Minikh attempted to support Peter III and resist Catherine II in the court upheaval of 1762]. At that time the Orlovs got honour and glory, while my grandfather got into prison and into quarantine, and our stern kin then quietened down; and I was born a bourgeois.

Beneath my heraldic seal I have buried a heap of documents, and I do not hobnob with the new aristocracy, and I have subdued the arrogance of my blood; I'm just a writer and a poet, I'm simply Pushkin, not Musin [the Musin-Pushkin branch of the family was given the title of Count], I am not a rich man, not a courtier; I am my own master: I am a bourgeois.

Post Scriptum

Решил Фиглярин, сидя дома,
Что черный дед мой Ганнибал
Был куплен за бутылку рома
И в руки шкиперу попал.

Сей шкипер был тот шкипер славный,
Кем наша двинулась земля,
Кто придал мощно бег державный
Рулю родного корабля.

Сей шкипер деду был доступен,
И сходно купленный арап
Возрос усерден, неподкупен,
Царю наперсник, а не раб.

И был отец он Ганнибала,
Пред кем средь чесменских пучин
Громада кораблей вспылала,
И пал впервые Наварин.

Post Scriptum

Figlyarin [Pushkin's thinly disguised name for his enemy, the journalist Bulgarin, who had written an article about a poet in Spanish America who traced his ancestry to a Negro prince, whereas in fact the poet's ancestor had been bought by a sea-captain for a bottle of rum] decided, while sitting at home, that my black grandfather Gannibal had been bought for a bottle of rum and had fallen into the hands of a skipper.

This skipper was that same glorious skipper by whom our land was brought to life, who in his might gave majestic impulse to the helm of our native ship [i.e. Peter I].

My grandfather [in fact, great-great-grandfather, Abram] was close to this skipper, and like a purchased Negro he grew up zealous, incorruptible, a confidant of the Tsar, and not a slave.

And he was the father of the Gannibal before whom in the midst of the deeps of Chesme Bay the mass of ships burst into flame, and before whom Navarino first fell. [Ivan Abramovich Gannibal, the brother of Pushkin's maternal grandfather, took part in the battles of Navarino and Chesme Bay, 1770.]

Решил Фиглярин вдохновенный:
Я во дворянстве мещанин.
Что ж он в семье своей почтенной?
Он?... он в Мещанской дворянин.

КЛЕВЕТНИКАМ РОССИИ

О чем шумите вы, народные витии?
Зачем анафемой грозите вы России?
Что возмутило вас? волнения Литвы?
Оставьте: это спор славян между собою,
Домашний, старый спор, уж взвешенный
    судьбою,
Вопрос, которого не разрешите вы.

Уже давно между собою
Враждуют эти племена;
Не раз клонилась под грозою
То их, то наша сторона.

Inspired Figlyarin has decided that I am a bourgeois nobleman.
But what is he, in his highly-respected family? He? He is a
Bourgeois Street nobleman. [The brothel centre in St Petersburg:
Bulgarin was married to a prostitute, the niece of a brothel-keeper.]
                                                            [1830]

TO THE SLANDERERS OF RUSSIA
[*Written during the Polish rebellion of 1831, in answer to pro-Polish
utterances made by Lafayette and other deputies in the French
Chamber and by French journalists.*]
WHAT are you clamouring about, bards of the people? Why do
you threaten Russia with your curses? What has aroused you? The
disturbances in Lithuania? Leave all that alone: it is a quarrel of
Slavs amongst themselves, an old domestic quarrel already weighed
by Fate, a question which you will not solve.
  For long these peoples have been warring amongst themselves;
now their side, now our side has often bowed down beneath the

Кто устоит в неравном споре:
Кичливый лях, иль верный росс?
Славянские ль ручьи сольются в русском море?
Оно ль иссякнет? вот вопрос.

Оставьте нас: вы не читали
Сии кровавые скрижали;
Вам непонятна, вам чужда
Сия семейная вражда;
Для вас безмолвны Кремль и Прага;
Бессмысленно прельщает вас
Борьбы отчаянной отвага –
И ненавидите вы нас . . .

За что ж? ответствуйте: за то ли,
Что на развалинах пылающей Москвы
Мы не признали наглой воли
Того, под кем дрожали вы?
За то ль, что в бездну повалили
Мы тяготеющий над царствами кумир
И нашей кровью искупили
Европы вольность, честь и мир? . . .

storm. Who will survive in the unequal conflict – the arrogant Pole
or the true Russian? Shall Slav streams merge in the Russian sea?
Shall it dry up? That is the question.

Leave us alone: you have not read these bloody tables; this
family animosity is incomprehensible and strange to you; for you
the Kremlin and Praga [a suburb of Warsaw] are silent; you are
senselessly attracted by all that is valiant in this desperate struggle
– And you hate us . . .

And for what? Answer! Is it because in the ruins of blazing
Moscow we did not recognize the insolent will of him beneath
whom you trembled? Is it because we hurled into the abyss the
idol which towered threateningly over kingdoms, and with our
blood atoned for the freedom, honour, and peace of Europe?

Вы грозны на словах – попробуйте на деле!
Иль старый богатырь, покойный на постеле,
Не в силах завинтить свой измаильский штык?
Иль русского царя уже бессильно слово?
   Иль нам с Европой спорить ново?
   Иль русский от побед отвык?
Иль мало нас? Или от Перми до Тавриды,
От финских хладных скал до пламенной Кол-
     хиды,
    От потрясенного Кремля
    До стен недвижного Китая,
    Стальной щетиною сверкая,
    Не встанет русская земля? . . .
    Так высылайте ж к нам, витии,
    Своих озлобленных сынов:
    Есть место им в полях России,
    Среди нечуждых им гробов.

You menace us with words – just try to act! Is then the old
bogatyr [hero of Russian epic poems], now resting on his bed, not
strong enough to screw on his Ismailian bayonet? [The Turkish
fortress of Ismail was captured by Suvorov in 1790.] Is then the
word of the Russian Tsar already powerless? Is it then new for us
to argue with Europe? Has the Russian then grown unaccustomed
to victories? Are there then too few of us? From Perm to
Tavrida, from the chill Finnish crags to flaming Colchis, from the
shaken Kremlin to the walls of immovable China, shall not the
Russian land arise with steel bristles flashing? Then send us your
embittered sons, O bards: there is room for them in the fields of
Russia, in the midst of graves not unknown to them.

[1831]

ЭХО

Ревет ли зверь в лесу глухом,
Трубит ли рог, гремит ли гром,
Поет ли дева за холмом –
  На всякий звук
Свой отклик в воздухе пустом
  Родишь ты вдруг.

Ты внемлешь грохоту громов,
И гласу бури и валов,
И крику сельских пастухов –
  И шлешь ответ;
Тебе ж нет отзыва . . . Таков
  И ты, поэт!

Не дай мне Бог сойти с ума.
Нет, легче посох и сума;
  Нет, легче труд и глад.
Не то, чтоб разумом моим
Я дорожил; не то, чтоб с ним
  Расстаться был не рад:

THE ECHO

SHOULD a beast roar in the dense forest, a horn sound, thunder peal, a maiden sing beyond the hill – to every sound you at once bring forth your response in the empty air.

  You listen to the rumble of thunder and to the voice of the storm and the waves and to the cries of the village shepherds – and you send an answer; but to you there is no answering echo . . . Such is your nature too, O poet!

[1831]

GOD grant that I go not mad. No, easier to bear would be the vagabond's staff and scrip; easier toil and hunger. It is not that I value my mind; not that I would not be glad to part with it:

72

Когда б оставили меня
На воле, как бы резво я
   Пустился в темный лес!
Я пел бы в пламенном бреду,
Я забывался бы в чаду
   Нестройных, чудных грез.

И я б заслушивался волн,
И я глядел бы, счастья полн,
   В пустые небеса;
И силен, волен был бы я,
Как вихорь, роющий поля,
   Ломающий леса.

Да вот беда: сойди с ума,
И страшен будешь как чума,
   Как раз тебя запрут,
Посадят на цепь дурака
И сквозь решетку как зверка
   Дразнить тебя придут.

А ночью слышать буду я
Не голос яркий соловья,

Were I to be left in freedom, how swiftly would I run into the
dark forest! I would sing in fiery frenzy, I would abandon myself
in the fumes of wondrous, incoherent dreams.

And to my heart's content I would listen to the waves, and full
of happiness I would gaze at the empty heavens; and I would be
strong and free, like a gust of wind tearing over fields and smashing
down forests.

But here's the trouble: go mad, and men will fear you like the
plague and straightway lock you up and put you on the madman's
chain, and come and tease you through the bars as if you were a
small animal.

And at night I would not hear the clear voice of the nightingale

Не шум глухой дубров –
А крик товарищей моих,
Да брань смотрителей ночных,
Да визг, да звон оков.

Я думал, сердце позабыло
Способность легкую страдать,
Я говорил: тому, что было,
Уж не бывать! уж не бывать!
Прошли восторги, и печали,
И легковерные мечты . . .
Но вот опять затрепетали
Пред мощной властью красоты.

Отцы пустынники и жены непорочны,
Чтоб сердцем возлетать во области заочны,
Чтоб укреплять его средь дольних бурь и битв,
Сложили множество божественных молитв;

or the dull rustle of the leafy groves – but the screams of my companions and the curses of the night wardens, the shrieks and the rattle of chains.

[1833]

I THOUGHT my heart had forgotten the easy ability to suffer, and I said: what is past shall be no more! shall be no more! Gone are the raptures and the sorrows, and the dreams which I believed in all too easily . . . But lo, they have begun to stir again, before the mighty power of beauty.

[1835]

DESERT fathers and virtuous women, in order to fly up in their hearts to the invisible realms, in order to strengthen their hearts midst earthly storms and battles, composed a multitude of divine

Но ни одна из них меня не умиляет,
Как та, которую священник повторяет
Во дни печальные Великого поста;
Всех чаще мне она приходит на уста
И падшего крепит неведомою силой:
Владыко дней моих! дух праздности унылой,
Любоначалия, змеи сокрытой сей,
И празднословия не дай душе моей.
Но дай мне зреть мои, о Боже, прегрешенья,
Да брат мой от меня не примет осужденья,
И дух смирения, терпения, любви
И целомудрия мне в сердце оживи.

EXEGI MONUMENTUM

Я памятник себе воздвиг нерукотворный,
К нему не зарастет народная тропа,
Вознесся выше он главою непокорной
    Александрийского столпа.

prayers; but not one of them moves me as much as that which the priest repeats during the sad days of the Great Fast; more often than all others it comes to my lips, and when I have fallen it strengthens me with untold strength: O Lord of my days! Grant not unto my soul the spirit of melancholy idleness, the love of power, that hidden serpent, and empty talk. But let me behold, O God, my transgressions; let not my brother receive condemnation from me; and revive in my heart the spirit of humility, patience, love, and chastity.

[1836]

EXEGI MONUMENTUM

I HAVE erected a monument to myself, not built by hands; the track to it, trodden by the people, shall not be overgrown; it has raised its indomitable head higher than Alexander's column [the granite memorial to Alexander I in St Petersburg].

Нет, весь я не умру – душа в заветной лире
Мой прах переживет и тленья убежит –
И славен буду я, доколь в подлунном мире
    Жив будет хоть один пиит.

Слух обо мне пройдет по всей Руси великой,
И назовет меня всяк сущий в ней язык,
И гордый внук славян, и финн, и ныне дикой
    Тунгус, и друг степей калмык.

И долго буду тем любезен я народу,
Что чувства добрые я лирой пробуждал,
Что в мой жестокий век восславил я Свободу
    И милость к падшим призывал.

Веленью Божию, о муза, будь послушна,
Обиды не страшась, не требуя венца,
Хвалу и клевету приемли равнодушно
    И не оспоривай глупца.

No, I shall not die entirely – in my sacred lyre my soul shall out-live my dust and escape corruption – and I shall be famed as long as even one poet remains alive in the sublunary world.

The rumour of my fame shall pass through all great Russia and every people living in her shall speak my name – both the proud descendant of the Slavs, and the Finn, and now the wild Tungus and the Kalmyk, the friend of the steppes.

For a long time I shall be dear to the people for having roused noble thoughts with my lyre, for having glorified Freedom in my harsh age and called for mercy for the fallen.

Hearken, O muse, to the commandment of God; fearing not insult, asking for no crown, receive with equanimity both praise and calumny, and do not argue with a fool.

[1836]

ЦЫГАНЫ

Цыганы шумною толпой
По Бессарабии кочуют.
Они сегодня над рекой
В шатрах изодранных ночуют.
Как вольность, весел их ночлег
И мирный сон под небесами;
Между колесами телег,
Полузавешанных коврами,
Горит огонь; семья кругом
Готовит ужин; в чистом поле
Пасутся кони; за шатром
Ручной медведь лежит на воле.
Все живо посреди степей:
Заботы мирные семей,
Готовых с утром в путь недальний,
И песни жен, и крик детей,
И звон походной наковальни.
Но вот на табор кочевой
Нисходит сонное молчанье,
И слышно в тишине степной
Лишь лай собак да коней ржанье.

THE GIPSIES

THE gipsies wander in a clamorous throng through Bessarabia. Today they are spending the night above the river in their tattered tents. Like freedom, their camp site for the night is gay, and their sleep peaceful beneath the heavens. Between the wheels of the wagons, half covered-over with rugs, a fire burns; around it a family cooks its supper; in the open steppe the horses graze; behind a tent a tame bear lies in freedom. All is a-bustle in the midst of the steppe: the peaceful cares of the families ready to move off in the morning on their short journey, and the songs of the women, and the shouts of the children, and the ring of the travelling anvil. But now sleepy silence descends on the nomadic camp, and in the quiet of the steppe can be heard only the barking of dogs and the neighing of horses. Everywhere the lights are put

Огни везде погашены,
Спокойно все, луна сияет
Одна с небесной вышины
И тихий табор озаряет.
В шатре одном старик не спит;
Он перед углями сидит,
Согретый их последним жаром,
И в поле дальнее глядит,
Ночным подернутое паром.
Его молоденькая дочь
Пошла гулять в пустынном поле.
Она привыкла к резвой воле,
Она придет; но вот уж ночь,
И скоро месяц уж покинет
Небес далеких облака, –
Земфиры нет как нет; и стынет
Убогий ужин старика.

Но вот она. За нею следом
По степи юноша спешит;
Цыгану вовсе он неведом.
«Отец мой, – дева говорит, –

out, all is quiet, the moon shines alone from the height of heaven and sheds her light on the quiet camp. In one tent an old man is not asleep; he sits in front of the coals, warmed by their last heat, and gazes into the distant steppe, which is veiled by the night mist. His young daughter has gone off to walk in the deserted steppe. She is used to gay freedom, she will come back; but now it is already night and soon the moon will have left the clouds of the distant heavens; there is no sign of Zemfira, and the miserable supper of the old man grows cold.

But here she is. Following behind her, a youth hastens over the steppe; he is quite unknown to the gipsy. 'Father,' says the girl, 'I

Веду я гостя; за курганом
Его в пустыне я нашла
И в табор нá ночь зазвала.
Он хочет быть как мы цыганом;
Его преследует закон,
Но я ему подругой буду.
Его зовут Алеко – он
Готов идти за мною всюду».

Старик

Я рад. Останься до утра
Под сенью нашего шатра
Или пробудь у нас и доле,
Как ты захочешь. Я готов
С тобой делить и хлеб и кров.
Будь наш – привыкни к нашей доле,
Бродящей бедности и воле –
А завтра с утренней зарей
В одной телеге мы поедем;
Примись за промысел любой:
Железо куй иль песни пой
И селы обходи с медведем.

am bringing a guest: I found him in the waste land beyond the mound and I have called him to the camp to spend the night. He wants to be a gipsy like us; he is pursued by the law, but I will be his loved one. He is called Aleko; he is ready to follow me everywhere.'

OLD MAN: I am glad. Remain till morning in the shelter of our tent, or stay with us even longer, as you wish. I am ready to share with you both bread and shelter. Be one of us, accustom yourself to our lot, to wandering poverty and freedom; and tomorrow at the dawn of day we shall set off in one wagon; take up any pursuit you please: forge iron, or sing songs and go around the villages with the bear.

Алеко

Я остаюсь.

Зетфира

Он будет мой:
Кто ж от меня его отгонит?
Но поздно . . . месяц молодой
Зашел; поля покрыты мглой,
И сон меня невольно клонит . . .

*

Светло. Старик тихонько бродит
Вокруг безмолвного шатра.
«Вставай, Земфира: солнце всходит,
Проснись, мой гость! пора, пора! . . .
Оставьте, дети, ложе неги!» . . .
И с шумом высыпал народ;
Шатры разобраны; телеги
Готовы двинуться в поход.
Все вместе тронулось — и вот
Толпа валит в пустых равнинах.
Ослы в перекидных корзинах
Детей играющих несут;
Мужья и братья, жены, девы,
И стар и млад вослед идут;

ALEKO: I am staying.
ZEMFIRA: He shall be mine: who shall drive him from me? But
it is late . . . the new moon has set, the fields are covered with
mist, and against my will I am overpowered by sleep . . .

*

It is light. The old man quietly wanders around the silent tent.
'Get up, Zemfira, the sun is rising; wake up, my guest, it is time,
it is time! My children, leave your couch of bliss.' And with
clamour the people poured forth; the tents were struck; the
wagons were ready to move off on the journey; everything started

Крик, шум, цыганские припевы,
Медведя рев, его цепей
Нетерпеливое бряцанье,
Лохмотьев ярких пестрота,
Детей и старцев нагота,
Собак и лай и завыванье,
Волынки говор, скрып телег,
Все скудно, дико, все нестройно,
Но все так живо-неспокойно,
Так чуждо мертвых наших нег,
Так чуждо этой жизни праздной,
Как песнь рабов однообразной!

*

Уныло юноша глядел
На опустелую равнину
И грусти тайную причину
Истолковать себе не смел.

off at once – and now the crowd throngs in the barren plains. In baskets slung over their backs the donkeys carry playing children; husbands and brothers, wives, girls, both old and young follow behind; shouts, din, gipsy songs, the bear's roar, the impatient jingling of its chains, the medley of bright-coloured rags, the nakedness of children and old men, the barking and howling of dogs, the sound of pipes, the creaking of wagons – all is wretched, wild, all is confused, but it is all so brisk and restless, so foreign to our dead pleasures, so foreign to this empty life, which is as monotonous as the song of slaves!

*

Gloomily the young man gazed at the now-empty plain, and he did not dare to explain to himself the secret cause of his sorrow.

С ним черноокая Земфира,
Теперь он вольный житель мира,
И солнце весело над ним
Полуденной красою блещет;
Что ж сердце юноши трепещет?
Какой заботой он томим?

Птичка Божия не знает
Ни заботы, ни труда;
Хлопотливо не свивает
Долговечного гнезда;
В долгу ночь на ветке дремлет;
Солнце красное взойдет,
Птичка гласу Бога внемлет,
Встрепенется и поет.
За весной, красой природы,
Лето знойное пройдет –
И туман и непогоды
Осень поздняя несет:
Людям скучно, людям горе;
Птичка в дальные страны,
В теплый край, за сине море
Улетает до весны.

Black-eyed Zemfira is with him, now he is a free dweller of the world, and merrily the sun in all its midday beauty shines over him; but why does the young man's heart quake, by what care is he oppressed?

God's little bird knows neither care nor toil; it does not hustle to build a long-lasting nest; in the long night it slumbers on a branch; the fair sun arises and the little bird hearkens to the voice of God, ruffles its feathers and sings. After spring – the adornment of nature – sultry summer will pass, and late autumn brings both mist and bad weather: it is irksome and grievous for man; the little bird flies off until the spring to distant lands, to a warm clime beyond the blue sea.

Подобно птичке беззаботной
И он, изгнанник перелетный,
Гнезда надежного не знал
И ни к чему не привыкал.
Ему везде была дорога,
Везде была ночлега сень;
Проснувшись поутру, свой день
Он отдавал на волю Бога,
И жизни не могла тревога
Смутить его сердечну лень.
Его порой волшебной славы
Манила дальная звезда;
Нежданно роскошь и забавы
К нему являлись иногда;
Над одинокой головою
И гром нередко грохотал;
Но он беспечно под грозою
И в вёдро ясное дремал.
И жил, не признавая власти
Судьбы коварной и слепой;
Но Боже! как играли страсти
Его послушною душой!
С каким волнением кипели
В его измученной груди!

Like the little carefree bird, he too, a migratory exile, knew no
safe nest and could not accustom himself to anything. Everywhere
the road was open to him, everywhere there was shelter for a
night's rest; waking in the morning, he would hand over his day to
the will of God and life's anxiety could not disturb the sloth of his
heart. At times the distant star of magic fame enticed him; un-
expectedly luxury and amusements would sometimes come to him;
even thunder often rumbled above his lonely head; but he would
slumber free of care beneath the storm and in clear fine weather,
and he lived without acknowledging the power of cunning blind
Fate; but, God, how passions played with his docile soul! With
what tumult they seethed in his tormented breast! Was it long ago

Давно ль, надолго ль усмирели?
Они проснутся: погоди!

*

Земфира

Скажи, мой друг: ты не жалеешь
О том, что бросил навсегда?

Алеко

Что ж бросил я?

Земфира

Ты разумеешь:
Людей отчизны, города.

Алеко

О чем жалеть? Когда б ты знала,
Когда бы ты воображала
Неволю душных городов!
Там люди, в кучах за оградой,
Не дышат утренней прохладой,
Ни вешним запахом лугов;

---

that they abated and was it for long? They will awake: wait!

*

ZEMFIRA: Tell me, my friend, do you not regret what you have
given up for ever?
ALEKO: What have I given up?
ZEMFIRA: You know – the people of your fatherland, the cities.
ALEKO: What is there to regret? If you knew, if you could
imagine the lack of freedom of the stifling cities! There people in
crowds, enclosed behind a barrier, cannot breathe the morning
freshness nor the vernal scent of meadows; they are ashamed of

Любви стыдятся, мысли гонят,
Торгуют волею своей,
Главы пред идолами клонят
И просят денег да цепей.
Что бросил я? Измен волненье,
Предрассуждений приговор,
Толпы безумное гоненье
Или блистательный позор.

Земфира

Но там огромные палаты,
Там разноцветные ковры,
Там игры, шумные пиры,
Уборы дев там так богаты!...

Алеко

Что шум веселий городских?
Где нет любви, там нет веселий.
А девы... Как ты лучше их
И без нарядов дорогих,
Без жемчугов, без ожерелий!
Не изменись, мой нежный друг!
А я... одно мое желанье
С тобой делить любовь, досуг
И добровольное изгнанье!

love, they persecute thought, they barter their freedom, bow their heads before idols, and ask for money and chains. What have I given up? The excitement of betrayals, the decree of prejudices, the mad persecution of the crowd, or glittering disgrace.

ZEMFIRA: But there are vast chambers there, many-coloured rugs, games, noisy feasts, there the clothes of girls are so rich!

ALEKO: What are the noisy pleasures of the city? Where there is no love, there there are no pleasures; and the girls... How much better are you than they, even without costly clothes, without pearls, without necklaces! Change not, my sweet friend! And I... my one desire is to share with you love, leisure, and voluntary exile!

Старик

Ты любишь нас, хоть и рожден
Среди богатого народа.
Но не всегда мила свобода
Тому, кто к неге приучен.
Меж нами есть одно преданье:
Царем когда-то сослан был
Полудня житель к нам в изгнанье.
(Я прежде знал, но позабыл
Его мудреное названье.)
Он был уже летами стар,
Но млад и жив душой незлобной –
Имел он песен дивный дар
И голос, шуму вод подобный –
И полюбили все его,
И жил он на брегах Дуная,
Не обижая никого,
Людей рассказами пленяя;
Не разумел он ничего,
И слаб и робок был, как дети;
Чужие люди за него
Зверей и рыб ловили в сети;
Как мерзла быстрая река
И зимни вихри бушевали,

OLD MAN: You are fond of us, though you were born in the midst of a rich people; but freedom is not always dear to him who is accustomed to pleasures. Amongst us there is a legend: once a dweller of the South was sent off to us in exile by an emperor (I used to know his difficult name, but now I have forgotten it). He was already old in years, but young and lively in his gentle soul; he had the wondrous gift of song and a voice like the noise of the waters. And all grew fond of him, and he lived on the banks of the Danube, offending no one, captivating people with his stories. He did not understand anything, and he was weak and shy, as children are; strangers would catch wild animals and fishes for him in nets; when the swift river froze and the wintry gusts raged, they would

Пушистой кожей покрывали
Они святого старика;
Но он к заботам жизни бедной
Привыкнуть никогда не мог;
Скитался он иссохший, бледный,
Он говорил, что гневный бог
Его карал за преступленье . . .
Он ждал: придет ли избавленье.
И все несчастный тосковал,
Бродя по берегам Дуная,
Да горьки слезы проливал,
Свой дальный град воспоминая,
И завещал он, умирая,
Чтобы на юг перенесли
Его тоскующие кости,
И смертью – чуждой сей земли
Не успокоенные гости!

Алеко

Так вот судьба твоих сынов,
О Рим, о громкая держава! . . .
Певец любви, певец богов,
Скажи мне, что такое слава?

cover the holy old man with furry skins. But he could never grow accustomed to the cares of our poor life; he wandered around, withered, pale, said that an angry god was punishing him for a crime . . . he waited for deliverance to come. And all the time the unhappy man grieved, wandering along the banks of the Danube, and shed bitter tears, recalling his distant city; and as his last behest while dying he asked that his sorrowing bones be transferred to the South – his bones, the guests of this alien land, which were not laid to rest, even by death!

ALEKO: Such then the fate of your sons, O Rome, O glorious power! O singer of love, singer of the gods, tell me, what is glory?

Могильный гул, хвалебный глас,
Из рода в роды звук бегущий?
Или под сенью дымной кущи
Цыгана дикого рассказ?

★

Прошло два лета. Так же бродят
Цыганы мирною толпой;
Везде по-прежнему находят
Гостеприимство и покой.
Презрев оковы просвещенья,
Алеко волен, как они;
Он без забот и сожаленья
Ведет кочующие дни.
Все тот же он; семья все та же;
Он, прежних лет не помня даже,
К бытью цыганскому привык.
Он любит их ночлегов сени,
И упоенье вечной лени,
И бедный, звучный их язык.
Медведь, беглец родной берлоги,

The posthumous rumble of fame, the voice of praise, the sound which runs from generation to generation? Or the tale of a wild gipsy under the cover of his smoky tent?

★

Two years have passed. Still in the same way the gipsies wander in a peaceful throng. As usual they find hospitality and rest everywhere. Spurning the shackles of civilization, Aleko is free like them; he passes days of roaming without cares and regret. He is still the same person; the family is still the same one; not even remembering former years, he has become accustomed to the gipsy way of life. He loves the shelter of their nightly camp-sites and the rapture of everlasting indolence and their poor, sonorous tongue. The bear, a fugitive from its native lair, the shaggy guest of his

Косматый гость его шатра,
В селеньях, вдоль степной дороги,
Близ молдаванского двора
Перед толпою осторожной
И тяжко пляшет, и ревет,
И цепь докучную грызет;
На посох опершись дорожный,
Старик лениво в бубны бьет,
Алеко с пеньем зверя водит,
Земфира поселян обходит
И дань их вольную берет.
Настанет ночь; они все трое
Варят нежатое пшено;
Старик уснул – и всё в покое . . .
В шатре и тихо и темно.

*

Старик на вешнем солнце греет
Уж остывающую кровь;
У люльки дочь поет любовь.
Алеко внемлет и бледнеет.

tent, in the villages along the steppe-road, before a cautious crowd near a Moldavian homestead, dances ponderously and roars and gnaws its irritating chain; leaning on his traveller's staff, the old man lazily strikes his tambourine, Aleko leads the bear about with song, Zemfira goes around all the villagers and takes their voluntary tribute. Night falls; all three cook the unreaped millet; the old man has fallen asleep – and all is at peace . . . In the tent it is quiet and dark.

*

In the spring sunshine the old man warms his blood, which is already growing cold. By the cradle his daughter sings of love; Aleko listens and grows pale.

Земфира

Старый муж, грозный муж,
Режь меня, жги меня:
Я тверда; не боюсь
Ни ножа, ни огня.

Ненавижу тебя,
Презираю тебя;
Я другого люблю,
Умираю любя.

Алеко

Молчи. Мне пенье надоело,
Я диких песен не люблю.

Земфира

Не любишь? мне какое дело!
Я песню для себя пою.

Режь меня, жги меня;
Не скажу ничего;
Старый муж, грозный муж,
Не узнаешь его.

ZEMFIRA: Old husband, harsh husband, stab me, burn me: I am firm; I fear neither knife nor fire.

I hate you, I despise you; I love another; loving I die.

ALEKO: Be silent. I am sick of your singing; I do not like your wild songs.

ZEMFIRA: You do not like them? What do I care! I am singing this song for myself.

Stab me, burn me; I shall say nothing; old husband, harsh husband, you shall not recognize him.

Он свежее весны,
Жарче летнего дня;
Как он молод и смел!
Как он любит меня!

Как ласкала его
Я в ночной тишине!
Как смеялись тогда
Мы твоей седине!

Алеко

Молчи, Земфира! я доволен . . .

Земфира

Так понял песню ты мою?

Алеко

Земфира!

Земфира

Ты сердиться волен,
Я песню про тебя пою.
(*Уходит и поет: Старый муж и проч.*)

He is fresher than spring, hotter than a summer's day; how
young and daring he is! How he loves me!
How I caressed him in the quiet of night! How we laughed then
at your grey hairs!
ALEKO: Be silent, Zemfira! Enough —
ZEMFIRA: So you have understood my song?
ALEKO: Zemfira!
ZEMFIRA: You are free to be angry; I am singing this song about
you.
(*Goes off, singing 'Old husband' etc.*)

Старик

Так, помню, помню – песня эта
Во время наше сложена,
Уже давно в забаву света
Поется меж людей она.
Кочуя на степях Кагула,
Ее, бывало, в зимню ночь
Моя певала Мариула,
Перед огнем качая дочь.
В уме моем минувши лета
Час от часу темней, темней;
Но заронилась песня эта
Глубоко в памяти моей.

*

Все тихо; ночь. Луной украшен
Лазурныйi юга небосклон,
Старик Земфирой пробужден:
«О мой отец! Алеко страшен.
Послушай: сквозь тяжелый сон
И стонет, и рыдает он».

OLD MAN: Yes, I remember, I remember – that song was composed in our time; it has long been sung amongst people to amuse the world. While roaming on the Kagul steppes, my Mariyula used to sing it of a winter night, dandling her daughter before the fire. The bygone years grow hourly darker, darker in my mind; but that song has sunk deep in my memory.

*

All is quiet; it is night. The azure horizon of the south is adorned by the moon. The old man is awakened by Zemfira: 'O my father! Aleko scares me. Listen: in his heavy sleep he groans and sobs.'

Старик

Не тронь его. Храни молчанье.
Слыхал я русское преданье:
Теперь полунощной порой
У спящего теснит дыханье
Домашний дух; перед зарей
Уходит он. Сиди со мной.

Земфира

Отец мой! шепчет он: Земфира!

Старик

Тебя он ищет и во сне:
Ты для него дороже мира.

Земфира

Его любовь постыла мне.
Мне скучно; сердце воли просит –
Уж я . . . Но тише! слышишь? он
Другое имя произносит . . .

Старик

Чье имя?

OLD MAN: Do not touch him. Keep silence. I have heard of an old Russian belief: now at the midnight hour a local spirit cramps the breathing of a sleeping person; before dawn it departs. Sit with me.

ZEMFIRA: My father, he is whispering 'Zemfira!'

OLD MAN: Even in sleep he seeks you: for him you are dearer than the world.

ZEMFIRA: His love is hateful to me; I am bored, my heart craves freedom – I am already . . . But hush! Do you hear? He utters another name.

OLD MAN: Whose name?

Земфира

Слышишь? хриплый стон
И скрежет ярый!... Как ужасно!...
Я разбужу его...

Старик

Напрасно,
Ночного духа не гони –
Уйдет и сам...

Земфира

Он повернулся,
Привстал, зовет меня... проснулся –
Иду к нему – прощай, усни.

Алеко

Где ты была?

Земфира

С отцом сидела.
Какой-то дух тебя томил;
Во сне душа твоя терпела
Мученья; ты меня страшил:
Ты, сонный, скрежетал зубами
И звал меня.

ZEMFIRA: Do you hear? a hoarse groan and a furious gnashing of the teeth! How terrible! I will awaken him...

OLD MAN: It is no use. Do not chase away the night spirit – it will go away of itself.

ZEMFIRA: He has turned over, he has half-risen; he is calling me; he has woken up. I am going to him – Farewell; you go to sleep.

ALEKO: Where have you been?

ZEMFIRA: I have been sitting with my father. Some spirit has been torturing you; in your sleep your soul has been suffering torments; you frightened me: in your sleep you gnashed your teeth and called me.

Алеко

Мне снилась ты.
Я видел, будто между нами . . .
Я видел страшные мечты!

Земфира

Не верь лукавым сновиденьям.

Алеко

Ах, я не верю ничему:
Ни снам, ни сладким увереньям,
Ни даже сердцу твоему.

★

Старик

О чем, безумец молодой,
О чем вздыхаешь ты всечасно?
Здесь люди вольны, небо ясно,
И жены славятся красой.
Не плачь: тоска тебя погубит.

Алеко

Отец, она меня не любит.

ALEKO: I dreamed of you. I dreamed that between us . . . I dreamed terrible dreams.
ZEMFIRA: Do not believe deceptive dreams.
ALEKO: Ah, I believe nothing: neither dreams, nor sweet assurances, nor even your heart.

★

OLD MAN: What do you sigh about, young hothead, all the time? Here people are free, the sky is clear and the women are renowned for their beauty. Weep not, grief will be your downfall.
ALEKO: Father! She does not love me.

Старик

Утешься, друг: она дитя.
Твое унынье безрассудно:
Ты любишь горестно и трудно,
А сердце женское – шутя.
Взгляни: под отдаленным сводом
Гуляет вольная луна;
На всю природу мимоходом
Равно сиянье льет она.
Заглянет в облако любое,
Его так пышно озарит –
И вот – уж перешла в другое;
И то недолго посетит.
Кто место в небе ей укажет,
Примолвя: там остановись!
Кто сердцу юной девы скажет.
Люби одно, не изменись?
Утешься.

Алеко

Как она любила!
Как нежно преклонясь ко мне,
Она в пустынной тишине
Часы ночные проводила!

OLD MAN: Console yourself, my friend: she is a child. Your gloom is senseless: you love grievously and laboriously, whereas a woman's heart loves jestingly. Behold: beneath the distant vault the free moon wanders. While passing she pours her radiance on all nature alike. When she peeps into a cloud, she illumines it so splendidly – and now she has already moved to another cloud; and this one too she will not visit for long. Who shall show her her place in the sky, saying: stop there! Who shall say to the heart of a young girl: love one alone, do not alter? Console yourself.
ALEKO: How she loved! How tenderly she leaned towards me and spent the hours of night in the quiet of the wilderness! Full of

Веселья детского полна,
Как часто милым лепетаньем
Иль упоительным лобзаньем
Мою задумчивость она
В минуту разогнать умела! . . .
И что ж? Земфира неверна! . .
Моя Земфира охладела! . . .

Старик

Послушай: расскажу тебе
Я повесть о самом себе.
Давно, давно, когда Дунаю
Не угрожал еще москаль –
(Вот видишь, я припоминаю,
Алеко, старую печаль.)
Тогда боялись мы султана;
А правил Буджаком паша
С высоких башен Аккермана –
Я молод был; моя душа
В то время радостно кипела;
И ни одна в кудрях моих
Еще сединка не белела, –
Между красавиц молодых

childish joy, how often with her sweet prattle or ravishing kisses was she able to dispel my pensiveness in a moment! And what do I learn? Zemfira is unfaithful! My Zemfira has grown cold towards me!

OLD MAN: Listen: I will tell you a tale about myself. Long, long ago, when the Moskal [contemptuous for 'Russian'] was not yet threatening the Danube – (You see, Aleko, I recall an old sorrow) – then we feared the sultan; and a pasha ruled the Budzhak steppes from the high towers of Akkerman – I was young; my soul at that time seethed joyously; and in my locks not one grey hair was yet to be seen – among the young beauties there was one . . . And

Одна была . . . и долго ею,
Как солнцем, любовался я,
И наконец назвал моею . . .

Ах, быстро молодость моя
Звездой падучею мелькнула!
Но ты, пора любви, минула
Еще быстрее: только год
Меня любила Мариула.

Однажды близ Кагульских вод
Мы чуждый табор повстречали;
Цыганы те, свои шатры
Разбив близ наших у горы,
Две ночи вместе ночевали.
Они ушли на третью ночь, —
И, брося маленькую дочь,
Ушла за ними Мариула.
Я мирно спал; заря блеснула;
Проснулся я, подруги нет!
Ищу, зову – пропал и след.
Тоскуя, плакала Земфира,
И я заплакал – с этих пор
Постыли мне все девы мира;

for a long time I admired her like the sun, and at last called her my
own . . .

Ah, swiftly did my youth flash by like a falling star! But you, O
time of love, passed still quicker: only for a year did Mariyula love
me.

Once near the waters of Kagul we met an alien camp; those
gipsies, having pitched their tents near ours by the hill, spent two
nights together with us. They went off on the third night, and,
leaving her little daughter behind, Mariyula went off after them. I
was sleeping peacefully; dawn flashed; I woke up: my beloved was
not there! I look for her, call her – all trace has vanished. Pining,
Zemfira wept, and I wept too! Since that time all the girls of the

Меж ими никогда мой взор
Не выбирал себе подруги,
И одинокие досуги
Уже ни с кем я не делил.

Алеко

Да как же ты не поспешил
Тотчас вослед неблагодарной
И хищникам и ей коварной
Кинжала в сердце не вонзил?

Старик

К чему? вольнее птицы младость;
Кто в силах удержать любовь?
Чредою всем дается радость;
Что было, то не будет вновь.

Алеко

Я не таков. Нет, я не споря
От прав моих не откажусь!
Или хоть мщеньем наслажусь.
О нет! когда б над бездной моря
Нашел я спящего врага,
Клянусь, и тут моя нога

world have become abhorrent to me. Never has my glance chosen from among them a lover for myself, and I have no longer shared my lonely leisure with anyone.

ALEKO: But why did you not hasten after the ungrateful girl straightway and plunge a dagger in the hearts of the plunderers and the treacherous girl?

OLD MAN: For what purpose? Youth is freer than a bird. Who is strong enough to retain love? Joy is given to all in turn; what has been, will not be again.

ALEKO: I am not such a man. I will not renounce my rights without dispute! Or at least I will enjoy revenge. Oh no! Were I to find my enemy asleep over the depths of the sea, I swear that even then

Не пощадила бы злодея;
Я в волны моря, не бледнея,
И беззащитного б толкнул;
Внезапный ужас пробужденья
Свирепым смехом упрекнул,
И долго мне его паденья
Смешон и сладок был бы гул.

★

Молодой цыган
Еще одно . . . одно лобзанье . . .

Земфира
Пора: мой муж ревнив и зол.

Цыган
Одно . . . но доле! . . . на прощанье.

Земфира
Прощай, покамест не пришел.

Цыган
Скажи – когда ж опять свиданье?

my foot would not spare the villain. Not blanching, I would push
him, even though he were defenceless, into the waves of the sea;
I would rebuke the sudden terror of awakening with a fierce laugh,
and the sound of his fall would long make me laugh and would
sound sweet in my ears.

★

YOUNG GIPSY: One more . . . one more kiss!
ZEMFIRA: It is time! My husband is jealous and angry.
GIPSY: One more . . . but longer! For our parting.
ZEMFIRA: Farewell, before he comes.
GIPSY: Say – when shall we meet again?

Земфира

Сегодня, как зайдет луна,
Там, за курганом над могилой . . .

Цыган

Обманет! не придет она!

Земфира

Вот он! беги! . . . Приду, мой **милый**.

*

Алеко спит. В его уме
Виденье смутное играет;
Он, с криком пробудясь **во тьме**,
Ревниво руку простирает;
Но обробелая рука
Покровы хладные хватает —
Его подруга далека . . .
Он с трепетом привстал и внемлет . . .
Все тихо — страх его объемлет,
По нем текут и жар и хлад;
Встает он, из шатра выходит,
Вокруг телег, ужасен, бродит;

ZEMFIRA: Tonight, when the moon rises, there beyond **the mound,**
over the grave . . .
GIPSY: She will deceive me! She will not come!
ZEMFIRA: Here he is! Run! I will come, my dear one.

*

Aleko is asleep. In his mind a vague vision plays; waking with a
shout in the darkness, he jealously stretches out his hand; but his
hand, grown timid, clutches the cold coverlet — his beloved is far
off . . . With trepidation he half-rises and listens . . . All is quiet —
fear seizes him, both heat and cold run through his body. He gets
up, goes out of the tent, and with fearful mien wanders around the

Спокойно все; поля молчат;
Темно; луна зашла в туманы,
Чуть брезжит звезд неверный свет,
Чуть по росе приметный след
Ведет за дальные курганы:
Нетерпеливо он идет,
Куда зловещий след ведет.

  Могила на краю дороги
Вдали белеет перед ним . . .
Туда слабеющие ноги
Влачит, предчувствием томим,
Дрожат уста, дрожат колени,
Идет . . . и вдруг . . . иль это сон?
Вдруг видит близкие две тени
И близкий шепот слышит он –
Над обесславленной могилой.

1-й голос

Пора . . .

2-й голос

Постой . . .

wagons; all is peaceful; the steppe is silent; it is dark; the moon
has gone into the mists, the faltering light of the stars barely
glimmers, a barely perceptible track in the dew leads to beyond the
distant mounds; impatiently he goes where the ill-boding track
leads.

A grave by the side of the road shines white in the distance
before him . . . There he drags his weakening steps, oppressed by
foreboding; his lips tremble, his knees tremble . . . on he walks . . .
and suddenly . . . or is it a dream? Suddenly he sees close by two
shadows and hears close by the sound of whispering – over the
defamed grave.

FIRST VOICE: It is time . . .
SECOND VOICE: Wait . . .

1-й голос

Пора, мой милый.

2-й голос

Нет, нет, постой, дождемся дня.

1-й голос

Уж поздно.

2-й голос

Как ты робко любишь.
Минуту!

1-й голос

Ты меня погубишь.

2-й голос

Минуту!

1-й голос

Если без меня
Проснется муж?...

Алеко

Проснулся я.
Куда вы! не спешите оба;
Вам хорошо и здесь у гроба.

FIRST VOICE: It is time, my dear one.
SECOND VOICE: No, no, wait – let us wait till day.
FIRST VOICE: It is late.
SECOND VOICE: How timidly you love! One minute more!
FIRST VOICE: You will destroy me.
SECOND VOICE: One minute!
FIRST VOICE: What if my husband should wake without me?
ALEKO: I have awoken. Where are you both off to? Do not hasten;
it is just as pleasant for you here, by the grave.

Земфира

Мой друг, беги, беги . . .

Алеко

Постой!

Куда, красавец молодой?
Лежи!

(*Вонзает в него нож.*)

Земфира

Алеко!

Цыган

Умираю . . .

Земфира

Алеко, ты убьешь его!
Взгляни: ты весь обрызган кровью!
О, что ты сделал?

Алеко

Ничего.
Теперь дыши его любовью.

ZEMFIRA: My friend, run, run . . .
ALEKO: Stop! Where are you going, my handsome young fellow?
Lie there!

(*Thrusts his knife into him.*)

ZEMFIRA: Aleko!
GIPSY: I am dying . . .
ZEMFIRA: Aleko, you will kill him! Look: you are all bespattered
with blood! Oh, what have you done?
ALEKO: Nothing. Now breathe his love.

Земфира

Нет, полно, не боюсь тебя! –
Твои угрозы презираю,
Твое убийство проклинаю . . .

Алеко

Умри ж и ты!

(*Поражает ее.*)

Умру любя . . .

★

Восток, денницей озаренный,
Сиял. Алеко за холмом,
С ножом в руках, окровавленный
Сидел на камне гробовом.
Два трупа перед ним лежали;
Убийца страшен был лицом.
Цыганы робко окружали
Его встревоженной толпой.
Могилу в стороне копали.

ZEMFIRA: No, enough: I do not fear you! I despise your threats, I curse your murder . . .
ALEKO: Then die yourself!

(*Strikes her.*)

ZEMFIRA: I die loving . . .

★

The east, lit up by the morning-star, was shining. Beyond the mound Aleko sat on the tombstone with a knife in his hands and covered with blood. The two corpses lay before him; the murderer was terrible in aspect. Shyly the gipsies surrounded him in anxious throng. They were digging a grave on one side. In mournful train

Шли жены скорбной чередой
И в очи мертвых целовали.
Старик-отец один сидел
И на погибшую глядел
В немом бездействии печали;
Подняли трупы, понесли
И в лоно хладное земли
Чету младую положили.
Алеко издали смотрел
На все . . . когда же их закрыли
Последней горстию земной,
Он молча, медленно склонился
И с камня на траву свалился.

Тогда старик, приближась, рек:
«Оставь нас, гордый человек!
Мы дики; нет у нас законов,
Мы не терзаем, не казним –
Не нужно крови нам и стонов –
Но жить с убийцей не хотим . . .
Ты не рожден для дикой доли,
Ты для себя лишь хочешь воли;

the women walked and kissed the dead on the eyes. The old father
sat alone and gazed at his dead daughter in the dumb inertia of
grief; they picked up the corpses, carried them and laid the
young couple in the cold bosom of the earth. Aleko watched it all
from afar . . . And when they covered them with the last handful
of earth, he silently, slowly, bent down and fell from the stone on to
the grass.

Then the old man came up to him and said: 'Leave us, proud
man! We are wild, we have no laws, we do not torture men, we do
not put men to death – we have no need of blood and groans – but
with a murderer we do not wish to live. You were not born for the
wild way of life: only for yourself do you want freedom; your voice

Ужасен нам твой будет глас:
Мы робки и добры душою,
Ты зол и смел – оставь же нас,
Прости, да будет мир с тобою».

Сказал – и шумною толпою
Поднялся табор кочевой
С долины страшного ночлега.
И скоро все в дали степной
Сокрылось; лишь одна телега,
Убогим крытая ковром,
Стояла в поле роковом.
Так иногда перед зимою,
Туманной, утренней порою,
Когда подъемлется с полей
Станица поздних журавлей
И с криком вдаль на юг несется,
Пронзенный гибельным свинцом,
Один печально остается,
Повиснув раненым крылом.
Настала ночь; в телеге темной
Огня никто не разложил,
Никто под крышею подъемной
До утра сном не опочил.

will be terrible to us: we are timid and good at heart, you are evil
and bold – so leave us; farewell, may peace be with you.'

He spoke – and in a clamorous throng the nomadic camp rose
from the vale of the terrible night's resting-place. And soon all was
hidden in the distant steppe. Only one wagon, covered with a
wretched rug, stood in the fateful field. Thus sometimes before
winter in the misty morning-time, when a flock of late cranes rises
up from the fields and with a cry flies swiftly southwards into the
distance, one, pierced by the fatal lead, remains sadly behind with
its wounded wing hanging. Night came; in the dark wagon no one
lit a fire, no one beneath its folding hood fell asleep before morning.

Эпилог

Волшебной силой песнопенья
В туманной памяти моей
Так оживляются виденья
То светлых, то печальных дней.

В стране, где долго, долго брани
Ужасный гул не умолкал,
Где повелительные грани
Стамбулу русский указал,
Где старый наш орел двуглавый
Еще шумит минувшей славой,
Встречал я посреди степей
Над рубежами древних станов
Телеги мирные цыганов,
Смиренной вольности детей.
За их ленивыми толпами
В пустынях часто я бродил,
Простую пищу их делил
И засыпал пред их огнями.
В походах медленных любил
Их песен радостные гулы –
И долго милой Мариулы
Я имя нежное твердил.

Epilogue

Thus by the magic strength of song are visions brought to life in
my misty memory, visions now of bright, now of sad days.

   In the land where for a long, long time the dreadful din of war
was not silent, where the Russian showed his imperious frontiers
to Stambul, where the departed glory of our old two-headed eagle
still resounds, there I met amid the steppes, over the boundaries
of ancient camps, the peaceful wagons of the gipsies, children of
humble freedom. Behind their lazy crowds I often wandered in the
wildernesses, shared their simple food, and fell asleep before their
fires. In their slow journeys I loved the cheerful ring of their songs
and for a long time I repeated the tender name of sweet Mariyula.

Но счастья нет и между вами,
Природы бедные сыны! . . .
И под издранными шатрами
Живут мучительные сны,
И ваши сени кочевые
В пустынях не спаслись от бед,
И всюду страсти роковые,
И от судеб защиты нет.

БОРИС ГОДУНОВ

[*Из 7-й сцены*]

Достиг я высшей власти;
Шестой уж год я царствую спокойно.
Но счастья нет моей душе. Не так ли
Мы смолоду влюбляемся и алчем
Утех любви, но только утолим
Сердечный глад мгновенным обладаньем,
Уж, охладев, скучаем и томимся? . . .
Напрасно мне кудесники сулят
Дни долгие, дни власти безмятежной –

But there is no happiness even amongst you, poor sons of nature! And beneath your tattered tents there are tormenting dreams, and your nomadic shelters in the wildernesses have not escaped disasters, and everywhere there are fateful passions, and from the Fates there is no defence.

BORIS GODUNOV

rom Scene 7: Tsar Boris's monologue]

I HAVE reached supreme power; now for the sixth year I rule in peace. But my soul has no happiness. Is it not thus that from early youth we fall in love and hunger for the joys of love, but only quench the hunger of our hearts with momentary possession, and, growing cold, already become bored, and languish? Vainly do the sorcerers promise me long days, days of untroubled power. Neither

Ни власть, ни жизнь меня не веселят;
Предчувствую небесный гром и горе.
Мне счастья нет. Я думал свой народ
В довольствии, во славе успокоить,
Щедротами любовь его снискать –
Но отложил пустое попеченье:
Живая власть для черни ненавистна,
Они любить умеют только мертвых.
Безумны мы, когда народный плеск
Иль ярый вопль тревожит сердце наше!
Бог насылал на землю нашу глад,
Народ завыл, в мученьях погибая;
Я отворил им житницы, я злато
Рассыпал им, я им сыскал работы –
Они ж меня, беснуясь, проклинали!
Пожарный огнь их домы истребил,
Я выстроил им новые жилища.
Они ж меня пожаром упрекали!
Вот черни суд: ищи ж ее любви.
В семье моей я мнил найти отраду,
Я дочь мою мнил осчастливить браком –
Как буря, смерть уносит жениха . . .

power nor life gladden me; I have a presentiment of heaven's thunder and sorrow. For me there is no happiness. I thought to calm my people with prosperity and glory, to win their love with generous gifts – but I have put aside that vain care: power alive is hateful to the rabble – they only know how to love the dead. We are mad if the applause or the wild yell of the people disturbs our heart! God sent famine to our land, and the people, dying in agony, began to moan; I opened the granaries for them, I scattered gold in their midst, I found them work – but raging they cursed me! A conflagration destroyed their homes, I built them new dwellings. But they blamed me for the fire! This is the judgement of the rabble! Seek, then, its love! Within my family I thought I would find joy. I thought I would make my daughter happy by marriage – like a storm, death carries off her bridegroom . . . And now

И тут молва лукаво нарекает
Виновником дочернего вдовства
Меня, меня, несчастного отца! . . .
Кто ни умрет, я всех убийца тайный:
Я ускорил Феодора кончину,
Я отравил свою сестру царицу,
Монахиню смиренную . . . всё я!
Ах! чувствую: ничто не может нас
Среди мирских печалей успокоить;
Ничто, ничто . . . едина разве совесть.
Так, здравая, она восторжествует
Над злобою, над темной клеветою. –
Но если в ней единое пятно,
Единое, случайно завелося,
Тогда – беда! как язвой моровой
Душа сгорит, нальется сердце ядом,
Как молотком стучит в ушах упрек,
И все тошнит, и голова кружится,
И мальчики кровавые в глазах . . .
И рад бежать, да некуда . . . ужасно!
Да, жалок тот, в ком совесть нечиста.

rumour cunningly proclaims me guilty of my daughter's widow-
hood, me, her hapless father . . . Whoever dies, I am the secret
murderer of them all: I hastened Feodor's end, I poisoned the
Tsaritsa my sister, the humble nun . . . Always it is I! Ah, I feel
that nothing can soothe is in the midst of worldly sorrows;
nothing, nothing . . . except conscience alone. Thus, when it is
clear, it will triumph over evil, over dark calumny. But if one stain,
one single stain, should by chance appear on it, then woe! the soul
will burn up as though afflicted by the plague, the heart will fill
with poison, reproach beats like a hammer in the ears, and always
there is nausea, and the head spins, and before the eyes are infants
dripping with blood . . . and flight would be welcome, but there is
nowhere to flee to . . . Oh, horror! Verily he is to be pitied whose
conscience is unclean.

[*Из 10–й сцены*]

Ух, тяжело! . . . дай дух переведу . . .
Я чувствовал: вся кровь моя в лицо
Мне кинулась — и тяжко опускалась . . .
Так вот зачем тринадцать лет мне сряду
Все снилося убитое дитя!
Да, да — вот что! теперь я понимаю.
Но кто же он, мой грозный супостат?
Кто на меня? Пустое имя, тень —
Ужели тень сорвет с меня порфиру,
Иль звук лишит детей моих наследства?
Безумец я! чего ж я испугался?
На призрак сей подуй — и нет его.
Так решено: не окажу я страха, —
Но презирать не должно ничего . . .
Ох, тяжела ты, шапка Мономаха!

[*From Scene 10: Boris's concluding monologue. Boris has just learned that a Pretender, claiming to be Dimitri, the murdered son of Ivan IV, has appeared in Cracow. According to Pushkin, Boris was responsible for Dimitri's murder.*]

Ah, how grievous . . . Let me get my breath . . . I felt all my blood rush to my face — and painfully drain away . . . So that is why for thirteen years on end I have always dreamed of the murdered child! Yes, yes, that is it! Now I understand. But who is he, my dread foe? Who is against me? An empty name, a shade — can it be that a shade shall tear the purple from me or a sound deprive my children of their heritage? A madman am I! What, indeed, am I afraid of? Blow on this phantom — and it is no more. Thus it is resolved: I will show no fear — but I must neglect nothing . . . Oh, heavy lies the crown of Monomakh!

[*Ночь. Сад. Фонтан.*]

Самозванец
(*входит*)

Вот и фонтан; она сюда придет.
Я, кажется, рожден не боязливым;
Перед собой вблизи видал я смерть,
Пред смертию душа не содрогалась.
Мне вечная неволя угрожала,
За мной гнались – я духом не смутился
И дерзостью неволи избежал.
Но что ж теперь теснит мое дыханье?
Что значит сей неодолимый трепет?
Иль это дрожь желаний напряженных?
Нет – это страх. День целый ожидал
Я тайного свидания с Мариной,
Обдумывал все то, что ей скажу,
Как обольщу ее надменный ум,
Как назову московскою царицей, –
Но час настал – и ничего не помню.

[*Scene 13: the Pretender, a runaway monk from Muscovy who claims to be Ivan IV's son Dimitri, has recently appeared in Poland, where he has raised an army to march against Tsar Boris. He is in love with Marina, the daughter of the Polish magnate Mnishek.*]

Night. A Garden. A Fountain.

PRETENDER (*enters*): Here at last is the fountain; she will come here. I was not born a coward, it seems; close before me I have seen death; my soul did not shudder in the presence of death. Everlasting captivity has threatened me; I have been pursued – I did not falter in spirit, and by dint of boldness I avoided captivity. But what is it now that constricts my breathing? What does this unconquerable trembling mean? Is this then the quivering of tense desires? No, it is fear. All day I have waited for this secret meeting with Marina, pondered over all that I would say to her, how I would beguile her haughty mind and call her Tsaritsa of Moscow – but the hour has come – and I remember nothing. I

Не нахожу затверженных речей;
Любовь мутит мое воображенье . . .
Но что-то вдруг мелькнуло . . . шорох . . .
тише . . .
Нет, это свет обманчивой луны,
И прошумел здесь ветерок.

Марина

(входит)

Царевич!

Самозванец

Она! . . Вся кровь во мне остановилась.

Марина

Димитрий! Вы?

Самозванец

Волшебный, сладкий голос!

(Идет к ней.)

Ты ль наконец? Тебя ли вижу я,
Одну со мной, под сенью тихой ночи?

cannot recall the speeches which I learned by heart; love dulls my imagination . . . But something has just suddenly flashed . . . there is a rustle . . . hush . . . No, it was the light of the deceptive moon and a breeze that rustled here.

MARINA (*enters*): Tsarevich!

PRETENDER: It is she! All my blood within me has stopped flowing.

MARINA: Dimitri! You?

PRETENDER: Sweet bewitching voice!

(*Goes to her.*)

Is it you at last? Is it you I see, alone with me beneath the shelter

Как медленно катился скучный день!
Как медленно заря вечерня гасла!
Как долго ждал во мраке я ночном!

Марина

Часы бегут, и дорого мне время –
Я здесь тебе назначила свиданье
Не для того, чтоб слушать нежны речи
Любовника. Слова не нужны. Верю,
Что любишь ты; но слушай: я решилась
С твоей судьбой и бурной и неверной
Соединить судьбу мою; то вправе
Я требовать, Димитрий, одного:
Я требую, чтоб ты души своей
Мне тайные открыл теперь надежды,
Намеренья и даже опасенья;
Чтоб об руку с тобой могла я смело
Пуститься в жизнь – не с детской слепотой,
Не как раба желаний легких мужа,
Наложница безмолвная твоя,
Но как тебя достойная супруга,
Помощница московского царя.

of quiet night? How slowly the dull day rolled by! How slowly the
sunset died away! How long I have waited in the dark of night!
MARINA: The hours run by, and time is precious to me – I granted
you a meeting here not in order to listen to the tender speeches of a
lover. Words are not necessary. I believe that you love me; but
listen: I have decided to join my destiny with your stormy unsure
destiny; so I have the right to demand one thing, Dimitri: I demand
that you now disclose to me the secret hopes, intentions, and even
fears of your soul, so that hand in hand with you I may set forth
boldly on life's path – not with childish blindness, not as the slave
of my husband's light desires, not as your silent mistress, but as a
wife worthy of you, the helpmeet of the Tsar of Moscow.

Самозванец

О, дай забыть хоть на единый час
Моей судьбы заботы и тревоги!
Забудь сама, что видишь пред собой
Царевича. Марина! зри во мне
Любовника, избранного тобою,
Счастливого твоим единым взором.
О, выслушай моления любви,
Дай высказать все то, чем сердце полно.

Марина

Не время, князь. Ты медлишь – и меж тем
Приверженность твоих клевретов стынет,
Час от часу опасность и труды
Становятся опасней и труднее,
Уж носятся сомнительные слухи,
Уж новизна сменяет новизну;
А Годунов свои приемлет меры . . .

Самозванец

Что Годунов ? во власти ли Бориса
Твоя любовь, одно мое блаженство ?
Нет, нет. Теперь гляжу я равнодушно
На трон его, на царственную власть.

PRETENDER: Oh, let us forget just for one hour the cares and
anxieties of my destiny! Forget that you see before you the
Tsarevich. Marina! Behold in me a lover chosen by yourself, who
is made happy by one single glance from you. Oh, listen to my
prayers of love; let me utter all that fills my heart.
MARINA: This is not the time, Prince. You dally – and meanwhile
the devotion of your followers grows cool; dangers and difficulties
become hourly more dangerous and more difficult. Already dubious
rumours fly around, already new tidings replace old, while Godunov is taking his measures . . .
PRETENDER: What of Godunov ? Is your love, my only happiness,
in Godunov's power ? No, no. Now with indifference I regard his

Твоя любовь . . . что без нее мне жизнь,
И славы блеск, и русская держава?
В глухой степи, в землянке бедной – ты,
Ты заменишь мне царскую корону,
Твоя любовь . . .

Марина

Стыдись; не забывай
Высокого, святого назначенья:
Тебе твой сан дороже должен быть
Всех радостей, всех обольщений жизни,
Его ни с чем не можешь ты равнять.
Не юноше кипящему, безумно
Плененному моею красотой,
Знай: отдаю торжественно я руку
Наследнику московского престола,
Царевичу, спасенному судьбой.

Самозванец

Не мучь меня, прелестная Марина,
Не говори, что сан, а не меня
Избрала ты. Марина! ты не знаешь,

throne, his royal power. Your love . . . Without it what for me is life, the glitter of glory and the realm of Russia? On the barren steppe, in a wretched mud-hut, you will replace for me the royal crown; your love . . .

MARINA: Shame! Do not forget your lofty, sacred destiny: your rank should be dearer to you than all the joys and all the allurements of life. You cannot compare it with anything. Know this: not to a youth seething with passion and madly captivated by my beauty, but to the heir of the throne of Moscow, the Tsarevich, saved by fate, do I solemnly give my hand.

PRETENDER: Do not torment me, fair Marina; do not say that it is my rank and not me that you have chosen. Marina! You do not

Как больно тем ты сердце мне язвишь –
Как! ежели . . . о страшное сомненье! –
Скажи: когда б не царское рожденье
Назначила слепая мне судьба;
Когда б я был не Иоаннов сын,
Не сей давно забытый миром отрок, –
Тогда б . . . тогда б любила ль ты меня?

Марина

Димитрий ты и быть иным не можешь;
Другого мне любить нельзя.

Самозванец

           Нет! полно:
Я не хочу делиться с мертвецом
Любовницей, ему принадлежащей.
Нет, полно мне притворствовать! скажу
Всю истину; так знай же: твой Димитрий
Давно погиб, зарыт – и не воскреснет;
А хочешь ли ты знать, кто я таков?
Изволь, скажу: я бедный черноризец;
Монашеской неволею скучая,
Под клобуком, свой замысел отважный
Обдумал я, готовил миру чудо –

know how sorely you thus wound my heart – What! If . . . O dreadful doubt! Say: if blind fate had not assigned to me royal birth, if I were not the son of Ivan, not that child so long forgotten by the world – then . . . then would you love me?
MARINA: Dimitri, you cannot be another; I could not love another.
PRETENDER: No! Enough: I do not wish to share with a dead man a lover who belongs to him. No, enough of my pretending! I will tell you the whole truth; know, then, that your Dimitri perished long ago, is buried – and will not rise again; and do you want to know who I am? Well then, I'll tell you. I am a poor monk; bored with monastic servitude, while beneath the cowl, I pondered my

И наконец из келии бежал
К украинцам, в их буйные курени,
Владеть конем и саблей научился;
Явился к вам; Димитрием назвался
И поляков безмозглых обманул.
Что скажешь ты, надменная Марина?
Довольна ль ты признанием моим?
Что ж ты молчишь?

Марина

О стыд! о горе мне!

(*Молчание.*)

Самозванец
(*тихо*)

Куда завлек меня порыв досады!
С таким трудом устроенное счастье
Я, может быть, навеки погубил.
Что сделал я, безумец? –

bold scheme, I prepared a miracle for the world – and at last I fled from my cell to the Ukrainians, to their wild *kureni* [Cossack settlements or camps]; I learned to master horse and sabre; I came to your people; I called myself Dimitri and deceived the brainless Poles. What say you, proud Marina? Are you satisfied with my confession? Why are you silent?

MARINA: O shame! O woe is me!

(*Silence.*)

PRETENDER (*sotto voce*): Where has my gust of anger carried me? Perhaps I have for ever destroyed the happiness contrived with such toil. Madman, what have I done?

(Вслух)

Вижу, вижу:
Стыдишься ты не княжеской любви.
Так вымолви ж мне роковое слово;
В твоих руках теперь моя судьба,
Реши: я жду

(Бросается на колени.)

Марина

Встань, бедный самозванец.
Не мнишь ли ты коленопреклоненьем,
Как девочки доверчивой и слабой
Тщеславное мне сердце умилить?
Ошибся, друг: у ног своих видала
Я рыцарей и графов благородных;
Но их мольбы я хладно отвергала
Не для того, чтоб беглого монаха . . .

Самозванец

(встает)

Не презирай младого самозванца;
В нем доблести таятся, может быть,
Достойные московского престола,
Достойные руки твоей бесценной . . .

(Aloud)

I see it, I see it: you are ashamed of love that is not princely. Say
to me, then, the fateful word. In your hands my destiny now lies.
Decide: I wait.

(Falls on his knees.)

MARINA: Arise, miserable Pretender. Surely you do not think that
you can move my vain heart with genuflexions, as though I were
a weak trusting girl? You are mistaken, my friend: at my feet I
have seen knights and noble counts; but I did not coldly scorn
their supplications so that a runaway monk . . .

PRETENDER (*rises*): Do not scorn the young Pretender; in him
perhaps there lie hidden virtues worthy of the throne of Moscow,
worthy of your priceless hand . . .

Марина
Достойные позорной петли, дерзкий!

Самозванец
Виновен я; гордыней обуянный,
Обманывал я Бога и царей,
Я миру лгал; но не тебе, Марина,
Меня казнить; я прав перед тобою.
Нет, я не мог обманывать тебя.
Ты мне была единственной святыней,
Пред нейже я притворствовать не смел.
Любовь, любовь ревнивая, слепая,
Одна любовь принудила меня
Все высказать.

Марина
Чем хвалится, безумец!
Кто требовал признанья твоего?
Уж если ты, бродяга безымянный,
Мог ослепить чудесно два народа,
Так должен уж по крайней мере ты
Достоин быть успеха своего
И свой обман отважный обеспечить
Упорною, глубокой, вечной тайной.
Могу ль, скажи, предаться я тебе,

MARINA: Worthy of a shameful noose, insolent fellow!
PRETENDER: I am to blame. Seized with pride, I deceived both
God and Tsars. I lied to the world; but it is not for you, Marina,
to punish me; I am innocent before you. No, I could not deceive you.
To me you were the only sacred thing, to whom I did not dare
pretend. Love, jealous, blind love, love alone forced me to say all.
MARINA: What does he boast of, the madman? Who asked for
your confession? If indeed you, a nameless vagrant, could miracu-
lously blind two nations, then at least you ought to be worthy of
your success, and ⸱cure your bo⸱ deception by stubborn, deep,

Могу ль, забыв свой род и стыд девичий,
Соединить судьбу мою с твоею,
Когда ты сам с такою простотой,
Так ветрено позор свой обличаешь?
Он из любви со мною проболтался!
Дивлюся: как перед моим отцом
Из дружбы ты доселе не открылся,
От радости пред нашим королем
Или еще пред паном Вишневецким
Из верного усердия слуги.

Самозванец

Клянусь тебе, что сердца моего
Ты вымучить одна могла признанье.
Клянусь тебе, что никогда, нигде,
Ни в пиршестве за чашею безумства,
Ни в дружеском, заветном разговоре,
Ни под ножом, ни в муках истязаний
Сих тяжких тайн не выдаст мой язык.

eternal secrecy. Tell me, can I commit myself to you, can I, forgetting my birth and my virgin modesty, join my destiny with yours, when you yourself, with such simplicity, so thoughtlessly, betray your shame? For love's sake he has let out his secret to me! I am amazed that for friendship's sake you have not so far revealed yourself to my father, or for joy's sake to our king, or, yet again, for the sake of a true servant's zeal, to Pan Wiśniowiecki!

PRETENDER: I swear to you that only you could extort my heart's confession. I swear to you that at no time, in no place, neither at a feast while drinking the cup of folly, nor in friendly, intimate conversation, nor beneath the knife, nor in the agony of torture, shall my tongue betray these grave secrets.

Марина

Клянешься ты! итак, должна я верить –
О, верю я! – но чем, нельзя ль узнать,
Клянешься ты? не именем ли Бога,
Как набожный приимыш езуитов?
Иль честию, как витязь благородный,
Иль может быть, единым царским словом,
Как царский сын? не так ли? говори.

Димитрий
(*гордо*)

Тень Грозного меня усыновила,
Димитрием из гроба нарекла,
Вокруг меня народы возмутила
И в жертву мне Бориса обрекла –
Царевич я. Довольно, стыдно мне
Пред гордою полячкой унижаться. –
Прощай навек. Игра войны кровавой,
Судьбы моей обширные заботы
Тоску любви, надеюсь, заглушат.
О как тебя я стану ненавидеть,
Когда пройдет постыдной страсти жар!
Теперь иду – погибель иль венец

MARINA: You swear! So, I must believe – Oh, I believe! But what, may I not know, do you swear by? Is it not by God's name, as a pious foster-child of the Jesuits? Or by honour, as a noble knight? Or perhaps by a single royal word, as the son of a Tsar? Is it not so? Speak.
DIMITRI (*proudly*): The shade of [Ivan] the Terrible has adopted me, has from the grave named me Dimitri, has stirred up the peoples around me and has destined Boris to be my victim – I am the Tsarevich. Enough. It is shameful for me to debase myself before a proud Polish woman. Farewell for ever. The game of bloody war, the vast cares of my destiny, will, I hope, deaden the pain of love. Oh, how I shall hate you when the heat of shameful passion abates! Now I go – ruin or a crown awaits my head in

Мою главу в России ожидает,
Найду ли смерть, как воин в битве честной,
Иль как злодей на плахе площадной,
Не будешь ты подругою моею,
Моей судьбы не разделишь со мною;
Но – может быть, ты будешь сожалеть
Об участи, отвергнутой тобою.

Марина

А если я твой дерзостный обман
Заранее пред всеми обнаружу?

Самозванец

Не мнишь ли ты, что я тебя боюсь?
Что более поверят польской деве,
Чем русскому царевичу? – Но знай,
Что ни король, ни папа, ни вельможи
Не думают о правде слов моих.
Димитрий я иль нет – что им за дело?
Но я предлог раздоров и войны.
Им это лишь и нужно, и тебя,
Мятежница! поверь, молчать заставят.
Прощай.

Russia. Whether I meet death as a warrior in honourable battle or as a criminal upon the block in public, you shall not be my consort, you shall not share my destiny with me; but – perhaps you will regret the lot you have rejected.

MARINA: And what if I expose your bold deceit to everyone beforehand?

PRETENDER: Surely you do not think that I am afraid of you? That a Polish girl will be believed more readily than the Russian Tsarevich? But know that neither King, nor Pope, nor magnates think about the truth of my words. Whether I am Dimitri or not – what is it to them? I am the pretext for conflicts and war. That is all they need; and you, rebellious one, believe me, they will force to be silent. Farewell.

Марина

Постой, царевич. Наконец
Я слышу речь не мальчика, но мужа.
С тобою, князь, она меня мирит.
Безумный твой порыв я забываю
И вижу вновь Димитрия. Но – слушай:
Пора, пора! проснись, не медли боле;
Веди полки скорее на Москву –
Очисти Кремль, садись на трон московский,
Тогда за мной шли брачного посла;
Но – слышит Бог – пока твоя нога
Не оперлась на тронные ступени,
Пока тобой не свержен Годунов,
Любви речей не буду слушать я.

(Уходит.)

Самозванец

Нет – легче мне сражаться с Годуновым
Или хитрить с придворным езуитом,
Чем с женщиной – черт с ними; мочи нет.
И путает, и вьется, и ползет,
Скользит из рук, шипит, грозит и жалит.

MARINA: Stay, Tsarevich. At last I hear the words not of a boy but of a man. These words reconcile me to you, Prince. I forget your headstrong outburst and I see again Dimitri. But listen: the time has come! Awake, tarry no longer; lead your armies with all haste on Moscow – purge the Kremlin, sit upon the throne of Moscow; then send a nuptial envoy to fetch me; but – God is my witness – until your foot rests on the steps of the throne, until Godunov is overthrown by you, I shall not listen to words of love.

(Exit.)

PRETENDER: No – it were easier for me to fight with Godunov or to play cunning with a Jesuit at court, than with a woman – the devil take them; I have no strength to fight them. She entangles, and twists, and crawls, and slips from the hands, hisses, threatens,

Змея! змея! – Недаром я дрожал.
Она меня чуть-чуть не погубила.
Но решено: заутра двину рать.

[*Москва. Царские Палаты.*
Борис, Басманов.]
Царь
Он побежден, какая польза в том?
Мы тщетною победой увенчались.
Он вновь собрал рассеянное войско
И нам со стен Путивля угрожает.
Что делают меж тем герои наши?
Стоят у Кром, где кучка казаков
Смеются им из-под гнилой ограды.
Вот слава! нет, я ими недоволен,
Пошлю тебя начальствовать над ними;
Не род, а ум поставлю в воеводы;
Пускай их спесь о местничестве тужит;
Пора презреть мне ропот знатной черни
И гибельный обычай уничтожить.

stings. Serpent! Serpent! Not for nothing did I tremble. She very nearly ruined me. But I have decided: tomorrow morning I move my army.

[*Scene 20: Boris has just heard the news that the Pretender has been beaten by the Russians at the battle of Sevsk, January 1605.*]

Moscow, the Palace of the Tsar,
Boris, Basmanov.

TSAR: He is defeated – what benefit lies therein? We have been crowned with an empty victory. He has again collected his scattered army and is threatening us from the walls of Putivl. What are our heroes doing in the meantime? They are standing by Kromy, where a handful of Cossacks laughs at them from the cover of their rotting parapet. There's glory for you! No, I am displeased with them; I shall send you to be in command of them; not birth but brains shall I appoint to lead my troops; let their pride grieve for *mestnichestvo* [the system whereby precedence was established according to birth and previous service]; it is time for me to disdain the murmur of the high-born rabble and to destroy that ruinous custom.

Басманов

Ах, государь, стократ благословен
Тот будет день, когда Разрядны книги
С раздорами, с гордыней родословной
Пожрет огонь.

Царь

                День этот недалек;
Лишь дай сперва смятение народа
Мне усмирить.

Басманов

                Что на него смотреть;
Всегда народ к смятенью тайно склонен:
Так борзый конь грызет свои бразды;
На власть отца так отрок негодует;
Но что ж? конем спокойно всадник правит,
И отроком отец повелевает.

Царь

Конь иногда сбивает седока,
Сын у отца не вечно в полной воле.

BASMANOV: Ah, sovereign, a hundredfold blessèd will be the day
when fire devours the Books of Precedence together with their
squabbles and their genealogical pride.

TSAR: That day is not far off; only first let me suppress the insurrection of the people.

BASMANOV: Why worry about the people? They are always
secretly inclined to insurrection: thus does a swift steed champ the
bit; thus does a boy chafe at his father's power. And what is the
result? The rider calmly controls his steed, and the father governs
his son.

TSAR: Sometimes the steed throws the rider, and the son does not
always submit to his father's will. Only with unslumbering severity

Лишь строгостью мы можем неусыпной
Сдержать народ. Так думал Иоанн,
Смиритель бурь, разумный самодержец,
Так думал и его свирепый внук.
Нет, милости не чувствует народ:
Твори добро – не скажет он спасибо;
Грабь и казни – тебе не будет хуже.

(*Входит боярин.*)

Что?

Боярин

Привели гостей иноплеменных.

Царь

Иду принять; Басманов, погоди.
Останься здесь: с тобой еще мне нужно
Поговорить.

(*Уходит.*)

can we restrain the people. So thought Ioann [Ivan III], the
subduer of storms, the wise autocrat; so too thought his fierce
grandson [Ivan IV]. No, the people do not appreciate kindness: do
good – they will not thank you; plunder and execute – it will be
none the worse for you.

(*Enter a boyar.*)

What is it?
BOYAR: The foreign merchants have been brought in.
TSAR: I go to receive them. Basmanov, wait. Stay here: I must talk
with you further.

(*Exit.*)

Басманов

Высокий дух державный.
Дай Бог ему с Отрепьевым проклятым
Управиться, и много, много он
Еще добра в России сотворит.
Мысль важная в уме его родилась.
Не надобно ей дать остыть. Какое
Мне поприще откроется, когда
Он сломит рог боярству родовому!
Соперников во брани я не знаю;
У царского престола стану первый . . .
И может быть . . . Но что за чудный шум?

(*Тревога. Бояре, придворные служители в беспорядке
бегут, встречаются и шепчутся.*)

Один

За лекарем!

Другой

Скорее к патриарху.

Третий

Царевича, царевича зовет!

BASMANOV: High sovereign spirit! God grant that he may get the better of the accursed Otrepyev [the Pretender], and he will do much, much further good in Russia. A noble thought has taken birth within his mind. It must not be allowed to grow cold. What a career will then be open to me when he breaks the horn of the hereditary aristocracy! I know no rivals in war; I shall be closest to the Tsar's throne . . . And perhaps . . . But what is that strange noise?

(*Alarm. Enter boyars and court attendants running in disorder. They meet and whisper.*)

ONE ATTENDANT: Send for a physician!
A SECOND: Go quickly to the Patriarch!
A THIRD: The Tsarevich, he is calling for the Tsarevich!

Четвертый

Духовника!

Басманов

Что сделалось такое?

Пятый

Царь занемог.

Шестой

Царь умирает.

Басманов
Боже!

Пятый

На троне он сидел и вдруг упал –
Кровь хлынула из уст и из ушей.

*(Царя выносят на стуле; все царское семейство, все
бояре.)*

Царь

Подите все – оставьте одного
Царевича со мною.

(Все удаляются.)

A FOURTH: Call his confessor!
BASMANOV: What has happened?
A FIFTH: The Tsar has fallen ill.
A SIXTH: The Tsar is dying.
BASMANOV: O God!
A FIFTH: He was sitting on the throne and suddenly fell – blood
gushed from his mouth and ears.
    (The Tsar is brought in on a chair; all the Tsar's family,
        all the boyars).
TSAR: Let all go hence – leave the Tsarevich alone with me.
    (Exeunt all.)

Умираю;
Обнимемся, прощай, мой сын: сейчас
Ты царствовать начнешь . . . о Боже, Боже!
Сейчас явлюсь перед Тобой – и душу
Мне некогда очистить покаяньем.
Но чувствую – мой сын, ты мне дороже
Душевного спасенья . . . так и быть!
Я подданным рожден и умереть
Мне подданным во мраке б надлежало;
Но я достиг верховной власти . . . чем?
Не спрашивай. Довольно: ты невинен,
Ты царствовать теперь по праву станешь.
Я, я за все один отвечу Богу . . .
О милый сын, не обольщайся ложно,
Не ослепляй себя ты добровольно –
В дни бурные державу ты приемлешь:
Опасен он, сей чудный самозванец,
Он именем ужасным ополчен . . .
Я, с давних лет в правленье искушенный,
Мог удержать смятенье и мятеж;
Передо мной они дрожали в страхе;
Возвысить глас измена не дерзала.

I am dying; let us embrace. Farewell, my son: now you will begin to rule . . . O God, O God! Straightway I shall appear before Thee – and I have no time to purify my soul with penitence. But I feel, my son, that you are dearer to me than the salvation of my soul . . . So be it! I was born a subject and it would be meet that in obscurity I should die a subject; but I reached supreme power . . . How? Do not ask. Enough! You are innocent, you will now begin to rule according to your right. I, I alone, will answer to God for everything . . . O my dear son, be not falsely deceived, blind not yourself of your own free will – in stormy days you assume power: he is dangerous, this strange Pretender, he is armed with a fearful name. Long tested in the art of ruling, I have been able to restrain uprising and revolt; before me they trembled with fear; treachery did not dare to raise its voice. But how will you, a young,

Но ты, младой, неопытный властитель,
Как управлять ты будешь под грозой,
Тушить мятеж, опутывать измену?
Но Бог велик! Он умудряет юность,
Он слабости дарует силу . . . слушай:
Советника, во-первых, избери
Надежного, холодных, зрелых лет,
Любимого народом – а в боярах
Почтенного породой или славой –
Хоть Шуйского. Для войска нынче нужен
Искусный вождь: Басманова пошли
И с твердостью снеси боярский ропот.
Ты с малых лет сидел со мною в Думе,
Ты знаешь ход державного правленья;
Не изменяй теченья дел. Привычка –
Душа держав. Я ныне должен был
Восстановить опалы, казни – можешь
Их отменить; тебя благословят,
Как твоего благословляли дядю,
Когда престол он Грозного приял.
Со временем и понемногу снова
Затягивай державные бразды.

inexperienced sovereign, rule during the storm, quench rebellion, entangle treachery? But God is great. He makes youth wise, He grants strength to weakness . . . Listen: first of all choose a reliable counsellor, of cool, ripe years, loved by the people and respected amongst the boyars for birth and renown – say Shuisky. For the army a skilled leader is now needed: send Basmanov, and endure with firmness the grumbling of the boyars. Since your early years you have sat with me in the Council, you know the way the state is ruled; do not change the course of procedure. Custom is the very soul of states. Recently I have had to restore disgraces, executions – you may revoke them; they will bless you as they blessed your uncle when he took the throne of [Ivan] the Terrible. In time, and little by little, draw in the reins of government afresh.

Теперь ослабь, из рук не выпуская . . .
Будь милостив, доступен к иноземцам,
Доверчиво их службу принимай.
Со строгостью храни устав церковный;
Будь молчалив; не должен царский голос
На воздухе теряться по-пустому;
Как звон святой, он должен лишь вещать
Велику скорбь или великий праздник.
О милый сын, ты входишь в те лета,
Когда нам кровь волнует женский лик.
Храни, храни святую чистоту
Невинности и гордую стыдливость:
Кто чувствами в порочных наслажденьях
В младые дни привыкнул утопать,
Тот, возмужав, угрюм и кровожаден,
И ум его безвременно темнеет.
В семье своей будь завсегда главою;
Мать почитай, но властвуй сам собою.
Ты муж и царь; люби свою сестру,
Ты ей один хранитель остаешься.

Now slacken them without letting them go from your hands . . .
Be gracious, accessible to foreigners; accept their service trustfully.
Strictly observe the Church's rules; be taciturn; the Tsar's voice
should not be lost in the air in vain; like the ringing of a sacred bell,
it should announce only great sorrow or great rejoicing. O my dear
son, you are coming to those years when a woman's face excites
our blood. Keep, keep the sacred purity of innocence and proud
modesty: he who in his young days is used to luxuriating sensually
in vicious delights will be surly and bloodthirsty when he reaches
man's estate, and his mind untimely darkens. In your family
always be the head; honour your mother, but be your own master.
You are both man and Tsar; love your sister; you are the only
protector left to her.

Феодор

(на коленях)

Нет, нет – живи и царствуй долговечно:
Народ и мы погибли без тебя.

Царь

Все кончено – глаза мои темнеют,
Я чувствую могильный хлад . . .

*(Входит патриарх, святители, за ними все бояре.
Царицу ведут под руки, царевна рыдает.)*

Кто там?

А! схима . . . так! святое постриженье . . .
Ударил час, в монахи царь идет –
И темный гроб моею будет кельей . . .
Повремени, владыко патриарх,
Я царь еще: внемлите вы, бояре:
Се тот, кому приказываю царство;
Целуйте крест Феодору . . . Басманов,
Друзья мои . . . при гробе вас молю
Ему служить усердием и правдой!
Он так еще и млад и непорочен . . .
Клянетесь ли?

FEODOR (*kneeling*): No, no! Live and rule long: the people and we are done for without you.
TSAR: All is finished – my eyes grow dark, I feel the coldness of the grave . . .

(Enter Patriarch, bishops, behind them all the boyars. The Tsaritsa is led in, supported on either side; the Tsarevna sobs.)

Who is there? Ah! The *skhima* [the supreme monastic order] . . . so! The sacred tonsure . . . The hour has struck; the Tsar becomes a monk – and a dark grave shall be my cell . . . Wait but an instant, lord Patriarch, I am still Tsar: hearken to me, boyars: this is he to whom I hand over the kingdom; kiss the cross in allegiance to Feodor . . . Basmanov, my friends . . . at the very grave I pray to you to serve him with zeal and truth! He is still so young and so unsullied . . . Do you swear?

Бояре

Клянемся.

Царь

Я доволен.
Простите ж мне соблазны и грехи
И вольные и тайные обиды . . .
Святый отец, приближься, я готов.

(*Начинается обряд пострижения. Женщин в
обмороке выносят.*)

[*Ставка.
Басманов вводит Пушкина.*]

Басманов

Войди сюда и говори свободно.
Итак, тебя ко мне он посылает?

BOYARS: We swear.
TSAR: I am content. Forgive me my transgressions and my sins,
the offences I have committed wittingly and the secret ones . . .
Holy father, approach. I am ready.

(*The ceremony of the tonsure begins. Women are carried out
swooning.*)

[*Scene 21: May 1605. Boris is dead. His son Feodor is Tsar. Pushkin,
an adherent of the Pretender, tries to persuade Basmanov, Commander-
in-chief of the Muscovite army, to transfer his allegiance to the
Pretender, who is about to march on Moscow.*]

*Headquarters
Basmanov leads in Pushkin.*

BASMANOV: Come in here and speak freely. So he [the Pre-
tender] sends you to me?

Пушкин

Тебе свою он дружбу предлагает
И первый сан по нем в московском царстве.

Басманов

Но я и так Феодором высоко
Уж вознесен. Начальствую над войском,
Он для меня презрел и чин разрядный,
И гнев бояр – я присягал ему.

Пушкин

Ты присягал наследнику престола
Законному; но если жив другой,
Законнейший? . .

Басманов

    Послушай, Пушкин, полно,
Пустого мне не говори; я знаю,
Кто он такой.

PUSHKIN: He offers you his friendship and the first rank after himself in the realm of Muscovy.
BASMANOV: But as it is I have already been raised up high by
Feodor. I am in command of the army: for me he has scorned
both rank, established by the Book of Precedence, and the boyars'
wrath. I have sworn allegiance to him.
PUSHKIN: You swore allegiance to the lawful heir to the throne;
but what if there should be alive another still more lawful?
BASMANOV: Listen, Pushkin, that is enough: speak no more
nonsense to me; I know who he is.

Пушкин

Россия и Литва
Димитрием давно его признали,
Но, впрочем, я за это не стою.
Быть может, он Димитрий настоящий,
Быть может, он и самозванец. Только
Я ведаю, что рано или поздно
Ему Москву уступит сын Борисов.

Басманов

Пока стою за юного царя,
Дотоле он престола не оставит;
Полков у нас довольно, слава Богу!
Победою я их одушевлю,
А вы, кого против меня пошлете?
Не казака ль Карелу? али Мнишка?
Да много ль вас, всего-то восемь тысяч.

Пушкин

Ошибся ты: и тех не наберешь –
Я сам скажу, что войско наше дрянь,
Что казаки лишь только селы грабят,
Что поляки лишь хвастают да пьют,
А русские . . . да что и говорить . . .

PUSHKIN: Russia and Lithuania have long recognized him as Dimitri; however, I do not insist on that. Perhaps he is the real Dimitri, perhaps he is just a Pretender. Only this I know, that sooner or later the son of Boris will yield Moscow to him.

BASMANOV: As long as I defend the young Tsar, so long he shall not leave the throne; we have sufficient forces, thank God! I shall inspire them with victory; and you – whom will you send against me? Not Karela the Cossack? Or Mnishek? And are there many of you? Why, a mere eight thousand.

PUSHKIN: You are mistaken: you will not find even that number of them – I myself say it, our army is rubbish, the Cossacks merely plunder villages, the Poles merely boast and drink, while the Russians . . . there's no denying it . . . With you I'll not dissemble;

Перед тобой не стану я лукавить;
Но знаешь ли, чем сильны мы, Басманов?
Не войском, нет, не польскою помогой,
А мнением; да! мнением народным.
Димитрия ты помнишь торжество
И мирные его завоеванья,
Когда везде без выстрела ему
Послушные сдавались города,
А воевод упрямых чернь вязала?
Ты видел сам, охотно ль ваши рати
Сражались с ним; когда же? при Борисе!
А нынче ль? . . . Нет, Басманов, поздно
    спорить
И раздувать холодный пепел брани:
Со всем твоим умом и твердой волей
Не устоишь; не лучше ли тебе
Дать первому пример благоразумный,
Димитрия царем провозгласить
И тем ему навеки удружить?
Как думаешь?

Басманов
Узнаете вы завтра.

---

but do you know what we are strong in, Basmanov? Not in our
army, no, not in Polish aid, but in opinion – yes! In popular
opinion. You recall the triumph of Dimitri and his peaceful
conquests, when everywhere submissive cities surrendered to him
without a shot and the rabble bound the stubborn generals? You
yourself have seen and know how willingly your armies fought
against him; yes, but when? During Boris's reign! But now?
No, Basmanov, it is too late to argue and to fan the cold embers of
war: with all your intelligence and firm will, you will not resist;
were it not better for you to be the first to give a sensible example,
to proclaim Dimitri Tsar, and thereby to do him a lasting service?
What do you think?
BASMANOV: You shall know tomorrow.

Пушкин

Решись.

Басманов

Прощай.

Пушкин

Подумай же, Басманов.

(*Уходит.*)

Басманов

Он прав, он прав; везде измена зреет –
Что делать мне? Ужели буду ждать,
Чтоб и меня бунтовщики связали
И выдали Отрепьеву? Не лучше ль
Предупредить разрыв потока бурный
И самому . . . Но изменить присяге!
Но заслужить бесчестье в род и род!
Доверенность младого венценосца
Предательством ужасным заплатить . . .
Опальному изгнаннику легко
Обдумывать мятеж и заговор,

PUSHKIN: Make up your mind!
BASMANOV: Farewell.
PUSHKIN: Think on it well, Basmanov.
(*Exit.*)
BASMANOV: He is right, he is right; everywhere treason ripens –
what am I to do? Shall I really wait for the rebels to bind me too
and hand me over to Otrepyev [the Pretender]? Would it not be
better to forestall the stormy burst of the torrent, and myself . . .
But to betray my oath! To incur dishonour in the eyes of generation after generation! To requite the trust of my young crown-
bearing master with terrible treachery . . . It is easy for a disgraced
exile to ponder rebellion and conspiracy – but for me, for me, my

Но мне ли, мне ль, любимцу государя . . .
Но смерть . . . но власть . . . но бедствия
народны . . .

(*Задумывается.*)

Сюда! кто там?

(*Свищет.*)

Коня! Трубите сбор.

ЕВГЕНИЙ ОНЕГИН
Глава Первая

I

«Мой дядя самых честных правил,
Когда не в шутку занемог,
Он уважать себя заставил
И лучше выдумать не мог.
Его пример другим наука;

sovereign's favourite . . . But death . . . but power . . . but the
sufferings of the people . . .

(*Ponders.*)

Come here! Who's there?

(*Whistles.*)

My horse! Sound the trumpet for assembly!

YEVGENY ONEGIN
Chapter One

I

'WHEN my uncle, a man of the highest principles, fell seriously ill,
he made himself respected and could have thought out no better
way; his example is a lesson to others. But, my God, what a bore

Но, Боже мой, какая скука
С больным сидеть и день и ночь,
Не отходя ни шагу прочь!
Какое низкое коварство
Полуживого забавлять,
Ему подушки поправлять,
Печально подносить лекарство,
Вздыхать и думать про себя:
Когда же черт возьмет тебя!»

II

Так думал молодой повеса,
Летя в пыли на почтовых,
Всевышней волею Зевеса
Наследник всех своих родных.
Друзья Людмилы и Руслана!
С героем моего романа
Без предисловий, сей же час
Позвольте познакомить вас:
Онегин, добрый мой приятель,
Родился на брегах Невы,
Где, может быть, родились вы

to sit with a sick man day and night without going so much as a pace away! What low cunning to amuse someone half-alive, to adjust his pillows, with gloomy countenance to bring him his medicine, to sigh and to think to oneself "When will the devil take you?"'

II

So thought our young rake, flying in a post-chaise through the dust, the heir, by the highest will of Zeus, of all his relatives. Friends of Ruslan and Lyudmila [Pushkin's epic poem printed in 1820], allow me to introduce you forthwith, without any foreword, to the hero of my novel. My good friend Onegin was born on the banks of the Neva, where perhaps you, my reader, were born or

Или блистали, мой читатель;
Там некогда гулял и я:
Но вреден север для меня.

III

Служив отлично благородно,
Долгами жил его отец,
Давал три бала ежегодно
И промотался наконец.
Судьба Евгения хранила:
Сперва *Madame* за ним ходила,
Потом *Monsieur* ее сменил.
Ребенок был резов, но мил.
Monsieur l'Abbé, француз убогой,
Чтоб не измучилось дитя,
Учил его всему шутя,
Не докучал моралью строгой,
Слегка за шалости бранил
И в Летний сад гулять водил.

where you shone! Once I too lived a carefree life there: but the north is inimical to me [Pushkin was exiled to the south in 1820].

III

Having served most impeccably, his father lived by his debts, gave three balls a year, and finally squandered away his money. Fate preserved Yevgeny. First of all *Madame* looked after him, then *Monsieur* replaced her. The child was lively but lovable. *Monsieur l'Abbé*, a paltry Frenchman, taught him everything in a joking manner so that the child should not become exhausted, and did not bore him with stern moralizing, but scolded him gently for his pranks and took him walking in the Summer Gardens.

IV

Когда же юности мятежной
Пришла Евгению пора,
Пора надежд и грусти нежной,
Monsieur прогнали со двора.
Вот мой Онегин на свободе;
Острижен по последней моде,
Как *dandy* лондонский одет –
И наконец увидел свет.
Он по-французски совершенно
Мог изъясняться и писал;
Легко мазурку танцевал
И кланялся непринужденно;
Чего ж вам больше? Свет решил,
Что он умен и очень мил.

V

Мы все учились понемногу
Чему-нибудь и как-нибудь,
Так воспитаньем, слава Богу,
У нас немудрено блеснуть.
Онегин был по мненью многих

IV

But when the age of rebellious youth came to Yevgeny – the time of hopes and tender sorrow – *Monsieur* was given the sack. And now my Onegin is free; his hair is cut in the latest fashion; he is dressed like a London dandy – and at last he made his début in society. He could express himself perfectly in French, and write it too; with ease he danced the Mazurka and unconstrainedly he bowed. What more do you want? Society decided that he was intelligent and very charming.

V

We have all learned – each of us a little – something or other and somehow or other. And so, thank God, it is not difficult with us to make a brilliant display of education. Onegin was, in the opinion

(Судей решительных и строгих)
Ученый малый, но педант:
Имел он счастливый талант
Без принужденья в разговоре
Коснуться до всего слегка,
С ученым видом знатока
Хранить молчанье в важном споре
И возбуждать улыбку дам
Огнем нежданных эпиграмм.

VI

Латынь из моды вышла ныне:
Так, если правду вам сказать,
Он знал довольно по-латыне,
Чтоб эпиграфы разбирать,
Потолковать об Ювенале,
В конце письма поставить *vale*,
Да помнил, хоть не без греха,
Из Энеиды два стиха.
Он рыться не имел охоты
В хронологической пыли
Бытописания земли:
Но дней минувших анекдоты
От Ромула до наших дней
Хранил он в памяти своей.

of many (unhesitating and stern judges), a learned fellow, but a crank. He had the happy art of gently touching on everything in conversation without constraint, and, with the learned air of an expert, keeping silence in a weighty argument and arousing the ladies' smiles by the fire of unexpected epigrams.

VI

Latin nowadays has gone out of fashion: to tell you the truth, he knew enough Latin to decipher epigraphs, to talk about Juvenal, to put *vale* at the end of a letter, and he remembered – though not faultlessly – a couple of lines from the *Aeneid*. He had no inclination to rummage in the chronological dust of the history of our land: but he kept in his memory anecdotes of bygone days, from Romulus to our own time.

XLV

Условий света свергнув бремя,
Как он, отстав от суеты,
С ним подружился я в то время.
Мне нравились его черты,
Мечтам невольная преданность,
Неподражательная странность
И резкий, охлажденный ум.
Я был озлоблен, он угрюм;
Страстей игру мы знали оба;
Томила жизнь обоих нас;
В обоих сердца жар угас;
Обоих ожидала злоба
Слепой Фортуны и людей
На самом утре наших дней.

XLVI

Кто жил и мыслил, тот не может
В душе не презирать людей;
Кто чувствовал, того тревожит
Призра́к невозвратимых дней:

[*Stanzas VII-XLIV: Yevgeny's life in St Petersburg is described –
his visits to balls, to the theatre, to restaurants, his attempts to dispel
boredom by writing and reading.*]

XLV

Having cast off, like him, the burden of society's conventions and
having set vanity aside, I made friends with him at that time. I
liked his features, his instinctive addiction to dreaming, his inimi-
table oddity, and his sharp cool mind. I was embittered, he was
sullen; we both knew the play of passions; life oppressed us both;
in both of us the heart's flame had burned out; the malice of blind
Fortune and of men awaited us both in the very morn of our days.

XLVI

He who has lived and pondered cannot in his heart but despise
people; he who has experienced emotions is disturbed by the

Тому уж нет очарований,
Того змия воспоминаний,
Того раскаянье грызет.
Все это часто придает
Большую прелесть разговору.
Сперва Онегина язык
Меня смущал; но я привык
К его язвительному спору,
И к шутке, с желчью пополам,
И злости мрачных эпиграмм.

XLVII

Как часто летнею порою,
Когда прозрачно и светло
Ночное небо над Невою,
И вод веселое стекло
Не отражает лик Дианы,
Воспомня прежних лет романы,
Воспомня прежнюю любовь,
Чувствительны, беспечны вновь,
Дыханьем ночи благосклонной
Безмолвно упивались мы!

phantom of irrevocable days, no longer feels fascination, is gnawed at by the serpent of memories and by repentance. All this often lends great charm to conversation. At first Onegin's tongue embarrassed me; but I grew used to his caustic arguments and to his jokes mixed half and half with spleen, and to the spitefulness of his grim epigrams.

XLVII

How often in summer-time, when the night sky above the Neva is transparent and light and when the merry mirror of the waters does not reflect Diana's face – how often, recalling romances of former years, recalling former love, sensitive once more, carefree once more, we silently relished the breath of kindly night! Just as the

Как в лес зеленый из тюрьмы
Перенесен колодник сонный,
Так уносились мы мечтой
К началу жизни молодой.

XLVIII

С душою, полной сожалений,
И опершися на гранит,
Стоял задумчиво Евгений,
Как описал себя пиит.
Все было тихо; лишь ночные
Перекликались часовые,
Да дрожек отдаленный стук
С Мильонной раздавался вдруг;
Лишь лодка, веслами махая,
Плыла по дремлющей реке:
И нас пленяли вдалеке
Рожок и песня удалая . . .
Но слаще, средь ночных забав,
Напев Торкватовых октав!

sleepy convict is transferred from his prison to a green forest, so were we carried away in our dreams to the beginning of our young life.

XLVIII

With his heart full of regrets and leaning on the granite parapet, Yevgeny stood pensively, just as the poet described himself. [A reference to N. M. Muravyev's poem 'To the Goddess of the Neva'.] All was quiet; only the night watchmen called to each other; and suddenly one could hear the distant clatter of a drozhky from Milyonnaya Street; only a boat with waving oars floated along the slumbering river. And in the distance the horn band and spirited song entranced us . . . But sweeter, midst the joys of night, is the melody of Torquato's *ottava rima*!

Глава Вторая

XI

В пустыне, где один Евгений
Мог оценить его дары,
Господ соседственных селений
Ему не нравились пиры;
Бежал он их беседы шумной.
Их разговор благоразумный
О сенокосе, о вине,
О псарне, о своей родне,
Конечно, не блистал ни чувством,
Ни поэтическим огнем,
Ни остротою, ни умом,
Ни общежития искусством;
Но разговор их милых жен
Гораздо меньше был умен.

[*Chapter 1, Stanza XLIX, to Chapter 2, Stanza X: a short digression on Italy follows. Onegin and Pushkin part company. Onegin's uncle dies and Onegin becomes a country squire. He is just as bored in the country as he was in the town. A young poet, Vladimir Lensky, arrives and settles in the neighbourhood.*]

Chapter 2

XI

In the wilderness, where only my Yevgeny could appreciate his gifts, he did not like the feasts of the lords of the neighbouring villages; he avoided their noisy chatter. Their sensible conversation about hay-making, wine, hounds, and their relatives did not of course shine with either emotion, or poetic fire, or humour, or intelligence, or the art of social intercourse. Yet the conversation of their dear wives was far less clever still.

XII

Богат, хорош собою, Ленский
Везде был принят как жених;
Таков обычай деревенский;
Все дочек прочили своих
За *полурусского соседа*;
Взойдет ли он, тотчас беседа
Заводит слово стороной
О скуке жизни холостой;
Зовут соседа к самовару,
А Дуня разливает чай;
Ей шепчут: «Дуня, примечай!»
Потом приносят и гитару:
И запищит она (Бог мой!):
Приди в чертог ко мне златой! . . .

XIII

Но Ленский, не имев, конечно,
Охоты узы брака несть,
С Онегиным желал сердечно
Знакомство покороче свесть.

XII

Rich and handsome, Lensky was everywhere received as an eligible bachelor; such is the country custom; everyone planned for their daughters to marry their *half-Russian neighbour*; as soon as he came into a room, straightway the conversation would begin to turn obliquely on the boredom of bachelor life; they would call their neighbour to the samovar and, while Dunya was pouring out tea, they would whisper to her: 'Dunya, note him!' Then they would bring the guitar and she would squeak (my God!): '*Come into my golden chamber!*' [A very popular aria from a contemporary opera.]

XIII

But Lensky, having of course no wish to bear the bonds of wedlock, heartily desired to make his relationship with Onegin more

Они сошлись. Волна и камень,
Стихи и проза, лед и пламень
Не столь различны меж собой.
Сперва взаимной разнотой
Они друг другу были скучны;
Потом понравились; потом
Съезжались каждый день верхом
И скоро стали неразлучны.
Так люди (первый каюсь я)
От *делать нечего* друзья.

XIV

Но дружбы нет и той меж нами.
Все предрассудки истребя,
Мы почитаем всех нулями,
А единицами – себя.
Мы все глядим в Наполеоны;
Двуногих тварей миллионы
Для нас орудие одно;
Нам чувство дико и смешно.
Сноснее многих был Евгений;
Хоть он людей, конечно, знал
И вообще их презирал, –

intimate. They became close friends. Wave and stone, verse and prose, ice and flame were not so different in themselves. At first they bored each other with their mutual disparity; then they took to one another; then they met each day on horseback, and soon they became inseparable. So people (and I am the first to admit it) become friends from having nothing to do.

XIV

But even that friendship does not exist between us; destroying all prejudices, we consider all people to be nonentities, but ourselves to be the entities. We all strive to become Napoleons. The millions of two-legged creatures are for us merely a weapon; for us emotion is strange and amusing. More tolerable than many was Onegin. Although of course he knew people and in general despised them –

Но (правил нет без исключений)
Иных он очень отличал
И вчуже чувство уважал.

XXII

Она поэту подарила
Младых восторгов первый сон,
И мысль об ней одушевила
Его цевницы первый стон.
Простите, игры золотые!
Он рощи полюбил густые,
Уединенье, тишину,
И ночь, и звезды, и луну,
Луну, небесную лампаду,
Которой посвящали мы
Прогулки средь вечерней тьмы,
И слезы, тайных мук отраду . . .
Но нынче видим только в ней
Замену тусклых фонарей.

still (there are no rules without exceptions) some people he preferred, and in his detachment he respected emotion.

[*Chapter 2, Stanzas XV–XXI: Lensky has fallen in love with Olga,
the daughter of a neighbouring landowner.*]

XXII

She [Olga] gave the poet the first dream of youth's raptures, and
thoughts of her inspired the first lament from his pipes. Farewell,
golden games! He began to find delight in dense thickets, in seclusion, in tranquillity, and in the night, the stars, the moon – the
moon, that heavenly lamp, to which we used to dedicate our walks
in the evening darkness and our tears, our consolation in secret
sorrows . . . But now in the moon we merely see a substitute for
dim lanterns.

XXIII

Всегда скромна, всегда послушна,
Всегда как утро весела,
Как жизнь поэта простодушна,
Как поцелуй любви мила;
Глаза, как небо, голубые,
Улыбка, локоны льняные,
Движенья, голос, легкий стан,
Всё в Ольге . . . но любой роман
Возьмите и найдете верно
Ее портрет: он очень мил,
Я прежде сам его любил,
Но надоел он мне безмерно.
Позвольте мне, читатель мой,
Заняться старшею сестрой.

XXIV

Ее сестра звалась Татьяна . . .
Впервые именем таким
Страницы нежные романа
Мы своевольно освятим.
И что ж? оно приятно, звучно;
Но с ним, я знаю, неразлучно
Воспоминанье старины

XXIII

Ever modest, ever obedient, ever merry as the morn, simple as a poet's life, sweet as a kiss of love; her eyes – blue as the sky, her smile, her flaxen locks, her movements, her voice, her slender figure – all this is in Olga . . . But take any novel and for sure you will find her portrait. It is very sweet, and I myself once loved such portraits; but then I became completely bored with them. Allow me, dear reader, to occupy myself with her elder sister.

XXIV

Her sister was called Tatyana . . . For the first time we will deliberately hallow the tender pages of a novel with such a name. And why not? It is pleasant, it sounds well, but with it, I know, are

Иль девичьей! Мы все должны
Признаться: вкусу очень мало
У нас и в наших именах
(Не говорим уж о стихах);
Нам просвещенье не пристало,
И нам досталось от него
Жеманство, – больше ничего.

XXV

Итак, она звалась Татьяной.
Ни красотой сестры своей,
Ни свежестью ее румяной
Не привлекла б она очей.
Дика, печальна, молчалива,
Как лань лесная боязлива,
Она в семье своей родной
Казалась девочкой чужой.
Она ласкаться не умела
К отцу, ни к матери своей;
Дитя сама, в толпе детей
Играть и прыгать не хотела
И часто целый день одна
Сидела молча у окна.

inseparably linked recollections of the olden days or of the servant-maids' quarters! We must all admit that we have precious little taste even in our names – to say nothing of our verse. Enlightenment does not suit us, and all that we have got from it is affectation – and nothing else.

XXV

And so she was called Tatyana. She had not the beauty of her sister, nor her rosy freshness to attract the eye. Shy, sad, silent, timid as a forest deer, in her own family she seemed a stranger. She did not know how to be affectionate with her father or with her mother; herself a child, she had no wish to play or skip amongst the crowd of children, and often she would sit the whole day long in silence by the window.

Глава Третья

XXXII

Татьяна то вздохнет, то охнет;
Письмо дрожит в ее руке;
Облатка розовая сохнет
На воспаленном языке.
К плечу головушкой склонилась,
Сорочка легкая спустилась
С ее прелестного плеча . . .
Но вот уж лунного луча
Сиянье гаснет. Там долина
Сквозь пар яснеет. Там поток
Засеребрился; там рожок
Пастуший будит селянина.
Вот утро: встали все давно,
Моей Татьяне все равно.

[Chapter 2, *Stanza XXVI, to Chapter 3, Stanza XXXI: the character and habits of Tatyana and her family, the Larins, are described. Onegin is introduced to the Larins by Lensky and Tatyana falls in love with him. She tells her nanny, and writes a letter to Onegin admitting her love for him.*]

Chapter 3

XXXII

Tatyana now sighs, now groans; the letter trembles in her hand; the pink wafer dries on her feverish tongue. She lets her head fall on her shoulder. Her light chemise slips from her exquisite shoulder. But now already the moonbeam's radiance dies out. There in the distance the valley becomes clear through the mist; there the torrent sparkles like silver, and the shepherd's horn wakes the villagers. Morning has come. Everyone has long been up – but to my Tatyana it is all one.

XXXIII

Она зари не замечает,
Сидит с поникшею главой
И на письмо не напирает
Своей печати вырезной.
Но, дверь тихонько отпирая,
Уж ей Филипьевна седая
Приносит на подносе чай.
«Пора, дитя мое, вставай:
Да ты, красавица, готова!
О пташка ранняя моя!
Вечор уж как боялась я!
Да, слава Богу, ты здорова!
Тоски ночной и следу нет,
Лицо твое как маков цвет».

XXXIV

— Ах! няня, сделай одолженье. —
«Изволь, родная, прикажи».
— Не думай . . . право . . . подозренье . . .
Но видишь . . . ах! не откажи. —
«Мой друг, вот Бог тебе порука».
— Итак, пошли тихонько внука
С запиской этой к О . . . к тому . . .

XXXIII

She does not notice the dawn; she sits with her head bowed and does not press her engraved signet upon the letter. But quietly opening the door grey-haired Filipyevna brings her her tea upon a tray. 'It's time, my child – get up: but you are already dressed, my fair one! O my early little bird! Oh, how frightened I was yesterday evening! But you are well, thank God! There is no sign of last night's sorrow – your face is like the colour of a poppy.'

XXXIV

'O nanny, do me a favour.' 'Of course, my darling, just tell me.' 'Don't think . . . indeed . . . suspicion . . . But you see . . . Oh, don't say no!' 'My dear, I swear to you by God!' 'Well then, send your grandson on the quiet with this note to O . . . to the one . . .

К соседу . . . да велеть ему,
Чтоб он не говорил ни слова,
Чтоб он не называл меня . . . –
«Кому же, милая моя?
Я нынче стала бестолкова.
Кругом соседей много есть;
Куда мне их и перечесть».

XXXV

– Как недогадлива ты, няня! –
«Сердечный друг, уж я стара,
Стара; тупеет разум, Таня;
А то, бывало, я востра,
Бывало, слово барской воли . . .»
– Ах, няня, няня! до того ли?
Что нужды мне в твоем уме?
Ты видишь, дело о письме
К Онегину. – «Ну, дело, дело.
Не гневайся, душа моя,
Ты знаешь, непонятна я . . .
Да что ж ты снова побледнела?»
– Так, няня, право ничего.
Пошли же внука своего.

to the neighbour . . . and tell him – not to say a word, not to
mention my name . . .' 'To whom, my dear? I have become slow-
witted nowadays. There are so many neighbours round here; how
on earth can I even count them all!'

XXXV

'How slow you are at guessing, nanny!' 'My darling friend, I am
old, indeed I am old: my mind grows dull, Tanya; yet once I was
keen-witted, once one word only of the master's wish . . .' 'Oh,
nanny, nanny! What has that to do with it? What need have I of
your wits? You see, it's about a letter to Onegin.' 'Well then, all
right, all right. Do not be angry, my darling, you know that I am
hard of understanding . . . But why have you grown pale again?'
'It's nothing, nanny, really nothing. Now send your grandson.'

XXXVIII

И между тем душа в ней ныла,
И слез был полон томный взор.
Вдруг топот! . . . кровь её застыла.
Вот ближе! скачут . . . и на двор
Евгений! «Ах!» — и легче тени
Татьяна прыг в другие сени,
С крыльца на двор, и прямо в сад,
Летит, летит; взглянуть назад
Не смеет; мигом обежала
Куртины, мостики, лужок,
Аллею к озеру, лесок,
Кусты сирен переломала,
По цветникам летя к ручью.
И, задыхаясь, на скамью

[Chapter 3, Stanzas XXXVI–XXXVII: There is no answer to the letter. Lensky visits the Larins and tells them that Onegin is coming in the evening. Tatyana waits for him.]

XXXVIII

Meanwhile her heart ached and her languorous eyes were full of tears. Suddenly the clatter of horses' hoofs! Her blood froze. Nearer and nearer! The horses are galloping . . . and Yevgeny drives into the courtyard! 'Ah!' she cries, and lighter than a shadow Tatyana jumps into the other entrance hall, from the porch to the courtyard, and straight into the garden she flies, she flies; she does not dare to look back; in an instant she ran through borders, across small bridges, a little field, down the avenue leading to the lake, through a copse, breaking down lilac shrubs, flying over flower-beds towards the brook – and gasping for breath, upon the bench . . .

XXXIX

Упала . . .
            «Здесь он! здесь Евгений!
О Боже! что подумал он!»
В ней сердце, полное мучений,
Хранит надежды темный сон;
Она дрожит и жаром пышет,
И ждет: нейдет ли? Но не слышит.
В саду служанки, на грядах,
Сбирали ягоду в кустах
И хором по наказу пели
(Наказ, основанный на том,
Чтоб барской ягоды тайком
Уста лукавые не ели
И пеньем были заняты:
Затея сельской остроты!)

Глава Четвертая

XI

Но, получив посланье Тани,
Онегин живо тронут был:

XXXIX

. . . she fell . . . 'He's here! Yevgeny's here! O God! What did
he think!' Her heart, full of torment, harbours an obscure dream
of hope; she trembles and burns with excitement, and waits: is he
not coming? But she hears nothing. In the garden on the beds the
servant girls were picking berries among the bushes and were
singing in chorus by order (an order designed to stop their sly
mouths from secretly eating the master's berries, and to occupy
them with singing: a true invention of provincial cunning!).

[*Chapter 3, Stanza XL, to Chapter 4, Stanza X: Onegin meets
Tatyana in the garden. Pushkin describes his early amorous successes
and his attitude to women.*]

Chapter 4

XI

But having received Tatyana's epistle Onegin was deeply touched:

Язык девических мечтаний
В нем думы роем возмутил;
И вспомнил он Татьяны милой
И бледный цвет и вид унылый;
И в сладостный, безгрешный сон
Душою погрузился он.
Быть может, чувствий пыл старинный
Им на минуту овладел;
Но обмануть он не хотел
Доверчивость души невинной.
Теперь мы в сад перелетим,
Где встретилась Татьяна с ним.

XII

Минуты две они молчали,
Но к ней Онегин подошел
И молвил: «Вы ко мне писали,
Не отпирайтесь. Я прочел
Души доверчивой признанья,
Любви невинной излиянья;
Мне ваша искренность мила,
Она в волненье привела
Давно умолкнувшие чувства;

the language of girlish reveries stirred up within him whole swarms of thoughts; and he remembered dear Tatyana's pale complexion and her despondent air. And he plunged his soul into a deep sinless dream. Perhaps the old ardour of his feelings seized him for a moment; but he did not wish to deceive the trustfulness of an innocent soul. And now we will fly across into the garden where Tatyana met him.

XII

For about two minutes they were silent, but Onegin came up to her and said: 'You have written to me, do not deny it. I read the admissions of your trustful soul, the confessions of your innocent love; your sincerity touches me; it has set astir feelings which have

Но вас хвалить я не хочу;
Я за нее вам отплачу
Признаньем также без искусства;
Примите исповедь мою:
Себя на суд вам отдаю.

XIII

Когда бы жизнь домашним кругом
Я ограничить захотел;
Когда б мне быть отцом, супругом
Приятный жребий повелел;
Когда б семейственной картиной
Пленился я хоть миг единый, —
То, верно б, кроме вас одной
Невесты не искал иной.
Скажу без блесток мадригальных:
Нашед мой прежний идеал,
Я, верно б, вас одну избрал
В подруги дней моих печальных,
Всего прекрасного в залог,
И был бы счастлив . . . сколько мог!

long been silent; but I do not wish to praise you; I will repay you for it with an avowal just as artless; accept my confession. I put myself on trial before you.

XIII

'Had I wished to confine my life to the domestic round; had some pleasant fate ordered me to be a father and a husband; had I just for one second been captivated by the picture of family life – then, in truth, I would have sought no other bride than you alone. I will say this without any madrigalian flashes: finding in you the ideal of my youth, I would truly have chosen you alone to be the companion of my sad days, as a pledge of all that is beautiful, and I would have been happy . . . in so far as I could!

XIV

Но я не создан для блаженства;
Ему чужда душа моя;
Напрасны ваши совершенства:
Их вовсе недостоин я.
Поверьте (совесть в том порукой),
Супружество нам будет мукой.
Я, сколько ни любил бы вас,
Привыкнув, разлюблю тотчас;
Начнете плакать: ваши слезы
Не тронут сердца моего,
А будут лишь бесить его.
Судите ж вы, какие розы
Нам заготовит Гименей
И, может быть, на много дней!

XV

Что может быть на свете хуже
Семьи, где бедная жена
Грустит о недостойном муже,
И днем и вечером одна;

XIV

'But I was not made for bliss; my soul is alien to it; your perfections are in vain: I am completely unworthy of them. Believe me (my conscience is a guarantee of this), marriage would be torment for us. However much I loved you, I would fall out of love with you as soon as I got used to you; you would begin to weep; your tears would not touch my heart but would only enrage it. Judge now yourself what roses Hymen would prepare for us – and perhaps for many a day!

XV

'What can be worse on earth than a family in which the poor wife sorrows for her unworthy husband and is alone day and night; in

Где скучный муж, ей цену зная
(Судьбу, однако ж, проклиная),
Всегда нахмурен, молчалив,
Сердит и холодно-ревнив!
Таков я. И того ль искали
Вы чистой, пламенной душой,
Когда с такою простотой,
С таким умом ко мне писали?
Ужели жребий вам такой
Назначен строгою судьбой?

XVI

Мечтам и годам нет возврата;
Не обновлю души моей . . .
Я вас люблю любовью брата
И, может быть, еще нежней.
Послушайте ж меня без гнева:
Сменит не раз младая дева
Мечтами легкие мечты;
Так деревцо свои листы
Меняет с каждою весною.
Так, видно, небом суждено.
Полюбите вы снова: но . . .

which the bored husband, knowing her true value (yet cursing fate) is always gloomy, silent, angry, and coldly jealous! Such would I be. And was it such a man that you sought with your pure passionate soul when you wrote to me with such simplicity, such intelligence? Can it be that such a lot was prescribed for you by stern fate?

XVI

'Daydreams and years have no return; I cannot renew my soul . . . I love you with a brother's love, and perhaps even more tenderly. But listen to me without anger: a young girl will many a time replace one light reverie with another; thus a sapling changes its leaves each spring. Thus it is clearly ordained by heaven. You will

Учитесь властвовать собою;
Не всякий вас, как я, поймет;
К беде неопытность ведет».

XXIV

Увы, Татьяна увядает,
Бледнеет, гаснет и молчит!
Ничто ее не занимает,
Ее души не шевелит.
Качая важно головою,
Соседы шепчут меж собою:
Пора, пора бы замуж ей!...
Но полно. Надо мне скорей
Развеселить воображенье
Картиной счастливой любви.
Невольно, милые мои,
Меня стесняет сожаленье;
Простите мне: я так люблю
Татьяну милую мою!

fall in love anew: but . . . learn to have mastery over yourself; not
everyone will understand you as I have done; inexperience leads
to misfortune.'

[*Chapter 4, Stanzas XVII–XXIII: Tatyana listens to Onegin in
silence and goes back to the house with him. After a digression on love
and friendship, Pushkin describes the effects of the meeting on Tatyana.*]

XXIV

Alas, Tatyana fades away, grows pale and dim and silent! Nothing
occupies her or stirs her soul. Gravely shaking their heads, the
neighbours whisper amongst themselves: 'It's time, high time she
got married!' But that's enough. I must now quickly cheer the
imagination with a picture of happy love. I cannot help but feel
oppressed by pity, my dear ones; forgive me; I so love my dear
Tatyana!

XXV

Час от часу плененный боле
Красами Ольги молодой,
Владимир сладостной неволе
Предался полною душой.
Он вечно с ней. В ее покое
Они сидят в потемках двое;
Они в саду, рука с рукой,
Гуляют утренней порой;
И что ж? Любовью упоенный,
В смятенье нежного стыда,
Он только смеет иногда,
Улыбкой Ольги ободренный,
Развитым локоном играть
Иль край одежды целовать.

XXVI

Он иногда читает Оле
Нравоучительный роман,
В котором автор знает боле
Природу, чем Шатобриан,
А между тем две, три страницы
(Пустые бредни, небылицы,

XXV

Hourly more captivated by the charms of young Olga, Vladimir abandoned himself with all his soul to sweet captivity. He is always with her. In her chamber the two sit in darkness; of a morning they stroll hand in hand in the garden; and what is the result? Enraptured by love, in the confusion of tender bashfulness, he only dares sometimes, emboldened by Olga's smile, to play with an untwined ringlet of her hair or to kiss the hem of her dress.

XXVI

Sometimes he reads to Olga an edifying novel in which the author knows nature better than Chateaubriand does, while from time to time he blushingly skips two or three pages – empty rubbish,

Опасные для сердца дев)
Он пропускает, покраснев.
Уединясь от всех далеко,
Они над шахматной доской,
На стол облокотясь, порой
Сидят, задумавшись глубоко,
И Ленский пешкою ладью
Берёт в рассеянье свою.

XL

Но наше северное лето,
Карикатура южных зим,
Мелькнёт и нет: известно это,
Хоть мы признаться не хотим.
Уж небо осенью дышало,
Уж реже солнышко блистало,
Короче становился день,
Лесов таинственная сень
С печальным шумом обнажалась,
Ложился на поля туман,
Гусей крикливых караван

fairy-tales, dangerous for the hearts of young girls. At times, retiring far from all the others, they sit over the chess board, leaning on the table, plunged deep in thought, and Lensky absent-mindedly takes his own castle with a pawn.

[Chapter 4, Stanzas XXVII–XXIX: a digression on the poetry written by Lensky to Olga follows. Pushkin then returns to Onegin and describes his carefree life in the country.]

XL

But our northern summer flashes by and is gone – a caricature of southern winters. This is well known, though we do not like to admit it. Already the sky breathed autumn, and ever rarer shone the sun; the days were growing shorter; the mysterious shade of the forests was baring itself with mournful sound; mist settled upon the fields, and the caravan of clamorous geese moved

XL

Тянулся к югу: приближалась
Довольно скучная пора;
Стоял ноябрь уж у двора.

XLI

Встает заря во мгле холодной;
На нивах шум работ умолк;
С своей волчихою голодной
Выходит на дорогу волк;
Его почуя, конь дорожный
Храпит – и путник осторожный
Несется в гору во весь дух;
На утренней заре пастух
Не гонит уж коров из хлева,
И в час полуденный в кружок
Их не зовет его рожок;
В избушке распевая, дева
Прядет, и, зимних друг ночей,
Трещит лучинка перед ней.

XLII

И вот уже трещат морозы
И серебрятся средь полей . . .
(Читатель ждет уж рифмы розы;

southwards: that rather boring time was drawing near – November was already at hand.

XLI

Dawn arises in a cold mist; the sound of work in the cornfields has grown silent; the wolf and his hungry she-wolf come out on to the road; the passing horse scents him and snorts, and the wary traveller rushes uphill at full speed; at dawn the herdsman no longer drives his cows from the shed, nor does his horn call them into a ring at midday; singing in her cottage the maiden spins, and the splinter – the friend of winter nights – crackles before her.

XLII

And now the brittle-hard frosts have set in, shining silver amidst the fields . . . (the reader is already expecting the rhyme 'roses'

На, вот возьми ее скорей!)
Опрятней модного паркета
Блистает речка, льдом одета.
Мальчишек радостный народ
Коньками звучно режет лед;
На красных лапках гусь тяжелый,
Задумав плыть по лону вод,
Ступает бережно на лед,
Скользит и падает; веселый
Мелькает, вьется первый снег,
Звездами падая на брег.

Глава Пятая

1

В тот год осенняя погода
Стояла долго на дворе,
Зими ждала, ждала природа.
Снег выпал только в январе
На третье в ночь. Проснувшись рано,
В окно увидела Татьяна

[rhymes with 'frosts' in Russian]; here you are then, take it quickly!). Neater than a fashionable parquet floor the river gleams, clad in ice. The joyful crowd of boys with hissing sound cut the ice with their skates; the heavy goose on its red web feet, having decided to swim upon the bosom of the waters, steps care-fully on to the ice, slips, and falls; the merry first snow flickers and swirls, falling like stars upon the bank.

[Chapter 4, Stanzas XLIII-LI: Lenski, who is to marry Olga in a fortnight, tells Onegin that he is invited to Tatyana's name-day party. Onegin agrees to go.]

Chapter 5

1

That year the autumn weather long dragged on; nature waited and waited for winter. But the first snow fell only in January – on the night of the third. Waking early, through the window Tatyana saw

Поутру побелевший двор,
Куртины, кровли и забор,
На стеклах легкие узоры,
Деревья в зимнем серебре,
Сорок веселых на дворе
И мягко устланные горы
Зимы блистательным ковром.
Всё ярко, всё бело кругом.

II

Зима!.. Крестьянин, торжествуя,
На дровнях обновляет путь;
Его лошадка, снег почуя,
Плетется рысью как-нибудь;
Бразды пушистые взрывая,
Летит кибитка удалая;
Ямщик сидит на облучке
В тулупе, в красном кушаке.
Вот бегает дворовый мальчик,
В салазки *жучку* посадив,
Себя в коня преобразив;
Шалун уж заморозил пальчик:
Ему и больно и смешно,
А мать грозит ему в окно . . .

the courtyard, which had grown white in the early morning, the flower-beds, the roofs, and the fence, and the delicate patterns on the windowpanes, the trees in their winter silver, the cheerful magpies in the courtyard, and the hills softly strewn with their shining carpet of winter. All around was bright, all was white.

II

Winter! The peasant with joyful heart renews his journeys on his sledge; his little horse, scenting the snow, jogs along at a trot; the dashing *kibítka* flies by, digging up the powdery furrows; the coach-man sits on the box in his sheepskin coat and crimson belt. Here the house-boy runs to and fro, having put his dog Zhúchka on his toboggan and turned himself into a horse. The little rascal's fingers are already frost-bitten: it's painful, yet it makes him laugh, while his mother wags her finger at him through the window . . .

III

Но, может быть, такого рода
Картины вас не привлекут:
Все это низкая природа;
Изящного не много тут.
Согретый вдохновенья богом,
Другой поэт роскошным слогом
Живописал нам первый снег
И все оттенки зимних нег;
Он вас пленит, я в том уверен,
Рисуя в пламенных стихах
Прогулки тайные в санях;
Но я бороться не намерен
Ни с ним покамест, ни с тобой,
Певец Финляндки молодой!

XI

И снится чудный сон Татьяне.
Ей снится, будто бы она
Идет по снеговой поляне,
Печальной мглой окружена;

III

But perhaps such pictures do not attract you: all this [you will say]
is base nature; there is not much that is graceful here. Warmed by
the god of inspiration, another poet has painted for us with luxuri-
ous style the year's first snow and all the shades of winter's joys
[Vyazemsky, 'First Snow']; he captivates you, I am sure of it, by
drawing secret sledge-rides in his fiery verses; but I do not intend
to compete either with him yet awhile, or with you, singer of the
young Finnish maid [E. A. Baratynsky, 'Eda']!

[*Chapter 5, Stanzas IV-X: On the evening before her name-day
Tatyana goes to bed.*]

XI

And Tatyana dreams a wondrous dream. She dreams that she is
walking through a snowy glade, surrounded by a gloomy mist;

В сугробах снежных перед нею
Шумит, клубит волной своею
Кипучий, темный и седой
Поток, не скованный зимой;
Две жердочки, склеены льдиной,
Дрожащий, гибельный мосток,
Положены через поток;
И пред шумящею пучиной,
Недоумения полна,
Остановилася она.

XII

Как на досадную разлуку,
Татьяна ропщет на ручей;
Не видит никого, кто руку
С той стороны подал бы ей;
Но вдруг сугроб зашевелился.
И кто ж из-под него явился?
Большой, взъерошенный медведь;
Татьяна *ах*! – а он реветь,
И лапу с острыми когтями
Ей протянул; она скрепясь

in the snow-drifts before her the seething, dark, grey torrent, no longer fettered by winter, resounds with swirling billows; two small stakes, stuck together by ice – a trembling, perilous little bridge – are laid across the torrent: and in front of the roaring abyss she stopped, full of bewilderment.

XII

Tatyana chafes at the stream, as at a grievous parting; she sees no one who might give her a hand from the other side; but suddenly the snowdrift shifted – and who appeared from beneath it? A large shaggy bear. 'Ah!' cried Tatyana; and he roared and stretched out to her a paw with sharp claws. Checking her fear, she

Дрожащей ручкой оперлась
И боязливыми шагами
Перебралась через ручей;
Пошла – и что ж? медведь за ней!

XIII

Она, взглянуть назад не смея,
Поспешный ускоряет шаг;
Но от косматого лакея
Не может убежать никак;
Кряхтя, валит медведь несносный;
Пред ними лес; недвижны сосны
В своей нахмуренной красе;
Отягчены их ветви все
Клоками снега; сквозь вершины
Осин, берез и лип нагих
Сияет луч светил ночных;
Дороги нет; кусты, стремнины
Метелью все занесены,
Глубоко в снег погружены.

leaned on it with trembling arm, and with timorous steps crossed over the stream; she started off, and what do you think? The bear followed her!

XIII

Not daring to look back, she hastens her hurried pace; but she simply cannot run away from her shaggy attendant; grunting, the horrid bear shambles on. Before them lies a forest; the pines are motionless in their sullen beauty. All their boughs are weighted down with clumps of snow. Through the tops of the naked aspens, beeches, and limes shine the rays of the stars of the night. There is no path; bushes and steeps have been covered by the snowstorm and are plunged deep in snow.

XIV

Татьяна в лес; медведь за нею;
Снег рыхлый по колено ей;
То длинный сук ее за шею
Зацепит вдруг, то из ушей
Златые серьги вырвет силой;
То в хрупком снеге с ножки милой
Увязнет мокрый башмачок;
То выронит она платок;
Поднять ей некогда; боится,
Медведя слышит за собой,
И даже трепетной рукой
Одежды край поднять стыдится;
Она бежит, он все вослед,
И сил уже бежать ей нет.

XV

Упала в снег; медведь проворно
Ее хватает и несет;
Она бесчувственно-покорна
Не шевельнется, не дохнет;
Он мчит ее лесной дорогой;
Вдруг – меж дерев шалаш убогой;

XIV

Tatyana enters the forest; the bear follows her; the crumbling snow is up to her knees; now a long branch suddenly catches her by the neck, now her golden ear-rings are violently torn from her ears; now her wet shoe gets stuck in the brittle snow and comes off her dear sweet foot; now she drops her handkerchief – she has no time to pick it up; she is afraid – she hears the bear behind her, and she does not even dare to lift the hem of her dress with trembling hand; she runs, and he keeps following her; and now she no longer has the strength to run.

XV

She fell into the snow; nimbly the bear seizes her and carries her; lifeless and submissive, she dares not move or breathe; he rushes her along the forest path; suddenly between the trees a wretched

Кругом все глушь; отвсюду он
Пустынным снегом занесен,
И ярко светится окошко,
И в шалаше и крик, и шум;
Медведь промолвил: «Здесь мой кум:
Погрейся у него немножко!»
И в сени прямо он идет
И на порог ее кладет.

XVI

Опомнилась, глядит Татьяна:
Медведя нет; она в сенях;
За дверью крик и звон стакана,
Как на больших похоронах;
Не видя тут ни капли толку,
Глядит она тихонько в щелку,
И что же видит?.. за столом
Сидят чудовища кругом:
Один в рогах с собачьей мордой,
Другой с петушьей головой,
Здесь ведьма с козьей бородой,
Тут остов чопорный и гордый,
Там карла с хвостиком, а вот
Полужуравль и полукот.

hut appears; all around is thick forest; on all sides the hut is covered with desolate snow, and the little window shines brightly, and in the hut there is noise and shouting; the bear said: 'Here my gossip lives: go and warm yourself for a little in his hut!' He goes straight into the entrance passage and sets her on the threshold.

XVI

Tatyana comes to and looks around: the bear has gone; she is in the entrance passage; behind the door are shouts and the ring of glasses, as at a great funeral feast. Seeing no sense at all in all this, she peeps stealthily through a crack – and what does she see? Monsters are sitting around a table: one has horns and a dog's muzzle, another has a cock's head; here sits a witch with a goat's beard, here an austere proud skeleton. There sits a dwarf with a little tail, and here a creature that is half-crane, half-cat.

XVII

Еще страшней, еще чуднее:
Вот рак верхом на пауке,
Вот череп на гусиной шее
Вертится в красном колпаке,
Вот мельница вприсядку пляшет
И крыльями трещит и машет;
Лай, хохот, пенье, свист и хлоп,
Людская молвь и конский топ!
Но что подумала Татьяна,
Когда узнала меж гостей
Того, кто мил и страшен ей,
Героя нашего романа!
Онегин за столом сидит
И в дверь украдкою глядит.

XVIII

Он знак подаст — и все хлопочут;
Он пьет — все пьют и все кричат;
Он засмеется — все хохочут;
Нахмурит брови — все молчат;
Он там хозяин, это ясно:
И Тане уж не так ужасно,

XVII

Still more terrifying, still more wondrous: here is a crab riding a spider; a skull on a goose's neck twists around in a red cap; a windmill dances squatting, rattles and waves its sails; barking, laughing, singing, whistling, banging, people talking and horses' hoofs clattering! But what did Tatyana think when amidst the guests she recognized him whom she loved and feared, the hero of our novel! Onegin sits at the table and glances furtively at the door.

XVIII

He gives a sign: and they all bustle; he drinks: they all drink and shout; he laughs: they all roar with laughter; he knits his brows: they are all silent. He is the master there – that is clear. Tanya no

И, любопытная, теперь
Немного растворила дверь . . .
Вдруг ветер дунул, загашая
Огонь светильников ночных;
Смутилась шайка домовых;
Онегин, взорами сверкая,
Из-за стола гремя встает;
Все встали; он к дверям идет.

XIX

И страшно ей; и торопливо
Татьяна силится бежать:
Нельзя никак; нетерпеливо
Метаясь, хочет закричать:
Не может; дверь толкнул Евгений:
И взорам адских привидений
Явилась дева; ярый смех
Раздался дико; очи всех,
Копыты, хоботы кривые,
Хвосты хохлатые, клыки,
Усы, кровавы языки,
Рога и пальцы костяные,
Всё указует на нее,
И все кричат: мое! мое!

longer felt so frightened, and in her curiosity she now opened the door a little . . . Suddenly a wind blew, quenching the flames of the night lamps; the band of goblins fell into confusion; Onegin with flashing eyes thunderously rises from the table; they all get up; he walks to the door.

XIX

But Tatyana is terrified, and she makes hasty efforts to run away: it is quite impossible; rushing impatiently hither and thither, she wants to cry out, but she cannot. Yevgeny pushed open the door and the girl appeared before the eyes of the hellish apparitions; a burst of wild and violent laughter rang out; the eyes of all, hoofs, crooked trunks, tufted tails, tusks, whiskers, bloody tongues, horns and bony fingers – all point at her and cry out: 'Mine! Mine!'

XX

Мое! – сказал Евгений грозно,
И шайка вся сокрылась вдруг;
Осталася во тьме морозной
Младая дева с ним сам-друг;
Онегин тихо увлекает
Татьяну в угол и слагает
Ее на шаткую скамью
И клонит голову свою
К ней на плечо; вдруг Ольга входит,
За нею Ленский; свет блеснул;
Онегин руку замахнул,
И дико он очами бродит,
И незваных гостей бранит;
Татьяна чуть жива лежит.

XXI

Спор громче, громче; вдруг Евгений
Хватает длинный нож, и вмиг
Повержен Ленский; страшно тени
Сгустились; нестерпимый крик
Раздался . . . хижина шатнулась . . .
И Таня в ужасе проснулась . . .

XX

'*Mine!*' said Yevgeny sternly, and suddenly all the band disappeared; the young girl remained alone with him in the frosty darkness; Onegin gently entices her into a corner, lays her on a rickety bench, and leans his head on her shoulder. Suddenly Olga comes in with Lensky following. Light flashes. Onegin waves his arms; his eyes rove wildly and he curses the uninvited guests; Tatyana lies there barely alive.

XXI

The argument grows louder and louder; suddenly Yevgeny seizes a long knife and in an instant Lensky is felled; frighteningly the shadows thickened; an intolerable cry rang out . . . The hut rocked . . . And Tanya awoke in terror . . . She looks around: it is

Глядит, уж в комнате светло;
В окне сквозь мерзлое стекло
Зари багряный луч играет;
Дверь отворилась. Ольга к ней,
Авроры северной алей
И легче ласточки, влетает;
«Ну, говорит, скажи ж ты мне,
Кого ты видела во сне?»

XXX

Сажают прямо против Тани,
И, утренней луны бледней
И трепетней гонимой лани,
Она темнеющих очей
Не подымает: пышет бурно
В ней страстный жар; ей душно, дурно;
Она приветствий двух друзей
Не слышит, слезы из очей
Хотят уж капать; уж готова
Бедняжка в обморок упасть;

already light in the room; through the window's frosted glass the purple ray of dawn flashes; the door opened. Olga flies in to her, rosier than the northern dawn and lighter than a swallow; 'Well,' she says, 'tell me now. Who did you dream of?'

[*Chapter 5, Stanzas XXII–XXIX: Tatyana tries in vain to interpret her dream from a dream-book. By the evening the house is full of guests. They go in to dinner. Lensky and Onegin enter.*]

XXX

They are seated directly opposite Tanya. And, paler than the morning moon and timider than the hunted deer, she does not lift her darkling eyes: the heat of passion blazes violently within her; she suffocates, feels faint; she does not hear the two friends' greetings; tears are just about to drop from her eyes; the poor girl is on the point of fainting; but her will and her power of reason

Но воля и рассудка власть
Превозмогли. Она два слова
Сквозь зубы молвила тишком
И усидела за столом.

XXXI

Траги-нервических явлений,
Девичьих обмороков, слез
Давно терпеть не мог Евгений:
Довольно их он перенес.
Чудак, попав на пир огромный,
Уж был сердит. Но, девы томной
Заметя трепетный порыв,
С досады взоры опустив,
Надулся он и, негодуя,
Поклялся Ленского взбесить
И уж порядком отомстить.
Теперь, заране торжествуя,
Он стал чертить в душе своей
Карикатуры всех гостей.

won the day. Quietly she uttered two words through her teeth and remained seated at the table.

XXXI

Yevgeny had long been unable to tolerate tragi-neurotic displays, girls' fainting fits and tears; he had put up with enough of them in his time. The odd fellow, arriving at the huge feast, was already angry. But noticing the languid maiden's sudden fit of trepidation, he lowered his glance in irritation and began to sulk, vowing in his indignation to enrage Lensky and to take fitting vengeance on him; and now, exulting in advance, he began in his mind to sketch out caricatures of all the guests.

XLI

Однообразный и безумный,
Как вихорь жизни молодой,
Кружится вальса вихорь шумный;
Чета мелькает за четой.
К минуте мщенья приближаясь,
Онегин, втайне усмехаясь,
Подходит к Ольге. Быстро с ней
Вертится около гостей,
Потом на стул ее сажает,
Заводит речь о том о сем;
Спустя минуты две потом
Вновь с нею вальс он продолжает;
Все в изумленье. Ленский сам
Не верит собственным глазам.

Глава Шестая

XVII

И вновь задумчивый, унылый
Пред милой Ольгою своей,

[Chapter 5, Stanzas XXXII–XL: later in the evening dancing begins.]

XLI

Monotonous and senseless, like a gust of young life, the noisy gust of the waltz whirls round; couple by couple the dancers flash by. Approaching the minute of revenge, Onegin, smiling secretly, goes up to Olga. Swiftly he spins with her around the guests, then seats her on a chair and starts talking of this and that. Then, a minute or two later, he continues the waltz with her afresh; all are amazed. Lensky himself cannot believe his eyes.

[Chapter 5, Stanza XLII, to Chapter 6, Stanza XVI: Lensky leaves the ball in anger. On the next day he challenges Onegin to a duel. Dissatisfied with his own conduct, Onegin nevertheless decides to fight. Lensky visits Olga.]

Chapter 6

XVII

And once again pensive and despondent in the presence of his

Владимир не имеет силы
Вчерашний день напомнить ей;
Он мыслит: «Буду ей спаситель.
Не потерплю, чтоб развратитель
Огнем и вздохов и похвал
Младое сердце искушал;
Чтоб червь презренный, ядовитый
Точил лилеи стебелек;
Чтобы двухутренний цветок
Увял еще полураскрытый».
Все это значило, друзья:
С приятелем стреляюсь я.

XVIII

Когда б он знал, какая рана
Моей Татьяны сердце жгла!
Когда бы ведала Татьяна,
Когда бы знать она могла,
Что завтра Ленский и Евгений
Заспорят о могильной сени;
Ах, может быть, ее любовь
Друзей соединила б вновь!

dear Olga, Vladimir has not the strength to remind her of the day before; he thinks: 'I shall be her saviour. I shall not permit the libertine to tempt her young heart with the fire of sighs and flattery, nor the despicable poisonous worm to nibble at the lily's slender stalk, nor shall I allow the flower on its second morn to fade away still half unfolded.' All this, my friends, meant 'I am going to fight a duel with my friend'.

XVIII

If only he had known what anguish burned my Tatyana's heart! Had Tatyana known, had it been possible for her to know, that on the morrow Lensky and Yevgeny were to dispute about the shadow of the grave – ah, perhaps her love would have united the two

Но этой страсти и случайно
Еще никто не открывал.
Онегин обо всем молчал;
Татьяна изнывала тайно;
Одна бы няня знать могла,
Да недогадлива была.

XIX

Весь вечер Ленский был рассеян,
То молчалив, то весел вновь;
Но тот, кто музою взлелеян,
Всегда таков: нахмуря бровь,
Садился он за клавикорды
И брал на них одни аккорды,
То, к Ольге взоры устремив,
Шептал: не правда ль? я счастлив.
Но поздно; время ехать. Сжалось
В нем сердце, полное тоской;
Прощаясь с девой молодой,
Оно как будто разрывалось.
Она глядит ему в лицо.
«Что с вами?» – Так. – И на крыльцо.

friends afresh! But as it happened no one had yet disclosed this passion. Onegin remained silent about it all; Tatyana pined away in secret; only her nanny might have known, but she was slow at guessing.

XIX

All evening Lensky was distraught – now silent, now cheerful again; but he who is nurtured by the muse is always like that: knitting his brow, he would sit down at the piano and would strike only chords on it; now he would turn his gaze on Olga and whisper: 'Is it not true? I am happy.' But it grew late; it was time to go. His grief-laden heart was wrung; when he parted from the young maiden it seemed as though it was bursting. She looked him in the face. 'What is the matter with you?' 'Oh, nothing.' And he went out on to the porch.

XX

Домой приехав, пистолеты
Он осмотрел, потом вложил
Опять их в ящик и, раздетый,
При свечке, Шиллера открыл;
Но мысль одна его объемлет;
В нем сердце грустное не дремлет:
С неизъяснимою красой
Он видит Ольгу пред собой.
Владимир книгу закрывает,
Берет перо; его стихи,
Полны любовной чепухи,
Звучат и льются. Их читает
Он вслух, в лирическом жару,
Как Дельвиг пьяный на пиру.

XXI

Стихи на случай сохранились;
Я их имею; вот они:
«Куда, куда вы удалились,
Весны моей златые дни?
Что день грядущий мне готовит?

XX

Arriving home, he examined the pistols, then he put them back again in their case, and, having undressed, he opened Schiller by the light of a candle; but one thought only absorbs his mind; his sorrowful heart does not slumber; in all her inexplicable beauty he sees Olga before him. Vladimir shuts his book and takes his pen; his verses, full of amorous rubbish, ring out and flow. He reads them aloud, in lyrical passion, like Delvig, drunken at a feast. [Baron Delvig, poet and school-friend of Pushkin.]

XXI

His verses have by chance survived; I have them; here they are: 'Whither, O whither have you gone, golden days of my youth? What has the coming day in store for me? In vain my gaze seeks

Его мой взор напрасно ловит,
В глубокой мгле таится он.
Нет нужды; прав судьбы закон.
Паду ли я, стрелой пронзенный,
Иль мимо пролетит она,
Все благо: бдения и сна
Приходит час определенный;
Благословен и день забот,
Благословен и тьмы приход!

XXII

Блеснет заутра луч денницы,
И заиграет яркий день;
А я, быть может, я гробницы
Сойду в таинственную сень,
И память юного поэта
Поглотит медленная Лета,
Забудет мир меня; но ты
Придешь ли, дева красоты,
Слезу пролить над ранней урной
И думать: он меня любил,

to grasp it; in the deep darkness it is concealed. There is no need; the law of Fate is right. Should I fall, pierced by an arrow, or should it fly past – it is all to the good; the appointed time for wakefulness and sleep comes; blessed is the day of cares – blessed, too, is the arrival of darkness!

XXII

'The ray of dawn will sparkle on the morrow and the bright day will shine; but I – perhaps I shall descend into the mysterious shadow of the tomb, and slow Lethe will swallow up the memory of the young poet. The world will forget me; but will you come, maiden of beauty, to shed a tear over my early urn and think "He

Он мне единой посвятил
Рассвет печальный жизни бурной! . .
Сердечный друг, желанный друг,
Приди, приди: я твой супруг! . . .»

XXIII

Так он писал *темно* и *вяло*
(Что романтизмом мы зовем,
Хоть романтизма тут нимало
Не вижу я; да что нам в том?)
И наконец перед зарею,
Склонясь усталой головою,
На модном слове *идеал*
Тихонько Ленский задремал;
Но только сонным обаяньем
Он позабылся, уж сосед
В безмолвный входит кабинет
И будит Ленского воззваньем:
«Пора вставать: седьмой уж час.
Онегин верно ждет уж нас».

loved me, to me alone he dedicated the sad dawn of his stormy
life"? Beloved friend, precious friend, come, Oh come! I am your
spouse!'

XXIII

Thus he wrote *darkly* and *limply* (we call it Romanticism, though
here I cannot see any Romanticism at all; but what has that to do
with us?), and at last, just before dawn, inclining his weary head,
Lensky quietly fell asleep on the fashionable word '*ideal*'; but no
sooner has he sunk into the oblivion of blissful sleep than his neighbour comes into his silent study and wakes Lensky up, calling:
'Time to get up: it's already past six. Onegin is sure to be already
waiting for us.'

XXVIII

Враги! Давно ли друг от друга
Их жажда крови отвела?
Давно ль они часы досуга,
Трапезу, мысли и дела
Делили дружно? Ныне злобно,
Врагам наследственным подобно,
Как в страшном, непонятном сне,
Они друг другу в тишине
Готовят гибель хладнокровно . . .
Не засмеяться ль им, пока
Не обагрилась их рука,
Не разойтиться ль полюбовно? . . .
Но дико светская вражда
Боится ложного стыда.

XXIX

Вот пистолеты уж блеснули,
Гремит о шомпол молоток.
В граненый ствол уходят пули,
И щелкнул в первый раз курок.

[*Chapter 6, Stanzas XXIV–XXVII: Onegin and Lensky with their
seconds, Guillot and Zaretsky, meet at the mill where the duel is to take
place.*]

XXVIII

Enemies! Was it so long ago that this thirst for blood separated
them from each other? Was it so long ago that they amicably
shared their hours of leisure, their board, their thoughts and deeds?
Now, filled with malice, just like hereditary enemies, as in a fearful,
incomprehensible dream, they prepare destruction for each other
calmly and in cold blood . . . Should they not burst out laughing
before their hands are stained with blood, should they not part in
friendship? But fashionable feuds are terribly afraid of false shame.

XXIX

But now their pistols have already flashed. The hammer knocks
against the ramrod. The bullets go into the faceted barrel and for

Вот порох струйкой сероватой
На полку сыплется. Зубчатый,
Надежно ввинченный кремень
Взведен еще. За ближний пень
Становится Гильо смущенный.
Плащи бросают два врага.
Зарецкий тридцать два шага
Отмерил с точностью отменной,
Друзей развел по крайний след,
И каждый взял свой пистолет.

XXX

«Теперь сходитесь».
            Хладнокровно,
Еще не целя, два врага
Походкой твердой, тихо, ровно
Четыре перешли шага,
Четыре смертные ступени.
Свой пистолет тогда Евгений,
Не преставая наступать,
Стал первый тихо подымать.
Вот пять шагов еще ступили,

the first time the cock is snapped. Now the powder is poured in a thin greyish stream on to the pan. The jagged flint, firmly screwed on, is raised once more. Confused, Guillot stands behind a nearby stump. The two enemies throw down their cloaks. Zaretsky measured out thirty-two paces with extreme accuracy, took the friends apart, each to the end mark, and both took their pistols.

XXX

'Now approach!' In cold blood the two enemies, not yet aiming, covered the four paces – the four fatal steps – with firm gait, calmly and evenly. Then, without ceasing to advance, Yevgeny first began calmly to raise his pistol. Now they have stepped five

И Ленский, жмуря левый глаз,
Стал также целить – но как раз
Онегин выстрелил . . . Пробили
Часы урочные: поэт
Роняет молча пистолет,

XXXI

На грудь кладет тихонько руку
И падает. Туманный взор
Изображает смерть, не муку.
Так медленно по скату гор,
На солнце искрами блистая,
Спадает глыба снеговая.
Мгновенным холодом облит,
Онегин к юноше спешит,
Глядит, зовет его . . . напрасно:
Его уж нет. Младой певец
Нашел безвременный конец!
Дохнула буря, цвет прекрасный
Увял на утренней заре,
Потух огонь на алтаре! . . .

more paces, and Lensky, screwing up his left eye, also began to aim – but at that very moment Onegin fired . . . The fateful hour struck: the poet, silently, drops his pistol . . .

XXXI

. . . quietly puts his hand on his breast, and falls. His misty glance portrays death, not agony. Thus a heap of snow falls slowly down a mountain slope with sparks flashing in the sun. Suffused with sudden cold, Onegin hastens to the young man, he looks at him, he calls him . . . in vain: he is no more. The young singer has found an untimely end! The storm wind blew, and the fair blossom faded at the dawn of day, the flame on the altar went out!

XXXVI

Друзья мои, вам жаль поэта:
Во цвете радостных надежд,
Их не свершив еще для света,
Чуть из младенческих одежд,
Увял! Где жаркое волненье,
Где благородное стремленье
И чувств и мыслей молодых,
Высоких, нежных, удалых?
Где бурные любви желанья,
И жажда знаний и труда,
И страх порока и стыда,
И вы, заветные мечтанья,
Вы, призрак жизни неземной,
Вы, сны поэзии святой!

XXXVII

Быть может, он для блага мира
Иль хоть для славы был рожден;
Его умолкнувшая лира

[*Chapter 6, Stanzas XXXII–XXXV: Onegin is shaken by Lensky's death. The body is taken away.*]

XXXVI

My friends, you are sorry for the poet: still in the bloom of joyful hopes, not yet having realized them for the world, barely out of the clothes of infancy, he faded away! Where is the passionate emotion, where is the noble flight of young, lofty, tender, dashing feelings and thoughts? Where are the stormy desires of love and the thirst for knowledge and toil, and the fear of vice and shame, and you, cherished reveries, you, phantom of unearthly life, you, dreams of sacred poetry!

XXXVII

Perhaps he was born for the good of the world or even for glory; his lyre, now silent, might have set a thunderous, uninterrupted

Гремучий, непрерывный звон
В веках поднять могла. Поэта,
Быть может, на ступенях света
Ждала высокая ступень.
Его страдальческая тень,
Быть может, унесла с собою
Святую тайну, и для нас
Погиб животворящий глас,
И за могильною чертою
К ней не домчится гимн времен,
Благословение племен.

XXXIX

А может быть и то: поэта
Обыкновенный ждал удел.
Прошли бы юношества лета:
В нем пыл души бы охдалел.
Во многом он бы изменился,
Расстался б с музами, женился,
В деревне, счастлив и рогат,

sound ringing throughout the ages. Perhaps a high rung on the ladder of the world awaited the poet. Perhaps his martyr's shade carried off with it the holy mystery, and for us a life-giving voice has become silent, and beyond the limit of the grave no hymn of ages, no blessing of the peoples will rush to greet that shade.

[*Stanza XXXVIII is defective.*]

XXXIX

And yet, perhaps, a normal fate might have awaited the poet. The years of youth would have passed: the ardour of the soul would have grown cold. He would have changed in many ways, he would have parted from the muses, married, and in the country, happy

Носил бы стеганый халат;
Узнал бы жизнь на самом деле,
Подагру б в сорок лет имел,
Пил, ел, скучал, толстел, хирел,
И наконец в своей постеле
Скончался б посреди детей,
Плаксивых баб и лекарей.

Глава Седьмая

X

Мой бедный Ленский! изнывая,
Не долго плакала она.
Увы! невеста молодая
Своей печали неверна.
Другой увлек ее вниманье,
Другой успел ее страданье
Любовной лестью усыпить,
Улан умел ее пленить,
Улан любим ее душою . . .
И вот уж с ним пред алтарем

though cuckolded, would have worn a quilted dressing-gown.
He would have come to know life as it really is, would have got
gout at forty, would have drunk, eaten, become bored, fat, and
ailing, and finally he would have died in his bed, surrounded by
children, tearful women, and doctors.

*[Chapter 6, Stanza XL, to Chapter 7, Stanza VII: A description
of Lensky's grave follows. After a lyrical digression we return to
Lensky's grave. Stanzas VIII and IX of Chapter 7, which describe
how Olga visited the grave, were omitted by Pushkin in the final
version.]*

Chapter 7

X

My poor Lensky! Though pining, Olga did not weep for long.
Alas! The betrothed maiden was unfaithful to her sorrow. Another
captured her attention, another succeeded in lulling her suffering
with amorous flattery, an Uhlan knew how to captivate her – in her
soul she loved an Uhlan . . . And now already she bashfully

Она стыдливо под венцом
Стоит с поникшей головою,
С огнем в потупленных очах,
С улыбкой легкой на устах.

XI

Мой бедный Ленский! за могилой
В пределах вечности глухой
Смутился ли, певец унылый,
Измены вестью роковой,
Или над Летой усыпленный
Поэт, бесчувствием блаженный,
Уж не смущается ничем,
И мир ему закрыт и нем? . . .
Так! равнодушное забвенье
За гробом ожидает нас.
Врагов, друзей, любовниц глас
Вдруг молкнет. Про одно именье
Наследников сердитый хор
Заводит непристойный спор.

stands with him before the altar beneath the marriage-crown, with head inclined, her lowered eyes burning and with a slight smile upon her lips.

XI

My poor Lensky! In the confines of remote eternity beyond the grave, was he, the melancholy bard, discountenanced by tidings of her fateful betrayal? Or is the poet, lulled o'er Lethe and blessedly unfeeling, no longer disturbed by aught, and is the world for him now closed and silent? Yes, indeed, indifferent oblivion awaits us beyond the grave. The voice of enemies, of friends, of lovers suddenly grows silent. Only about the inheritance does the angry choir of heirs start its unseemly argument.

[*Chapter 7, Stanzas XII–XIV: Tatyana sees Olga and her husband off. She is sad and lonely.*]

XV

Был вечер. Небо меркло. Воды
Струились тихо. Жук жужжал.
Уж расходились хороводы;
Уж за рекой, дымясь, пылал
Огонь рыбачий. В поле чистом,
Луны при свете серебристом,
В свои мечты погружена,
Татьяна долго шла одна.
Шла, шла. И вдруг перед собою
С холма господский видит дом,
Селенье, рощу под холмом
И сад над светлою рекою.
Она глядит – и сердце в ней
Забилось чаще и сильней.

XVI

Ее сомнения смущают:
«Пойду ль вперед, пойду ль назад? . . .
Его здесь нет. Меня не знают . . .
Взгляну на дом, на этот сад».

XV

It was evening. The sky was growing dark. The waters streamed quietly by. A beetle buzzed. Already the dancers were dispersing; already, beyond the river, a fisherman's fire burned and smoked. In the open field by the silvery light of the moon Tatyana walked long alone, plunged in her dreams. She walked on and on. And suddenly from a hill she sees before her the manor house, the village, the grove at the foot of the hill, and the garden above the bright river. She gazes – and her heart within her began to beat more often and more strongly.

XVI

Doubts confuse her: 'Shall I go on, shall I go back? He is not here. I am not known here . . . I will have a look at the house, at

И вот с холма Татьяна сходит,
Едва дыша; кругом обводит
Недоуменья полный взор . . .
И входит на пустынный двор.
К ней, лая, кинулись собаки.
На крик испуганный ея
Ребят дворовая семья
Сбежалась шумно. Не без драки
Мальчишки разогнали псов,
Взяв барышню под свой покров.

XXI

Татьяна с ключницей простилась
За воротами. Через день
Уж утром рано вновь явилась
Она в оставленную сень.
И в молчаливом кабинете,
Забыв на время все на свете,
Осталась наконец одна,
И долго плакала она.

this garden.' And now Tatyana comes down the hill, barely breathing; she casts around her a gaze full of bewilderment . . . and she enters the deserted courtyard. The dogs rushed barking towards her. At the sound of her frightened cry a whole family of servants' children gathered noisily around. Not without scuffling the boys chased the dogs away and took the young lady under their protection.

[*Chapter 7, Stanzas XVII–XX: Tatyana visits Onegin's study. She asks permission to return.*]

XXI

Tatyana said farewell to the housekeeper beyond the gate. A day later she again appeared early in the morning in the abandoned dwelling. And in the silent study, for a time forgetting everything in the world, she at last remained alone, and for a long time she

Потом за книги принялася.
Сперва ей было не до них,
Но показался выбор их
Ей странен. Чтенью предалася
Татьяна жадною душой;
И ей открылся мир иной.

XXII

Хотя мы знаем, что Евгений
Издавна чтенье разлюбил,
Однако ж несколько творений
Он из опалы исключил:
Певца Гяура и Жуана
Да с ним еще два—три романа,
В которых отразился век
И современный человек
Изображен довольно верно
С его безнравственной душой,
Себялюбивой и сухой,
Мечтанью преданной безмерно,
С его озлобленным умом,
Кипящим в действии пустом.

wept. Then she set about the books. At first she had no time for them; but then the choice of books seemed strange to her. With eager heart Tatyana abandoned herself to reading; and a new world was opened up to her.

XXII

Although we know that Yevgeny had long since ceased to love reading, still he excluded some works from banishment: the singer of the Giaour and Juan [Byron], and with him one or two more novels in which the age was reflected and modern man quite faithfully portrayed, with his amoral soul, self-loving and dry, utterly addicted to dreaming, with his embittered mind seething in vain activity.

XXIII

Хранили многие страницы
Отметку резкую ногтей;
Глаза внимательной девицы
Устремлены на них живей.
Татьяна видит с трепетаньем,
Какою мыслью, замечаньем
Бывал Онегин поражен,
В чем молча соглашался он.
На их полях она встречает
Черты его карандаша.
Везде Онегина душа
Себя невольно выражает
То кратким словом, то крестом,
То вопросительным крючком.

XXIV

И начинает понемногу
Моя Татьяна понимать
Теперь яснее – слава Богу –
Того, по ком она вздыхать
Осуждена судьбою властной:
Чудак печальный и опасный,

XXIII

Many a page kept the sharp imprint of his nail; on them the eyes of the attentive girl were keenly fixed. With trepidation Tatyana saw what thoughts, what remarks Yevgeny had been struck by, what he had agreed with in silence. On the margins of the pages she meets his pencil marks. Everywhere Yevgeny's soul cannot help expressing itself, now with a short word, now with a cross, now with a question mark.

XXIV

And now little by little my Tatyana begins to understand more clearly – thank God – the man for whom she was condemned to sigh by powerful fate: this gloomy, dangerous crank, this creation

Созданье ада иль небес,
Сей ангел, сей надменный бес,
Что ж он? Ужели подражанье,
Ничтожный призрак, иль еще
Москвич в Гарольдовом плаще,
Чужих причуд истолкованье,
Слов модных полный лексикон?...
Уж не пародия ли он?

XXVIII

Вставая с первыми лучами,
Теперь она в поля спешит
И, умиленными очами
Их озирая, говорит:
«Простите, мирные долины,
И вы, знакомых гор вершины,
И вы, знакомые леса;
Прости, небесная краса,
Прости, веселая природа;
Меняю милый, тихий свет

of hell or heaven, this angel, this haughty demon – what, then, is he? Can it be that he is an imitation, a worthless phantom, or yet again a Muscovite in Childe Harold's cloak, a reproduction of the vagaries of others, a dictionary full of fashionable words? Can it be that he is a parody?

[*Chapter 7, Stanzas XXV–XXVII: Tatyana's mother decides to take her to Moscow in the hopes of finding a fiancé. Tatyana is alarmed at the prospect.*]

XXVIII

Rising with the first rays, now she hurries to the fields, and gazing on them with tender eyes, she says: 'Farewell, peaceful valleys, and you, the tops of familiar hills, and you, familiar forests! Farewell, heavenly beauty, farewell, joyous nature! I am exchang-

На шум блистательных сует . . .
Прости ж и ты, моя свобода!
Куда, зачем стремлюся я?
Что мне сулит судьба моя?»

XXIX

Ее прогулки длятся доле.
Теперь то холмик, то ручей
Остановляют поневоле
Татьяну прелестью своей.
Она, как с давними друзьями,
С своими рощами, лугами
Еще беседовать спешит.
Но лето быстрое летит.
Настала осень золотая.
Природа трепетна, бледна,
Как жертва, пышно убрана . . .
Вот север, тучи нагоняя,
Дохнул, завыл – и вот сама
Идет волшебница зима.

ing the dear quiet world for the clamour of brilliant vanities. Farewell, too, my freedom! Whither am I hastening and why? What does my fate hold in store for me?'

XXIX

Her walks last longer. Tatyana cannot help stopping, captivated by the charm now of a hillock, now of a stream. She hurries yet again to converse with her groves, her meadows, as with old friends. But swift summer flies by. Golden autumn has come. Nature, quivering and pale, is luxuriantly bedecked like a sacrifice . . . Now the north wind, driving the clouds together, blew and howled – and here comes the sorceress Winter herself.

[*Chapter 7, Stanza XXX, to Chapter 8, Stanza XVI: They travel to Moscow. Tatyana is unable to get used to the atmosphere and is bored by society. She marries a general. Onegin cannot settle down after the duel and takes to aimless travelling. He turns up at a ball in Moscow and recognizes Tatyana.*]

Глава Восьмая

XVII

«Ужели, – думает Евгений: –
Ужель она? Но точно . . . Нет . . .
Как! из глуши степных селений . . .
И неотвязчивый лорнет
Он обращает поминутно
На ту, чей вид напомнил смутно
Ему забытые черты.
«Скажи мне, князь, не знаешь ты,
Кто там в малиновом берете
С послом испанским говорит?»
Князь на Онегина глядит.
– Ага! давно ж ты не был в свете.
Постой, тебя представлю я. –
«Да кто ж она?» – Жена моя. –

XVIII

«Так ты женат! не знал я ране!
Давно ли?» – Около двух лет. –
«На ком?» – На Лариной. – «Татьяне!»

Chapter 8

XVII

'Can it be,' thinks Yevgeny. 'Can it be she? But it's just like . . .
No . . . From the remote villages of the steppes!' And each
minute he trains his importunate lorgnette on the one whose aspect
reminded him vaguely of forgotten features. 'Tell me, Prince, do
you not know who that is over there in a crimson toque talking to
the Spanish ambassador?' The prince looks at Onegin. 'Aha, you
have been away from society for a long time! Wait, I'll introduce
you.' 'Yes, but who is she?' 'My wife.'

XVIII

'So you're married? I didn't know before! Have you been married
long?' 'About two years.' 'Who to?' 'A Larin.' 'Tatyana!'

– Ты ей знаком? – «Я им сосед».
– О, так пойдем же. – Князь подходит,
К своей жене и ей подводит
Родню и друга своего.
Княгиня смотрит на него . . .
И что ей душу ни смутило,
Как сильно ни была она
Удивлена, поражена,
Но ей ничто не изменило:
В ней сохранился тот же тон,
Был так же тих ее поклон.

XIX

Ей-ей! не то, чтоб содрогнулась
Иль стала вдруг бледна, красна . . .
У ней и бровь не шевельнулась;
Не сжала даже губ она.
Хоть он глядел нельзя прилежней,
Но и следов Татьяны прежней
Не мог Онегин обрести.
С ней речь хотел он завести
И – и не мог. Она спросила,
Давно ль он здесь, откуда он

'Does she know you?' 'I'm a neighbour of theirs.' 'Oh well, let's go then.' The prince goes to his wife and brings his relative and friend to her. The princess looks at him . . . And whatever stirred her soul, however great was her amazement and surprise, nothing betrayed her: she preserved exactly the same tone, her bow was just as serene.

XIX

In very truth, far from shuddering or suddenly becoming pale or crimson, she did not even move an eyebrow, nor did she even compress her lips. Although he gazed with all attention, Onegin could not find a single trace of the former Tatyana. He wanted to start a conversation with her and – and could not. She asked whether he had been here long, where he had come from, and

И не из их ли уж сторон?
Потом к супругу обратила
Усталый взгляд; скользнула вон . . .
И недвижим остался он.

XX

Ужель та самая Татьяна,
Которой он наедине,
В начале нашего романа,
В глухой, далекой стороне,
В благом пылу нравоученья,
Читал когда-то наставленья,
Та, от которой он хранит
Письмо, где сердце говорит,
Где всё наруже, всё на воле,
Та девочка . . . иль это сон? . . .
Та девочка, которой он
Пренебрегал в смиренной доле,
Ужели с ним сейчас была
Так равнодушна, так смела?

whether he had not come from their parts. Then she cast a weary glance at her husband; slipped out . . . and he remained immobile.

XX

Can it really be that same Tatyana to whom once, in the beginning of our novel, in those remote and distant parts, he recited admonishments *tête à tête* in the noble glow of moral exhortation? Can it be she, the writer of the letter he keeps, in which the heart speaks, in which everything is expressed, everything freely spoken – that same girl . . . or is this a dream? That same girl, whom he had scorned in her humble lot – could it now be that she was so indifferent, so unconstrained with him?

[*Chapter 8, Stanzas XXI–XLI: Onegin falls in love with Tatyana, but she pays no attention to him. He writes to her, but gets no answer. Winter passes, and in spring Onegin goes to Tatyana; he finds her reading a letter and crying; he falls at her feet.*]

XLII

Она его не подымает
И, не сводя с него очей,
От жадных уст не отымает
Бесчувственной руки своей . . .
О чем теперь ее мечтанье?
Проходит долгое молчанье,
И тихо наконец она:
«Довольно; встаньте. Я должна
Вам объясниться откровенно.
Онегин, помните ль тот час,
Когда в саду, в аллее нас
Судьба свела, и так смиренно
Урок ваш выслушала я?
Сегодня очередь моя.

XLIII

Онегин, я тогда моложе,
Я лучше, кажется, была,
И я любила вас; и что же?
Что в сердце вашем я нашла?
Какой ответ? одну суровость.
Не правда ль? Вам была не новость
Смиренной девочки любовь?

XLII

She does not raise him from his knees, and without taking her eyes from him she does not remove her impassive hand from his greedy lips . . . What does she dream of now? The long silence draws on, and at last she says quietly: 'Enough; get up. I must speak my mind to you with candour. Onegin, do you remember that hour when in the garden, in the alley, fate brought us together and I listened so humbly to your lecture? Today it is my turn.

XLIII

'Onegin, I was then younger, more beautiful, it seems, and I loved you; and well, what did I find in your heart? What answer? Only severity. Is it not true? Was the love of a humble girl no novelty to

И нынче – Боже! – стынет кровь,
Как только вспомню взгляд холодный
И эту проповедь . . . Но вас
Я не виню: в тот страшный час
Вы поступили благородно,
Вы были правы предо мной:
Я благодарна всей душой . . .

XLIV

Тогда – не правда ли? – в пустыне,
Вдали от суетной молвы,
Я вам не нравилась . . . Что ж ныне
Меня преследуете вы?
Зачем у вас я на примете?
Не потому ль, что в высшем свете
Теперь являться я должна;
Что я богата и знатна,
Что муж в сраженьях изувечен,
Что нас за то ласкает двор?
Не потому ль, что мой позор
Теперь бы всеми был замечен
И мог бы в обществе принесть
Вам соблазнительную честь?

you? And now – O God! – my blood grows cold as soon as I remember your chill glance and that sermon . . . But I do not blame you: in that dreadful hour you acted nobly, you were right in your attitude to me: with all my soul I am grateful . . .

XLIV

'Then – is it not true? – in the wilderness, far from empty Fame, you were not taken with me . . . Why then do you now pursue me? Why have you set your sights at me? Is it not because I must now appear in high society, because I am rich and of high rank, because my husband was crippled in battles and because the court favours us for that? Is it not because my disgrace would now be noticed by everybody and might bring you tempting renown in society?

XLV

Я плачу . . . если вашей Тани
Вы не забыли до сих пор,
То знайте: колкость вашей брани,
Холодный, строгий разговор,
Когда б в моей лишь было власти,
Я предпочла б обидной страсти
И этим письмам и слезам.
К моим младенческим мечтам
Тогда имели вы хоть жалость,
Хоть уважение к летам . . .
А нынче! – что к моим ногам
Вас привело? какая малость!
Как с вашим сердцем и умом
Быть чувства мелкого рабом?

XLVI

А мне, Онегин, пышность эта,
Постылой жизни мишура,
Мои успехи в вихре света,
Мой модный дом и вечера,
Что в них? Сейчас отдать я рада

XLV

'I weep . . . If you have not yet forgotten your Tanya, then know that if it were only within my power I would prefer the sting of your obloquy, your cold, severe discourse, to this offensive passion, to these letters and tears. Then at least you had pity on my childish reveries and at least you had respect for my years . . . But now! What has brought you to my feet? What a trifle! How, with your heart and your intelligence, can you be the slave of petty emotion?

XLVI

'But as for me, Onegin, this splendour, the tinsel of this hateful life, my successes in the whirl of society, my fashionable house and my soirées – what is there in them for me? At this moment I

Всю эту ветошь маскарада,
Весь этот блеск, и шум, и чад
За полку книг, за дикий сад,
За наше бедное жилище,
За те места, где в первый раз,
Онегин, видела я вас,
Да за смиренное кладбище,
Где нынче крест и тень ветвей
Над бедной нянею моей . . .

XLVII

А счастье было так возможно,
Так близко! . . . Но судьба моя
Уж решена. Неосторожно,
Быть может, поступила я:
Меня с слезами заклинаний
Молила мать; для бедной Тани
Все были жребии равны . . .
Я вышла замуж. Вы должны,
Я вас прошу, меня оставить;
Я знаю: в вашем сердце есть

would be glad to give all this shabby masquerade, all this glitter, noise, and vapour for a shelf of books, for a wild garden, for our poor dwelling, for those places where I saw you for the first time, Onegin, and for the humble graveyard, where now my poor nanny lies beneath a cross and the shade of branches . . .

XLVII

'Yet happiness was so possible, so close! But now my fate is already decided. I acted imprudently, perhaps: with tears and entreaties my mother implored me; for poor Tanya all lots were equal . . . I married. You must leave me, I beg you; I know that in your heart

И гордость и прямая честь.
Я вас люблю (к чему лукавить?),
Но я другому отдана;
Я буду век ему верна».

Отрывки из Путешествия Онегина
А там, меж хижинок татар . . .
Какой во мне проснулся жар!
Какой волшебною тоскою
Стеснялась пламенная грудь!
Но, муза! прошлое забудь.

Какие б чувства ни таились
Тогда во мне – теперь их нет:
Они прошли иль изменились . . .
Мир вам, тревоги прошлых лет!

there is both pride and true honour. I love you (why dissemble?)
but I am married to another; and I shall be true to him for ever.'

[*Chapter 8, Stanzas XLVIII–LI: Tatyana goes out of the room. Her
husband enters. At this point Pushkin leaves Onegin and says farewell
to his readers.*]

Extracts from Onegin's Journey

[*Originally planned as Chapter 8, but later replaced by the present
Chapter 8 and printed under the above title. Onegin travels from
Moscow to Nizhny Novgorod and thence to the Caucasus and the
Crimea. Pushkin recalls his own past.*]

AND there, amidst the Tatars' huts . . . what passion awoke in
me! By what enchanting melancholy was my ardent breast con-
stricted! But, O muse, forget the past!
    Whatever feelings were concealed within me at that time – now
they are no longer: they have passed or changed . . . Peace be
unto you, emotions of bygone years! At that time I thought I

В ту пору мне казались нужны
Пустыни, волн края жемчужны,
И моря шум, и груды скал,
И гордой девы идеал,
И безыменные страданья . . .
Другие дни, другие сны;
Смирились вы, моей весны
Высокопарные мечтанья,
И в поэтический бокал
Воды я много подмешал.

Иные нужны мне картины:
Люблю песчаный косогор,
Перед избушкой две рябины,
Калитку, сломанный забор,
На небе серенькие тучи,
Перед гумном соломы кучи
Да пруд под сенью ив густых,
Раздолье уток молодых;
Теперь мила мне балалайка
Да пьяный топот трепака
Перед порогом кабака.
Мой идеал теперь – хозяйка,
Мои желания – покой,
Да щей горшок, да сам большой.

needed wildernesses, the pearly crests of waves, and the sound of
the sea, and rocks piled high, and the 'ideal' of a proud maiden,
and nameless sufferings. Times change, dreams change: you have
grown calm, high-flown reveries of my spring, and I have poured
much water into my poetic goblet.

I need other pictures: I love a sandy hill-side, two rowan trees
before a little cottage, a wicker gate, a broken fence, little grey
clouds in the sky, heaps of straw in front of the threshing-floor –
and a pond beneath the shade of thick willows where young ducks
are free to swim at will; the balalaika and the drunken stamping of
the *trepak* dance before the tavern's threshold are what I now like.
My ideal is now a housewife; my desires are peace and quiet, and
a bowl of soup and myself my own master. [Russian saying.]

МОЦАРТ И САЛЬЕРИ

Сцена I

Комната.

Сальери

Все говорят: нет правды на земле.
Но правды нет — и выше. Для меня
Так это ясно, как простая гамма.
Родился я с любовию к искусству;
Ребенком будучи, когда высоко
Звучал орган в старинной церкви нашей,
Я слушал и заслушивался — слезы
Невольные и скадкие текли.
Отверг я рано праздные забавы;
Науки, чуждые музыке, были
Постылы мне; упрямо и надменно
От них отрекся я и предался
Одной музыке. Труден первый шаг
И скучен первый путь. Преодолел
Я ранние невзгоды. Ремесло
Поставил я подножием искусству;
Я сделался ремесленник: перстам

MOZART AND SALIERI

Scene One

A Room.

SALIERI: All men say there is no justice on earth. But there is no justice on high either. For me this is as clear as a simple scale. I was born with a love for art; while still a child, when the organ rang out high up in our ancient church, I listened and never wearied of listening, and tears flowed, involuntary and sweet. Early in life I rejected empty amusements; studies foreign to music were repugnant to me; obstinately and haughtily I forswore them and dedicated myself to music alone. The first step was difficult, the first path dull. I overcame early reverses. I set up craftsmanship as a pedestal for art; I became a craftsman: I lent an obedient, arid

Придал послушную, сухую беглость
И верность уху. Звуки умертвив,
Музыку я разъял, как труп. Поверил
Я алгеброй гармонию. Тогда
Уже дерзнул, в науке искушенный,
Предаться неге творческой мечты.
Я стал творить; но в тишине, но в тайне,
Не смея помышлять еще о славе.
Нередко, просидев в безмолвной келье
Два, три дня, позабыв и сон и пищу,
Вкусив восторг и слезы вдохновенья,
Я жег мой труд и холодно смотрел,
Как мысль моя и звуки, мной рожденны,
Пылая, с легким дымом исчезали.
Что говорю? Когда великий Глюк
Явился и открыл нам новы тайны
(Глубокие, пленительные тайны),
Не бросил ли я все, что прежде знал,
Что так любил, чему так жарко верил,
И не пошел ли бодро вслед за ним
Безропотно, как тот, кто заблуждался

agility to my fingers and sureness to my ear. Killing the sounds, I dissected music as if it were a corpse. I checked harmony by algebra. Then, experienced in science, at last I ventured to indulge in the joy of creative fantasy. I began to create, but on the quiet, in secret, not yet daring to dream of glory. Often, having sat in my silent cell for two or three days, forgetting both sleep and food, having tasted the rapture and tears of inspiration, I would burn my work and coldly watch my thoughts and the sounds which I had given birth to blaze and disappear in a wisp of smoke! What am I saying? When the great Gluck appeared and revealed to us new secrets (deep, fascinating secrets), did I not cast aside all that I had previously known, that I had so loved, that I had so ardently believed, and did I not follow firmly and boldly after him, uncomplaining, like a man who has got lost and is sent in a different

И встречным послан в сторону иную?
Усильным, напряженным постоянством
Я наконец в искусстве безграничном
Достигнул степени высокой. Слава
Мне улыбнулась; я в сердцах людей
Нашел созвучия своим созданьям.
Я счастлив был: я наслаждался мирно ·
Своим трудом, успехом, славой; также
Трудами и успехами друзей,
Товарищей моих в искусстве дивном.
Нет! никогда я зависти не знал,
О, никогда! – нижè, когда Пиччини
Пленить умел слух диких парижан,
Нижè, когда услышал в первый раз
Я Ифигении начальны звуки.
Кто скажет, чтоб Сальери гордый был
Когда-нибудь завистником презренным,
Змеей, людьми растоптанною, вживе
Песок и пыль грызущею бессильно?
Никто!... А ныне – сам скажу – я ныне
Завистник. Я завидую; глубоко,

direction by someone he meets? By vigorous, intense persistence I at last reached a high level within limitless art. Fame smiled on me; in the hearts of men I found harmony with my own creations. I was happy: in peace I enjoyed my toil, success, and fame, as well as the toil and the successes of my friends and comrades in this wondrous art. No, never did I know envy! Oh, never – neither when Piccini was able to captivate the ears of the boorish Parisians, nor when I heard for the first time the opening sounds of *Iphigenia*. Who will say that proud Salieri was ever a contemptible envier, a serpent trampled on by men yet, while still alive, impotently gnawing sand and dust? No one! But now – to myself I will say it – now I am envious. I envy; deeply, painfully, I envy.

Мучительно завидую. – О небо!
Где ж правота, когда священный дар,
Когда бессмертный гений – не в награду
Любви горящей, самоотверженья,
Трудов, усердия, молений послан –
А озаряет голову безумца,
Гуляки праздного? . . . О Моцарт, Моцарт!

(Входит Моцарт.)
        Моцарт

Ага! увидел ты! а мне хотелось
Тебя нежданной шуткой угостить.

        Сальери

Ты здесь! – Давно ль?

        Моцарт

        Сейчас. Я шел к тебе,
Нес кое-что тебе я показать;
Но, проходя перед трактиром, вдруг
Услышал скрыпку . . . Нет, мой друг,
        Сальери!

O heaven! Where is justice, when the sacred gift, when immortal genius is sent not to reward burning love, self-sacrifice, toil, ardour, supplications, but illumines the head of a madcap, of an idle rake? O Mozart, Mozart!

(Enter Mozart.)

MOZART: Aha! You saw me! And I wanted to treat you to an unexpected joke.
SALIERI: You here! Have you been here long?
MOZART: I have just come. I was on my way to see you and was bringing one or two things to show you; but passing in front of an inn, I suddenly heard a violin . . . No, Salieri, my friend! You

Смешнее отроду ты ничего
Не слыхивал . . . Слепой скрыпач в трактире
Разыгрывал voi che sapete. Чудо!
Не вытерпел, привел я скрыпача,
Чтоб угостить тебя его искусством.
Войди!

(*Входит слепой старик со скрыпкой.*)
Из Моцарта нам что-нибудь!

(*Старик играет арию из Дон-Жуана;
Моцарт хохочет.*)

Сальери
И ты смеяться можешь?

Моцарт

Ах, Сальери!
Ужель и сам ты не смеешься?

have never in all your life heard anything funnier! A blind fiddler
in the inn was playing *Voi che sapete.* Amazing! I could not
restrain myself, and I've brought the fiddler to treat you to his art.
Come in!

(*Enter a blind old man with his violin.*)
Play us something from Mozart!
(*The old man plays an aria from Don Juan; Mozart roars with
laughter.*)
SALIERI: And you can laugh?
MOZART: Ah, Salieri! Can it be that you are not laughing?

Сальери

Нет.
Мне не смешно, когда маляр негодный
Мне пачкает Мадонну Рафаэля,
Мне не смешно, когда фигляр презренный
Пародией бесчестит Алигьери.
Пошел, старик.

Моцарт

Постой же: вот тебе,
Пей за мое здоровье.

(*Старик уходит.*)

Ты, Сальери,
Не в духе нынче. Я приду к тебе
В другое время.

Сальери

Что ты мне принес?

SALIERI: No. I do not find it funny when a worthless wretched painter bedaubs a Raphael Madonna for me; I do not find it funny when a contemptible buffoon dishonours Alighieri with a parody. Be off, old man!
MOZART: Wait. Here you are: drink my health.

(*Exit old man.*)

Salieri, you are not in good spirits today. I will come to you some other time.
SALIERI: What have you brought me?

Моцарт

Нет – так; безделицу. Намедни ночью
Бессоница моя меня томила,
И в голову пришли мне две, три мысли.
Сегодня их я набросал. Хотелось
Твое мне слышать мненье; но теперь
Тебе не до меня.

Сальери

Ах, Моцарт, Моцарт!
Когда же мне не до тебя? Садись;
Я слушаю.

Моцарт

(*за фортепиано*)

Представь себе . . . кого бы?
Ну, хоть меня – немного помоложе;
Влюбленного – не слишком, а слегка –
С красоткой, или с другом – хоть с тобой,
Я весел . . . Вдруг: виденье гробовое,
Незапный мрак иль что-нибудь такое . . .
Ну слушай же.

(*Играет.*)

MOZART: Nothing – just a trifle. The other night my insomnia tormented me, and two or three ideas came into my head. Today I jotted them down. I wanted to hear your opinion; but you have no time for me now.

SALIERI: Ah, Mozart, Mozart! When don't I have time for you? Sit down. I am listening.

MOZART (*at the piano*): Imagine . . . Who? Well, say myself – a little younger; in love – not too much, but just a little; I'm with a pretty woman, or with a friend, say you; I'm merry . . . Suddenly a vision of the grave, sudden darkness, or something like that . . . Well now, listen.

(*Plays.*)

213

Сальери

Ты с этим шел ко мне
И мог остановиться у трактира
И слушать скрыпача слепого! – Боже!
Ты, Моцарт, недостоин сам себя.

Моцарт

Что ж, хорошо?

Сальери

Какая глубина!
Какая смелость и какая стройность!
Ты, Моцарт, бог, и сам того не знаешь;
Я знаю, я.

Моцарт

Ба! право? может быть . . .
Но божество мое проголодалось.

Сальери

Послушай: отобедаем мы вместе
В трактире Золотого Льва.

SALIERI: You were coming to me with this, and you could stop by an inn and listen to a blind fiddler? My God! Mozart, you are not worthy of yourself.
MOZART: Well? Is it good?
SALIERI: What depth! What boldness and what harmony! You are a god, Mozart, and you do not know it yourself. I do.
MOZART: Bah! Really? Perhaps . . . But my godhead is starving.
SALIERI: Listen: let us dine together at the Golden Lion.

Моцарт

Пожалуй;
Я рад. Но дай схожу домой сказать
Жене, чтобы меня она к обеду
Не дожидалась.

(Уходит.)

Сальери

Жду тебя; смотри ж.
Нет! не могу противиться я доле
Судьбе моей: я избран, чтоб его
Остановить — не то мы все погибли,
Мы все, жрецы, служители музыки,
Не я один с моей глухою славой . . .
Что пользы, если Моцарт будет жив
И новой высоты еще достигнет?
Подымет ли он тем еще искусство? Нет;
Оно падет, как он исчезнет:
Наследника нам не оставит он.
Что пользы в нем? Как некий херувим,
Он несколько занес нам песен райских,
Чтоб, возмутив бескрылое желанье
В нас, чадах праха, после улететь!
Так улетай же! чем скорей, тем лучше.

MOZART: All right; I'd like to. But let me go home and tell my wife not to expect me for dinner.

(Exit.)

SALIERI: I'll wait for you; mind you come . . . No! I can no longer resist my fate: I am chosen to stop him — otherwise we are all done for, all of us priests and servants of music, not merely I with my dim glory . . . What will it avail if Mozart is alive and reaches yet new heights? Will he raise art thereby? No! It will fall again when he disappears: he will leave us no heir. What use is there in him? Like some cherub he has brought us a few heavenly songs, only to fly away after stirring a wingless desire within us children of dust! So, fly away then! The quicker the better!

Вот яд, последний дар моей Изоры.
Осьмнадцать лет ношу его с собою –
И часто жизнь казалась мне с тех пор
Несносной раной, и сидел я часто
С врагом беспечным за одной трапезой,
И никогда на шепот искушенья
Не приклонился я, хоть я не трус,
Хотя обиду чувствую глубоко,
Хоть мало жизнь люблю. Все медлил я.
Как жажда смерти мучила меня,
Что умирать? я мнил: быть может, жизнь
Мне принесет незапные дары;
Быть может, посетит меня восторг
И творческая ночь и вдохновенье;
Быть может, новый Гайден сотворит
Великое – и наслажуся им . . .
Как пировал я с гостем ненавистным,
Быть может, мнил я, злейшего врага
Найду; быть может, злейшая обида
В меня с надменной грянет высоты –
Тогда не пропадешь ты, дар Изоры.
И я был прав! и наконец нашел

Here is a poison, the last gift of my Isora. For eighteen years I have been carrying it about with me – and often since then life has seemed to me an intolerable torment, and often I have sat at the same table with my carefree foe, and never have I yielded to the whisper of temptation, although I am no coward, although I feel the wrong deeply, although I have little love for life. I have always bided my time. When the thirst for death tormented me, I would think: 'Why die? Perhaps life will bring me unexpected gifts; perhaps rapture will visit me, and the creative night and inspiration; perhaps a new Haydn will create great things and I shall enjoy them . . .' When I feasted with a hated guest, I used to think; 'Perhaps I shall find a direr foe; perhaps a direr wrong will crash upon me from a lordly height – then you will not come amiss, O gift of Isora!' And I was right! At last I have found my foe, and

Я моего врага, и новый Гайден
Меня восторгом дивно упоил!
Теперь – пора! заветный дар любви,
Переходи сегодня в чашу дружбы.

Сцена II

Особая комната в трактире; фортепиано.
Моцарт и Сальери за столом.

Сальери

Что ты сегодня пасмурен?

Моцарт

Я? Нет!

Сальери

Ты, верно, Моцарт, чем-нибудь расстроен?
Обед хороший, славное вино,
А ты молчишь и хмуришься.

Моцарт

Признаться,
Мой Requiem меня тревожит.

a new Haydn has wondrously enraptured me with ecstasy! Now is the time! O sacred gift of love, enter today into the cup of friendship!

Scene Two

Private room at an inn: piano: Mozart and Salieri seated at table.
SALIERI: Why are you gloomy today?
MOZART: I? Not at all!
SALIERI: You are worried by something, Mozart, I am sure. A good dinner, fine wine, but you are silent and morose.
MOZART: I admit, my *Requiem* is worrying me.

Сальери

А?

Ты сочиняешь Requiem? Давно ли?

Моцарт

Давно, недели три. Но странный случай . . .
Не сказывал тебе я?

Сальери

Нет.

Моцарт

Так слушай.
Недели три тому, пришел я поздно
Домой. Сказали мне, что заходил
За мною кто-то. Отчего – не знаю,
Всю ночь я думал: кто бы это был?
И что ему во мне? Назавтра тот же
Зашел и не застал опять меня.
На третий день играл я на полу
С моим мальчишкой. Кликнули меня;
Я вышел. Человек, одетый в черном,
Учтиво поклонившись, заказал
Мне Requiem и скрылся. Сел я тотчас

SALIERI: Ah! You are writing a *Requiem*? Have you been at it long?
MOZART: Yes, about three weeks. But a strange occurrence . . .
Did I not tell you about it?
SALIERI: No.
MOZART: Well, listen. About three weeks ago I came home late.
I was told that someone had called for me. Why, I do not know,
but all night I thought: who can it have been? And what does he
want of me? On the next day the same man called, and again did
not find me at home. On the third day I was on the floor playing
with my little boy. I was called; I went out. A man, dressed in
black, bowed courteously, ordered a *Requiem* from me, and disappeared. I immediately sat down and began to write. And since

И стал писать – и с той поры за мною
Не приходил мой черный человек;
А я и рад: мне было б жаль расстаться
С моей работой, хоть совсем готов
Уж Requiem. Но между тем я . . .

Сальери

Что?

Моцарт

Мне совестно признаться в этом . . .

Сальери

В чем же?

Моцарт

Мне день и ночь покоя не дает
Мой черный человек. За мною всюду
Как тень он гонится. Вот и теперь
Мне кажется, он с нами сам—третей
Сидит.

that time my man in black has not come to me again; yet I am
glad: I would be loath to part with my work, although the *Requiem*
is quite ready now. But meanwhile I . . .
SALIERI: What?
MOZART: I am ashamed to admit it . . .
SALIERI: To admit what?
MOZART: Day and night my man in black gives me no rest. He
hunts me everywhere like a shadow. And even now he seems to be
sitting here with the two of us.

Сальери

И полно! что за страх ребячий?
Рассей пустую думу. Бомарше
Говаривал мне: «Слушай, брат Сальери,
Как мысли черные к тебе придут,
Откупори шампанского бутылку
Иль перечти ,,Женитьбу Фигаро"».

Моцарт

Да! Бомарше ведь был тебе приятель;
Ты для него «Тарара» сочинил,
Вещь славную. Там есть один мотив . . .
Я все твержу его, когда я счастлив . . .
Ла ла ла ла . . . Ах, правда ли, Сальери,
Что Бомарше кого-то отравил?

Сальери

Не думаю: он слишком был смешон
Для ремесла такого.

Моцарт

Он же гений,
Как ты да я. А гений и злодейство –
Две вещи несовместные. Не правда ль?

SALIERI: Enough! What childish fear is this? Dispel this empty thought. Beaumarchais used to say to me: 'Listen, brother Salieri, when black thoughts come to you, uncork a bottle of champagne or reread *The Marriage of Figaro.*'
MOZART: Yes! Beaumarchais was a friend of yours, of course; you composed *Tarare* for him, a glorious piece. There's one tune in it . . . I always repeat it when I'm happy . . . La-la, la-la . . . Oh, Salieri, is it true that Beaumarchais poisoned someone?
SALIERI: I think not: he was too humorous for such a trade.
MOZART: He is a genius, like you and me. And genius and villainy are two things that are incompatible. Isn't that so?

220

Сальери

Ты думаешь?

(*Бросает яд в стакан Моцарта.*)

Ну, пей же.

Моцарт

За твое
Здоровье, друг, за искренний союз,
Связующий Моцарта и Сальери,
Двух сыновей гармонии.

(*Пьет.*)

Сальери

Постой,
Постой, постой! . . . Ты выпил . . . без меня?

Моцарт

(*бросает салфетку на стол*)

Довольно, сыт я.

(*Идет к фортепиано.*)

Слушай же, Сальери,
Мой Requiem.

SALIERI: You think so?

(*Casts the poison into Mozart's glass.*)

Come, drink up!

MOZART: Your health, friend; to the true bond that links Mozart and Salieri, two sons of harmony.

(*Drinks.*)

SALIERI: Wait, wait, wait! You've drunk it! Without me?

MOZART (*throws his napkin on the table*): Enough. I have had my fill.

(*Goes to the piano.*)

Now, Salieri, listen to my *Requiem*.

(*Играет.*)

Ты плачешь?

Сальери

Эти слезы
Впервые лью: и больно и приятно,
Как будто тяжкий совершил я долг,
Как будто нож целебный мне отсек
Страдавший член! Друг Моцарт, эти слезы ...
Не замечай их. Продолжай, спеши
Еще наполнить звуками мне душу ...

Моцарт

Когда бы все так чувствовали силу
Гармонии! Но нет: тогда б не мог
И мир существовать; никто б не стал
Заботиться о нуждах низкой жизни;
Все предались бы вольному искусству.
Нас мало избранных, счастливцев праздных,
Пренебрегающих презренной пользой,
Единого прекрасного жрецов.
Не правда ль? Но я нынче нездоров,
Мне что-то тяжело; пойду засну.
Прощай же!

(*Plays.*)

You're weeping?

SALIERI: I shed these tears for the first time: I feel both pain and
pleasure, as though I had completed some grievous task, as though
the healing knife had cut off a suffering limb from me! Mozart,
my friend, these tears ... pay no attention to them. Continue,
hasten yet to fill my soul with sounds ...

MOZART: If only all men would so feel the strength of harmony!
But no: then the world could not even exist; no one would care for
the needs of ordinary life – all would give themselves up to free
art. There are few of us chosen ones, the idle happy ones who
neglect contemptible utility, the priests of beauty alone. Isn't that
true? But I am not well today. Something is making me feel ill; I'll
go and sleep. Farewell!

Сальери

До свиданья.

(*Один.*)

Ты заснешь
Надолго, Моцарт! Но ужель он прав,
И я не гений? Гений и злодейство
Две вещи несовместные. Неправда:
А Бонаротти? или это сказка
Тупой, бессмысленной толпы – и не был
Убийцею создатель Ватикана?

СКАЗКА О ЗОЛОТОМ ПЕТУШКЕ

Негде, в тридевятом царстве,
В тридесятом государстве,
Жил-был славный царь Дадон.
Смолоду был грозен он
И соседям то и дело
Наносил обиды смело;

SALIERI: Till we meet again.

(*Alone.*)

You will sleep long, Mozart! But can it be that he is right, and I am
not a genius? Genius and villainy are two things that are incompatible. It is not true: what of Buonarotti? Or is that a fiction of the
dull, senseless rabble – and was the builder of the Vatican not a
murderer after all?

THE TALE OF THE GOLDEN COCKEREL

SOMEWHERE in the thrice-ninth kingdom, in the thrice-tenth
realm [i.e. at the other end of the earth, in fairyland] lived the
glorious Tsar Dadon. From his youth he was formidable, and all
the time he boldly caused offence to his neighbours; but as old age

Но под старость захотел
Отдохнуть от ратных дел
И покой себе устроить.
Тут соседи беспокоить
Стали старого царя,
Страшный вред ему творя.
Чтоб концы своих владений
Охранять от нападений,
Должен был он содержать
Многочисленную рать.
Воеводы не дремали,
Но никак не успевали:
Ждут, бывало, с юга, глядь, –
Ан с востока лезет рать.
Справят здесь, – лихие гости
Идут от моря. Со злости
Инда плакал царь Дадон,
Инда забывал и сон.
Что и жизнь в такой тревоге!
Вот он с просьбой о помоге
Обратился к мудрецу,
Звездочету и скопцу.
Шлет за ним гонца с поклоном.

drew on, he conceived a desire to rest from warlike matters and to arrange a life of peace and quiet. But now his neighbours began to trouble the repose of the old Tsar, causing him terrible harm. In order to protect the limits of his possessions from attacks, he had to maintain a multitudinous army. His generals did not slumber, but they simply had not time for everything: they would be waiting for the enemy to come from the south – but no, from the east an army moves. They would repair the damage here – and evil guests come marching from the sea. And so Tsar Dadon would even weep with rage and even lose his sleep. What sort of life was that, in such anxiety! And so, with a request for help, he turned to a wise man, an astrologer and eunuch. He sends a courier to ask him to come.

Вот мудрец перед Дадоном
Стал и вынул из мешка
Золотого петушка.
«Посади ты эту птицу, —
Молвил он царю, — на спицу;
Петушок мой золотой
Будет верный сторож твой:
Коль кругом все будет мирно,
Так сидеть он будет смирно;
Но лишь чуть со стороны
Ожидать тебе войны,
Иль набега силы бранной,
Иль другой беды незваной,
Вмиг тогда мой петушок
Приподымет гребешок,
Закричит и встрепенется
И в то место обернется».
Царь скопца благодарит,
Горы золота сулит.
«За такое одолженье, —
Говорит он в восхищенье, —
Волю певую твою
Я исполню, как мою».

And now the wise man stood **before** Dadon and took from his bag a golden cockerel. 'Put this bird', he said to the Tsar, 'on a spire; my golden cockerel will be your true watchman: if all around is peaceful, then he will sit quietly; but no sooner shall a war, or a raid by an armed force, or any other untoward misfortune threaten you from any quarter, than in an instant my cockerel will raise his comb, crow, ruffle his feathers and turn in that direction.' The Tsar thanks the eunuch, promises mountains of gold. 'For such a service,' he says in delight, 'I will **grant** your first wish as though it were mine.'

Петушок с высокой спицы
Стал стеречь его границы.
Чуть опасность где видна,
Верный сторож как со сна
Шевельнется, встрепенется,
К той сторонке обернется
И кричит: «Кири-ку-ку.
Царствуй, лежа на боку!»
И соседи присмирели,
Воевать уже не смели:
Таковой им царь Дадон
Дал отпор со всех сторон!

Год другой проходит мирно;
Петушок сидит все смирно.
Вот однажды царь Дадон
Страшным шумом пробужден:
«Царь ты наш! отец народа! –
Возглашает воевода, –
Государь! проснись! беда!»
– Что такое, господа? –
Говорит Дадон, зевая, –
А?... Кто там?... беда какая? –

The cockerel began to guard his borders from a high spire. No sooner is danger seen anywhere, than the true watchman stirs himself as though waking from sleep, ruffles his feathers, turns in that direction and cries: 'Kiri-ku-ku. Take it easy as you rule!' And the neighbours quietened down, no longer did they dare to war: so fiercely Tsar Dadon repulsed them on all sides!

One year passes peacefully by, and then another; the cockerel sits quietly all the while. Then one day Tsar Dadon was woken by a terrible noise: 'Our Tsar! Father of the people!' the general cries out. 'Sovereign, awake! Disaster!' 'What is it, gentlemen?' says Dadon, yawning. 'Eh? Who's there? What disaster?' The

Воевода говорит:
«Петушок опять кричит;
Страх и шум во всей столице».
Царь к окошку, – ан на спице,
Видит, бьется петушок,
Обратившись на восток.
Медлить нечего: «Скорее!
Люди, нà конь! Эй, живее!»
Царь к востоку войско шлет,
Старший сын его ведет.
Петушок угомонился,
Шум утих, и царь забылся.

Вот проходит восемь дней,
А от войска нет вестей;
Было ль, не было ль сраженья, –
Нет Дадону донесенья.
Петушок кричит опять.
Кличит царь другую рать;
Сына он теперь меньшого
Шлет на выручку большого;
Петушок опять утих.
Снова вести нет от них!

general says: 'The cockerel is crowing again; there is fear and din throughout the whole capital.' The Tsar goes to the window – there indeed on the spire he sees the cockerel wildly fluttering, having turned towards the east. It's no use dallying: 'Quickly! Soldiers, to your horses! Make haste, make haste!' The Tsar sends his army eastward; his eldest son leads it. The cockerel quietened down, the din abated, and the Tsar dozed off again.

Eight days now go by, but there is no news from the army; has there or has there not been a battle? There is no message for Dadon. The cockerel crows again; the Tsar summons another army; now he sends his younger son to the rescue of his elder son; once more the cockerel became silent. Again there is no news from

Снова восемь дней проходят;
Люди в страхе дни проводят;
Петушок кричит опять,
Царь скликает третью рать
И ведет ее к востоку, —
Сам не зная, быть ли проку.

Войска идут день и ночь;
Им становится невмочь.
Ни побоища, ни стана,
Ни надгробного кургана
Не встречает царь Дадон.
«Что за чудо?» — мыслит он.
Вот осьмой уж день проходит,
Войско в горы царь приводит
И промеж высоких гор
Видит шелковый шатер.
Все в безмолвии чудесном
Вкруг шатра; в ущелье тесном
Рать побитая лежит.
Царь Дадон к шатру спешит . . .
Что за страшная картина!
Перед ним его два сына

them! Again eight days pass by; the people spend the days in fear;
once more the cockerel crows; the Tsar calls together a third army
and leads it eastwards, himself not knowing whether any good will
come of it.

The troops march day and night; they cannot stand it any more.
Tsar Dadon comes across neither battle nor camp nor burial
mound. 'What kind of wonder is this?' he thinks. And now
already the eighth day passes; the Tsar leads his army into the
mountains and in the midst of the high mountains he sees a silken
tent. All lies in wondrous silence around the tent; in a narrow
ravine the beaten army lies. Tsar Dadon hastens to the tent . . .
What a terrible picture! In front of him his two sons both lie dead

Без шеломов и без лат
Оба мертвые лежат,
Меч вонзивши друг во друга.
Бродят кони их средь луга,
По притоптанной траве,
По кровавой мураве . . .
Царь завыл: «Ох, дети, дети!
Горе мне! попались в сети
Оба наши сокола!
Горе! смерть моя пришла».
Все завыли за Дадоном,
Застонала тяжким стоном
Глубь долин, и сердце гор
Потряслося. Вдруг шатер
Распахнулся . . . и девица,
Шамаханская царица,
Вся сияя как заря,
Тихо встретила царя.
Как пред солнцем птица ночи,
Царь умолк, ей глядя в очи,
И забыл он перед ней
Смерть обоих сыновей.
И она перед Дадоном
Улыбнулась – и с поклоном
Его за руку взяла

without helmets and without armour, having plunged their swords into each other. In the middle of the meadow their horses wander over the trampled grass, over the bloody sward . . . The Tsar began to wail: 'Oh, my children, my children! Woe is me! Both our falcons have fallen into snares! Woe! My death has come!' All began to wail after Dadon; the depth of the valleys groaned with a grievous groan and the heart of the mountains was shaken. Suddenly the tent was flung wide open . . . and a maiden, the queen of Shemakha, all shining like the dawn, softly met the Tsar. Like a bird of night before the sun, the Tsar fell silent, looking her in the eyes, and in her presence he forgot the death of both his sons. And she smiled at Dadon and with a bow took him by the hand and

И в шатер свой увела.
Там за стол его сажала,
Всяким явством угощала,
Уложила отдыхать
На парчовую кровать.
И потом, неделю ровно,
Покорясь ей безусловно,
Околдован, восхищен,
Пировал у ней Дадон.

Наконец и в путь обратный
Со своею силой ратной
И с девицей молодой
Царь отправился домой.
Перед ним молва бежала,
Быль и небыль разглашала.
Под столицей, близ ворот,
С шумом встретил их народ, –
Все бегут за колесницей,
За Дадоном и царицей;
Всех приветствует Дадон . . .
Вдруг в толпе увидел он,
В сарачинской шапке белой,
Весь как лебедь поседелый,
Старый друг его, скопец.

led him off into her tent. There she sat him at a table, regaled him
with all kinds of food and laid him down to rest on a brocaded bed;
and then, for exactly a week, submitting to her unconditionally,
bewitched, enraptured, Dadon feasted with her.

At last the Tsar set off homewards on the return journey, with
his armed force and with the young maiden. Before him rumour
ran and noised abroad both truth and falsehood. Hard by the
capital, near the gates, the people met them with clamour. They all
run after the chariot, after Dadon and the queen; Dadon greets
them all . . . Suddenly in the crowd he saw – in a white Saracen
hat, with his hair all white like a swan – his old friend the eunuch.

«А, здорово, мой отец, –
Молвил царь ему, – что скажешь?
Подь поближе. Что прикажешь?»
– Царь! – ответствует мудрец, –
Разочтемся наконец.
Помнишь? за мою услугу
Обещался мне, как другу,
Волю первую мою
Ты исполнить, как свою.
Подари ж ты мне девицу,
Шамаханскую царицу. –
Крайне царь был изумлен.
«Что ты? – старцу молвил он, –
Или бес в тебя ввернулся,
Или ты с ума рехнулся?
Что ты в голову забрал?
Я, конечно, обещал,
Но всему же есть граница.
И зачем тебе девица?
Полно, знаешь ли кто я?
Попроси ты от меня
Хоть казну, хоть чин боярский,
Хоть коня с конюшни царской,
Хоть полцарства моего».

'Ah, greetings, good father!' said the Tsar to him. 'What have you to say? Come closer, what is your wish?' 'O Tsar,' answers the wise man, 'let us settle our accounts at last. Do you remember? For my services you promised me, as a friend, to fulfil my first wish as though it were your own. Well then, give me the maiden, the queen of Shemakha.' The Tsar was exceedingly amazed. 'What's that you say?' he said to the old man. 'Either a devil has got into you, or you have gone out of your mind. What has got into your head? Of course I promised, but there is a limit to everything. And what do you want the maiden for? Enough. Do you know who I am? Ask of me either my treasury, or the rank of boyar, or a horse from the royal stables, or, if you will, half my kingdom.' 'I

– Не хочу я ничего!
Подари ты мне девицу,
Шамаханскую царицу, –
Говорит мудрец в ответ.
Плюнул царь: «Так лих же: нет!
Ничего ты не получишь.
Сам себя ты, грешник, мучишь;
Убирайся, цел пока;
Оттащите старика!»
Старичок хотел заспорить,
Но с иным накладно вздорить;
Царь хватил его жезлом
По лбу; тот упал ничком,
Да и дух вон. – Вся столица
Содрогнулась, а девица –
Хи-хи-хи да ха-ха-ха!
Не боится, знать, греха.
Царь, хоть был встревожен сильно,
Усмехнулся ей умильно.
Вот – въезжает в город он . . .
Вдруг раздался легкий звон,
И в глазах у всей столицы
Петушок спорхнул со спицы,

wish for nought! Give me the maiden, the queen of Shemakha,'
says the wise man in reply. The Tsar spat: 'The devil take it, no!
You will get nothing. You torment yourself, you sinner – clear off,
while you are still whole; drag the old man away!' The old man
wanted to argue, but with some people it is disadvantageous to
pick a quarrel; the Tsar struck him on the forehead with his
sceptre; he fell down flat and his spirit departed. All the capital
shuddered – but the maiden cried: 'Hee, hee, hee!' and 'Ha, ha
ha!' She clearly has no fear of sin. The Tsar, although he was
extremely alarmed, smiled tenderly at her. And now he rides into
the town . . . Suddenly there was a light ringing sound and before
the eyes of the whole capital the cockerel fluttered down from its

К колеснице полетел
И царю на темя сел,
Встрепенулся, клюнул в темя
И взвился . . . и в то же время
С колесницы пал Дадон –
Охнул раз, – и умер он.
А царица вдруг пропала,
Будто вовсе не бывало.
Сказка ложь, да в ней намек!
Добрым молодцам урок.

МЕДНЫЙ ВСАДНИК

ПЕТЕРБУРГСКАЯ ПОВЕСТЬ

Вступление

На берегу пустынных волн
Стоял *он*, дум великих полн,
И вдаль глядел. Пред ним широко
Река неслася; бедный челн
По ней стремился одиноко.

spire, flew to the chariot, and sat on the top of the Tsar's head, ruffled its feathers, pecked at his pate, and soared up . . . And at that same time Dadon fell from his chariot – groaned once – and died. But the queen suddenly disappeared, as though she had never been there. The tale is not true, but there's a hint in it, a lesson for fine lads!

THE BRONZE HORSEMAN

(*A Tale of St Petersburg*)

Introduction

On the shore washed by the desolate waves *he* stood, full of lofty thoughts, and he gazed into the distance. Before him the broad river rushed by; on it in solitude sped a wretched skiff. Scattered

По мшистым, топким берегам
Чернели избы здесь и там,
Приют убогого чухонца;
И лес, неведомый лучам
В тумане спрятанного солнца,
Кругом шумел.

И думал он:
Отсель грозить мы будем шведу,
Здесь будет город заложен
Назло надменному соседу.
Природой здесь нам суждено
В Европу прорубить окно,
Ногою твердой стать при море.
Сюда по новым им волнам
Все флаги в гости будут к нам,
И запируем на просторе.

Прошло сто лет, и юный град,
Полнощных стран краса и диво,
Из тьмы лесов, из топи блат
Вознесся пышно, горделиво;
Где прежде финский рыболов,

here and there like black specks on the mossy, marshy banks were the huts, the shelter of the miserable Finn; and the forest, unknown to the rays of the mist-enshrouded sun, rustled all around.

And thus he thought: 'From here, we shall threaten the Swede; here a city shall be founded to spite our haughty neighbour. By nature we are fated here to cut a window through to Europe, to stand with firm foothold on the sea. Here, on waves unknown to them, ships of every flag will come to visit us, and we shall revel on the open sea.'

A hundred years have passed, and the young city, the adornment and marvel of the northern lands, has risen splendidly and proudly from the gloom of the forests and the swamp of the marshes; where

Печальный пасынок природы,
Один у низких берегов
Бросал в неведомые воды
Свой ветхий невод, ныне там
По оживленным берегам
Громады стройные теснятся
Дворцов и башен; корабли
Толпой со всех концов земли
К богатым пристаням стремятся;
В гранит оделася Нева;
Мосты повисли над водами;
Темно-зелеными садами
Ее покрылись острова,
И перед младшею столицей
Померкла старая Москва,
Как перед новою царицей
Порфироносная вдова.

Люблю тебя, Петра творенье,
Люблю твой строгий, стройный вид,
Невы державное теченье,
Береговой ее гранит,
Твоих оград узор чугунный,
Твоих задумчивых ночей
Прозрачный сумрак, блеск безлунный,

once the Finnish fisherman, Nature's sad stepson, alone on the low-lying banks cast his time-worn net into the unknown waters, there now huge harmonious palaces and towers crowd on the bustling banks; ships in their throngs speed from all ends of the earth to the rich quays; the Neva is clad in granite; bridges hang poised over her waters; her islands are covered with dark-green gardens. And before the younger capital ancient Moscow has paled, like a purple-clad widow before a new empress.

I love you, city of Peter's creation, I love your stern, harmonious aspect, the majestic flow of the Neva, her granite banks, the iron tracery of your railings, the transparent twilight and the moonless

Когда я в комнате моей
Пишу, читаю без лампады,
И ясны спящие громады
Пустынных улиц, и светла
Адмиралтейская игла,
И, не пуская тьму ночную
На золотые небеса,
Одна заря сменить другую
Спешит, дав ночи полчаса.
Люблю зимы твоей жестокой
Недвижный воздух и мороз,
Бег санок вдоль Невы широкой,
Девичьи лица ярче роз,
И блеск, и шум, и говор балов,
А в час пирушки холостой
Шипенье пенистых бокалов
И пунша пламень голубой.
Люблю воинственную живость
Потешных Марсовых полей,
Пехотных ратей и коней
Однообразную красивость,
В их стройно зыблемом строю
Лоскутья сих знамен победных,

gleam of your pensive nights, when in my room I write or read without a lamp, and the slumbering masses of your deserted streets shine clearly, and the Admiralty spire is luminous, and, without letting the dark of night on to the golden skies, one dawn hastens to relieve another, granting night a mere half-hour. I love the motionless air and the frost of your harsh winter, the sledges coursing along the broad Neva, the faces of girls brighter than roses, and the sparkle and noise and sound of voices at the balls, and, at the hour of the bachelor's feast, the hiss of foaming goblets and the pale-blue flame of punch. I love the warlike vivacity of the playing-fields of Mars [the parade-ground], the uniform beauty of the troops of infantry and of the horses, the tattered remnants of those victorious banners in their harmoniously swaying array, the

Сиянье шапок этих медных,
Насквозь простреленных в бою.
Люблю, военная столица,
Твоей твердыни дым и гром,
Когда полнощная царица
Дарует сына в царский дом,
Или победу над врагом
Россия снова торжествует,
Или, взломав свой синий лед,
Нева к морям его несет
И, чуя вешни дни, ликует.

Красуйся, град Петров, и стой
Неколебимо, как Россия,
Да умирится же с тобой
И побежденная стихия;
Вражду и плен старинный свой
Пусть волны финские забудут
И тщетной злобою не будут
Тревожить вечный сон Петра!

Была ужасная пора,
Об ней свежо воспоминанье . . .
Об ней, друзья мои, для вас
Начну свое повествованье.
Печален будет мой рассказ.

gleam of those bronze helmets, shot through in battle. O martial capital, I love the smoke and thunder of your fortress, when the northern empress presents a son to the royal house, or when Russia celebrates yet another victory over the foe, or when the Neva, breaking her blue ice, bears it to the seas and exults, scenting spring days.

Show your splendour, city of Peter, and stand unshakeable like Russia, so that even the conquered elements may make their peace with you; let the Finnish waves forget their enmity and ancient bondage, and let them not disturb the eternal sleep of Peter with their empty spite!

There was a dread time – the memory of it is still fresh . . . I will begin my narrative of it for you, my friends. My tale will be sad.

Часть Первая

Над омраченным Петроградом
Дышал ноябрь осенним хладом.
Плеская шумною волной
В края своей ограды стройной,
Нева металась, как больной
В своей постеле беспокойной.
Уж было поздно и темно;
Сердито бился дождь в окно,
И ветер дул, печально воя.
В то время из гостей домой
Пришел Евгений молодой . . .
Мы будем нашего героя
Звать этим именем. Оно
Звучит приятно; с ним давно
Мое перо к тому же дружно.
Прозванья нам его не нужно,
Хотя в минувши времена
Оно, быть может, и блистало
И под пером Карамзина
В родных преданьях прозвучало;
Но ныне светом и молвой
Оно забыто. Наш герой

Part One

Over darkened Petrograd November breathed its autumn chill.
With noisy waves splashing against the edges of her shapely
bounds, the Neva tossed like a sick man in his restless bed. It was
already late and dark; angrily the rain beat against the window and
the wind blew, sadly howling. At that time young Yevgeny came
home from visiting friends . . . We will call our hero by this
name. It sounds pleasant; furthermore, it has long been congenial
to my pen. We do not need his surname, although perhaps in
bygone days it even shone, and beneath the pen of Karamzin rang
forth in our native legends; but now it is forgotten by the world
and by fame. Our hero lives in Kolomna [a district of St Peters-

Живет в Коломне; где-то служит,
Дичится знатных и не тужит
Ни о почиющей родне,
Ни о забытой старине.

Итак, домой пришед, Евгений
Стряхнул шинель, разделся, лег.
Но долго он заснуть не мог
В волненье разных размышлений.
О чем же думал он? о том,
Что был он беден, что трудом
Он должен был себе доставить
И независимость и честь;
Что мог бы Бог ему прибавить
Ума и денег. Что ведь есть
Такие праздные счастливцы,
Ума недальнего, ленивцы,
Которым жизнь куда легка!
Что служит он всего два года;
Он также думал, что погода
Не унималась; что река
Все прибывала; что едва ли
С Невы мосты уже не сняли

burg]; he works in an office somewhere, he shuns the aristocracy and grieves neither for deceased relatives nor for forgotten times of old.

And so, having come home, Yevgeny tossed aside his cloak, undressed, lay down. But for a long time he was not able to fall asleep, in the turmoil of his divers thoughts. What, then, did he think about? About the fact that he was poor, that by toil he had to win for himself both independence and honour; that God might have granted him more brains and money; that after all there are lazy lucky folk, of limited brain, idlers, for whom life is oh so easy, that he had been a clerk for only two years; he also thought that the weather was not becoming calmer; that the river was still rising, and that as likely as not the bridges on the Neva had

И что с Парашей будет он
Дни на два, на три разлучен.
Евгений тут вздохнул сердечно
И размечтался, как поэт.

«Жениться? Мне? зачем же нет?
Оно и тяжело, конечно;
Но что ж, я молод и здоров,
Трудиться день и ночь готов;
Уж кое-как себе устрою
Приют смиренный и простой
И в нем Парашу успокою.
Пройдет, быть может, год-другой –
Местечко получу, Параше
Препоручу семейство наше
И воспитание ребят . . .
И станем жить, и так до гроба
Рука с рукой дойдем мы оба,
И внуки нас похоронят . . .»

Так он мечтал. И грустно было
Ему в ту ночь, и он желал,
Чтоб ветер выл не так уныло
И чтобы дождь в окно стучал
Не так сердито . . .

already been raised, and that for two or three days he would be separated from Parasha. At this point Yevgeny sighed from his very heart and fell to dreaming like a poet.

'Marry? Me? But why not? It would be hard, of course; but then I'm young and healthy, I'm ready to toil day and night; somehow or other I'll fix myself a humble, simple shelter and in it I'll let Parasha live a life of quiet. A year or two perhaps will pass, and I'll get a job and I'll hand over our family and the children's upbringing to Parasha . . . And we'll begin to live, and thus we'll both go hand in hand to the grave, and our grandchildren will bury us . . .'

Thus he mused. And he felt sad that night, and he wished the wind would not howl so gloomily and that the rain would not beat so angrily at the window . . .

Сонны очи
Он наконец закрыл. И вот
Редеет мгла ненастной ночи
И бледный день уж настает ...
Ужасный день!

Нева всю ночь
Рвалася к морю против бури,
Не одолев их буйной дури ...
И спорить стало ей невмочь ...
Поутру над ее брегами
Теснился кучами народ,
Любуясь брызгами, горами
И пеной разъяренных вод.
Но силой ветров от залива
Перегражденная Нева
Обратно шла, гневна, бурлива,
И затопляла острова,
Погода пуще свирепела,
Нева вздувалась и ревела,
Котлом клокоча и клубясь,
И вдруг, как зверь остервенясь,
На город кинулась. Пред нею
Все побежало, все вокруг

At last he closed his sleepy eyes. And now the darkness of the foul night thins out and the pale day already draws on ... That dreadful day!

All night the Neva rushed towards the sea against the storm, unable to overcome the madness of the winds ... and she could no longer endure the struggle ... In the morning swarms of people crowded on her banks, admiring the spray, the mountains and the foam of the maddened waters. But hemmed in by the strength of the winds from the gulf, the Neva went back again, angry, turbulent, and swamped the islands. The weather raged more fiercely, the Neva swelled up and roared, bubbling like a cauldron and swirling, and suddenly, with the frenzy of a beast, hurled herself upon the city. Everything ran before her, everything

Вдруг опустело – воды вдруг
Втекли в подземные подвалы,
К решеткам хлынули каналы,
И всплыл Петрополь, как тритон,
По пояс в воду погружен.

Осада! приступ! злые волны,
Как воры, лезут в окна. Челны
С разбега стекла бьют кормой.
Лотки под мокрой пеленой,
Обломки хижин, бревны, кровли,
Товар запасливой торговли,
Пожитки бледной нищеты,
Грозой снесенные мосты,
Гроба с размытого кладбища
Плывут по улицам!
     Народ
Зрит Божий гнев и казни ждет.
Увы! все гибнет: кров и пища!
Где будет взять?
     В тот грозный год
Покойный царь еще Россией

suddenly became deserted round about – suddenly the waters flowed into the cellars under ground, the canals surged up to the railings, and Petropolis floated up like Triton, plunged waist-high in the water.

Siege! Assault! The evil waves climb like thieves through the windows. Scudding boats smash the panes with their sterns. Hawkers' trays beneath their damp covers, fragments of huts, beams, roofs, the wares of thrifty trading, the chattels of pale poverty, bridges swept away by the storm, coffins from the inundated cemetery – all float along the streets!

The people gaze on the wrath of God and wait their doom. Alas! All is perishing: shelter and food – where shall they find them?

In that dread year the late Tsar still ruled Russia with glory. He

Со славой правил. На балкон,
Печален, смутен, вышел он
И молвил: «С Божией стихией
Царям не совладеть». Он сел
И в думе скорбными очами
На злое бедствие глядел.
Стояли стогны озерами,
И в них широкими реками
Вливались улицы. Дворец
Казался островом печальным.
Царь молвил – из конца в конец,
По ближним улицам и дальным
В опасный путь средь бурных вод
Его пустились генералы
Спасать и страхом обуялый
И дома тонущий народ.

Тогда, на площади Петровой,
Где дом в углу вознесся новый,
Где над возвышенным крыльцом
С подъятой лапой, как живые,
Стоят два льва сторожевые,
На звере мраморном верхом,
Без шляпы, руки сжав крестом,

came out on to the balcony, sad, troubled, and said: 'Tsars cannot master the divine elements.' He sat down and pensively gazed on the dire disaster with sorrowful eyes. The squares were now like lakes, and into them poured the streets in broad rivers. The palace seemed like a sad island. The Tsar spoke – from end to end, along streets near and far, his generals set off on their dangerous journey midst the storm waters, to save the people stricken with fear and drowning in their homes.

There, in Peter's square, where in the corner a new house towers up, where over the lofty porch two guardian lions stand like living creatures with upraised paw – there astride the marble beast, hatless, his arms tightly crossed, sat Yevgeny, motionless

Сидел недвижный, страшно бледный
Евгений. Он страшился, бедный,
Не за себя. Он не слыхал,
Как подымался жадный вал,
Ему подошвы подмывая,
Как дождь ему в лицо хлестал,
Как ветер, буйно завывая,
С него и шляпу вдруг сорвал.
Его отчаянные взоры
На край один наведены
Недвижно были. Словно горы,
Из возмущенной глубины
Вставали волны там и злились,
Там буря выла, там носились
Обломки . . . Боже, Боже! там —
Увы! близехонько к волнам,
Почти у самого залива —
Забор некрашенный, да ива
И ветхий домик: там оне,
Вдова и дочь, его Параша,
Его мечта . . . Или во сне
Он это видит? иль вся наша
И жизнь ничто, как сон пустой,
Насмешка неба над землей?

and fearfully pale. He was afraid, poor fellow, not for himself. He
did not hear the greedy billow rise, lapping his soles; he did not
feel the rain lash his face, nor the wind, wildly howling, suddenly
tear his hat from his head. His desperate gaze was firmly fixed on
one distant point. There, just like mountains, waves rose up from
the seething depths and raged, there the storm howled, there
wreckage rushed to and fro . . . O God, O God! There, alas, so
close to the waves, almost by the gulf itself – is an unpainted fence
and a willow and a small ramshackle house: there they live, the
widow and her daughter, his Parasha, his dream . . . Or is he
dreaming this? Or is all our life nothing but an empty dream,
heaven's mockery at earth?

И он, как будто околдован,
Как будто к мрамору прикован,
Сойти не может! Вкруг него
Вода и больше ничего!
И, обращен к нему спиною,
В неколебимой вышине,
Над возмущенною Невою
Стоит с простертою рукою
Кумир на бронзовом коне.

Часть Вторая

Но вот, насытясь разрушеньем
И наглым буйством утомясь,
Нева обратно повлеклась,
Своим любуясь возмущеньем
И покидая с небреженьем
Свою добычу. Так злодей,
С свирепой шайкою своей
В село ворвавшись, ломит, режет,
Крушит и грабит; вопли, скрежет,
Насилье, брань, тревога, вой!...
И, грабежом отягощенны,
Боясь погони, утомленны,
Спешат разбойники домой,
Добычу на пути роняя.

And he, as though bewitched, as though riveted to the marble,
cannot get down! Around him is water and nothing else! And with
back turned to him, on unshakeable eminence, over the turbulent
Neva, stands the Image with outstretched arm on his bronze horse.

Part Two

But now, satiated with destruction and wearied by her insolent
violence, the Neva drew back, revelling in the chaos she had
caused and nonchalantly abandoning her booty. Thus a marauder,
bursting into a village with his savage band, smashes, slashes,
shatters, and robs; shrieks, gnashing of teeth, violence, oaths, panic,
howls! And weighed down with their plunder, fearing pursuit,
exhausted, the robbers hasten home, dropping their plunder on the
way.

Вода сбыла, и мостовая
Открылась, и Евгений мой
Спешит, душою замирая,
В надежде, страхе и тоске
К едва смирившейся реке.
Но, торжеством победы полны,
Еще кипели злобно волны,
Как бы под ними тлел огонь,
Еще их пена покрывала,
И тяжело Нева дышала,
Как с битвы прибежавший конь.
Евгений смотрит: видит лодку;
Он к ней бежит как на находку;
И перевозчика зовет —
И перевозчик беззаботный
Его за гривенник охотно
Чрез волны страшные везет.

И долго с бурными волнами
Боролся опытный гребец,
И скрыться вглубь меж их рядами
Всечасно с дерзкими пловцами
Готов был челн — и наконец
Достиг он берега.

The water subsided and the roadway became visible, and my
Yevgeny in hope and fear and grief hastens with sinking heart to
the river, which has barely abated. But full of the triumph of
victory, the waves still seethed angrily, as though fire were smoulder-
ing beneath them; foam still covered them, and heavily the Neva
breathed, like a horse galloping home from battle. Yevgeny looks:
he sees a boat; he runs towards it as to some unexpected find; he
calls the ferryman, and the carefree ferryman for ten kopecks
willingly rows him over the dire waves.

And for long the experienced oarsman struggled with the stormy
waves, and all the time the skiff was on the point of plunging with
its rash crew into the depths between the ranges of the waves —
and at last he reached the bank.

Несчастный
Знакомой улицей бежит
В места знакомые. Глядит,
Узнать не может. Вид ужасный!
Все перед ним завалено;
Что сброшено, что снесено;
Скривились домики, другие
Совсем обрушились, иные
Волнами сдвинуты; кругом,
Как будто в поле боевом,
Тела валяются. Евгений
Стремглав, не помня ничего,
Изнемогая от мучений,
Бежит туда, где ждет его
Судьба с неведомым известьем,
Как с запечатанным письмом.
И вот бежит уж он предместьем,
И вот залив, и близок дом . . .
Что ж это ? . . .
Он остановился.
Пошел назад и воротился.
Глядит . . . идет . . . еще глядит.
Вот место, где их дом стоит;

The wretched Yevgeny runs down a familiar street to familiar places. He gazes and can recognize nothing. A terrible sight! All is piled up before him: this has been hurled down, that has been torn away; the little houses have become twisted, others have completely collapsed and others have been shifted by the waves; all around, as on a battlefield, corpses are strewn. Remembering nothing and exhausted by torments, Yevgeny rushes headlong to the place where Fate awaits him with tidings yet unknown, as with a sealed letter. And now he is already running through the suburb, and here is the bay, and close by is the house . . . But what is this ?

He stopped. He went back and turned. He looks . . . walks forward . . . looks again. Here is the place where their house stood;

Вот ива. Были здесь вороты –
Снесло их, видно. Где же дом?
И, полон сумрачной заботы,
Все ходит, ходит он кругом,
Толкует громко сам с собою –
И вдруг, ударя в лоб рукою,
Захохотал.
       Ночная мгла
На город трепетный сошла;
Но долго жители не спали
И меж собою толковали
О дне минувшем.
       Утра луч
Из-за усталых, бледных туч
Блеснул над тихою столицей
И не нашел уже следов
Беды вчерашней; багряницей
Уже прикрыто было зло.
В порядок прежний все вошло.
Уже по улицам свободным
С своим бесчувствием холодным
Ходил народ. Чиновный люд,

here is the willow. There were gates here – they have been swept away, evidently. But where is the house? And full of gloomy anxiety he walks and walks around and talks loudly to himself – and suddenly, striking his forehead with his hand, he burst out laughing.

The darkness of night came down upon the terror-stricken town; but for a long time its inhabitants could not sleep, and talked among themselves of the past day.

From behind the tired pale clouds the ray of morning shone over the quiet capital and found no traces of yesterday's disaster; the damage was already covered by dawn's purple mantle [or, perhaps, 'by the Tsar's purple mantle', i.e. by the measures taken by Alexander 1]. Everything returned to its former order. Already along the cleared streets the people were walking with cold im-

Покинув свой ночной приют,
На службу шел. Торгаш отважный,
Не унывая, открывал
Невой ограбленный подвал,
Сбираясь свой убыток важный
На ближнем выместить. С дворов
Свозили лодки.
                    Граф Хвостов,
Поэт, любимый небесами,
Уж пел бессмертными стихами
Несчастье невских берегов.

Но бедный, бедный мой Евгений . . .
Увы! его смятенный ум
Против ужасных потрясений
Не устоял. Мятежный шум
Невы и ветров раздавался
В его ушах. Ужасных дум
Безмолвно полон, он скитался.
Его терзал какой-то сон.
Прошла неделя, месяц – он
К себе домой не возвращался.

---

passiveness. Government officials, leaving their night's shelter, were on their way to work. The bold huckster, never despairing, was opening his cellar, which had been robbed by the Neva, intending to make good his grave loss at his neighbour's expense. Boats were being carted away from the courtyards.

Count Khvostov, the poet beloved of the heavens, in immortal verses already sang of the disaster of the Neva's banks. [D. I. Khvostov, a second-rate poet and a contemporary of Pushkin.]

But my poor, poor Yevgeny . . . Alas! his confused mind could not stand up to such terrible shocks. The tumultuous sound of the Neva and of the winds echoed in his ears. Filled with terrible thoughts, he wandered silently about. Some sort of dream tormented him. A week passed, a month – he did not return home. His

Его пустынный уголок
Отдал внаймы, как вышел срок,
Хозяин бедному поэту.
Евгений за своим добром
Не приходил. Он скоро свету
Стал чужд. Весь день бродил пешком,
И спал на пристани; питался
В окошко поданным куском.
Одежда ветхая на нем
Рвалась и тлела. Злые дети
Бросали камни вслед ему.
Нередко кучерские плети
Его стегали, потому
Что он не разбирал дороги
Уж никогда; казалось – он
Не примечал. Он оглушен
Был шумом внутренней тревоги.
И так он свой несчастный век
Влачил, ни зверь ни человек,
Ни то ни се, ни житель света,
Ни призрак мертвый . . .

                    Раз он спал
У невской пристани. Дни лета
Клонились к осени. Дышал

landlord, when the time ran out, leased his deserted nook to a poor poet. Yevgeny did not come to fetch his possessions. He soon became a stranger to the world. All day long he wandered on foot, while at night he slept on the embankment; he fed on morsels handed him through windows. The shabby clothes he wore were tattered and mouldy. Cruel children threw stones at him. Often the coachmen's whips lashed him, because he was no longer able to find his way; it seemed that he did not notice anything. He was deafened by the noise of inner turmoil. And so he dragged out his miserable life, neither beast nor man, neither this nor that, neither dweller in this world nor phantom of the dead . . .

Once he was sleeping on the Neva embankment. The days of summer were declining towards autumn. A foul wind was breath-

Ненастный ветер. Мрачный вал
Плескал на пристань, ропща пени
И бьясь об гладкие ступени,
Как челобитчик у дверей
Ему не внемлющих судей.
Бедняк проснулся. Мрачно было:
Дождь капал, ветер выл уныло,
И с ним вдали, во тьме ночной
Перекликался часовой . . .
Вскочил Евгений; вспомнил живо
Он прошлый ужас; торопливо
Он встал; пошел бродить, и вдруг
Остановился — и вокруг
Тихонько стал водить очами
С боязнью дикой на лице.
Он очутился под столбами
Большого дома. На крыльце
С подъятой лапой, как живые,
Стояли львы сторожевые,
И прямо в темной вышине
Над огражденною скалою
Кумир с простертою рукою
Сидел на бронзовом коне.

ing. The sullen wave splashed against the embankment, reproachfully grumbling and beating against the smooth steps, like a petitioner at the door of judges who do not hearken to him. The poor wretch woke up. It was dark: the rain dripped, the wind howled gloomily, and in the distance a watchman exchanged cries with it in the darkness of the night . . . Yevgeny started up; he vividly recalled the past terror; hastily he got up; he set off wandering, and suddenly he stopped — and slowly he began to cast his eyes around with wild fear on his face. He found himself at the foot of the pillars of the great house. On the porch the guardian lions stood like living creatures with upraised paw, and on his dark eminence, right over the railed-in rock, the Image sat on his bronze horse with outstretched arm.

Евгений вздрогнул. Прояснились
В нем страшно мысли. Он узнал
И место, где потоп играл,
Где волны хищные толпились,
Бунтуя злобно вкруг него,
И львов, и площадь, и того,
Кто неподвижно возвышался
Во мраке медною главой,
Того, чьей волей роковой
Под морем город основался . . .
Ужасен он в окрестной мгле!
Какая дума на челе!
Какая сила в нем сокрыта!
А в сем коне какой огонь!
Куда ты скачешь, гордый конь,
И где опустишь ты копыта?
О мощный властелин судьбы!
Не так ли ты над самой бездной
На высоте, уздой железной
Россию поднял на дыбы?

Кругом подножия кумира
Безумец бедный обошел

Yevgeny shuddered. His thoughts became terribly clear within him. He recognized the place where the flood had played, where the rapacious waves had crowded, angrily rioting around him, and also the lions, and the square, and him who motionlessly held his bronze head aloft in the darkness, him by whose fateful will the city was founded by the sea . . . Terrible was he in the surrounding gloom! What thought was on his brow! What strength was hidden within him! And in that steed what fire! Whither do you gallop, proud steed, and where will you plant your hoofs? O mighty master of Fate! Was it not thus that you, standing aloft on the very brink of the precipice, reared up Russia with your iron curb?

The poor madman walked around the pedestal of the Image and

И взоры дикие навел
На лик державца полумира.
Стеснилась грудь его. Чело
К решетке хладной прилегло,
Глаза подернулись туманом,
По сердцу пламень пробежал,
Вскипела кровь. Он мрачен стал
Пред горделивым истуканом
И, зубы стиснув, пальцы сжав,
Как обуянный силой черной,
«Добро, строитель чудотворный! –
Шепнул он, злобно задрожав, –
Ужо тебе!...» И вдруг стремглав
Бежать пустился. Показалось
Ему, что грозного царя,
Мгновенно гневом возгоря,
Лицо тихонько обращалось ...
И он по площади пустой
Бежит и слышит за собой –
Как будто грома грохотанье –
Тяжело-звонкое скаканье
По потрясенной мостовой.
И, озарен луною бледной,

brought wild looks to bear on the countenance of the ruler of half
the world. His breast contracted. His brow was pressed to the cold
railings, his eyes were covered over with darkness, flames ran
through his heart, his blood boiled. Sullenly he stood before the
haughty statue, and clenching his teeth and clasping tight his hands,
like one possessed by some dark power, he whispered, trembling
with wrath: 'All right then, builder of marvels! Just you wait!'
And suddenly he set off running at breakneck speed. It seemed to
him that the face of the dead Tsar, momentarily flaring up with
rage, was slowly turning ... And he runs across the empty square
and hears behind him – like the rumble of thunder – the ponderous
clangour of galloping hoofs over the shaken roadway. And lit up

Простерши руку в вышине,
За ним несется Всадник Медный
На звонко-скачущем коне;
И во всю ночь безумец бедный,
Куда стопы ни обращал,
За ним повсюду Всадник Медный
С тяжелым топотом скакал.

И с той поры, когда случалось
Идти той площадью ему,
В его лице изображалось
Смятенье. К сердцу своему
Он прижимал поспешно руку,
Как бы его смиряя муку,
Картуз изношенный сымал,
Смущенных глаз не подымал
И шел сторонкой.

        Остров малый
На взморье виден. Иногда
Причалит с неводом туда
Рыбак на ловле запоздалый
И бедный ужин свой варит,
Или чиновник посетит,
Гуляя в лодке в воскресенье,

by the pale moon, stretching out his hand aloft, the Bronze Horseman rushes after him on his clangorously galloping steed. And all night long, wherever the poor madman turned his step, the Bronze Horseman galloped after him with ponderous clatter.

And from that time on, whenever he happened to go by that square, confusion appeared upon his face. He would hastily press his hand to his heart, as though easing its torment, he would doff his tattered cap, he would not raise his troubled eyes, and would go by some roundabout way.

A little island can be seen off the shore. Sometimes a belated fisherman while out fishing will moor there with his net and cook his meagre supper there, or some civil servant, while boating on a

Пустынный остров. Не взросло
Там ни былинки. Наводненье
Туда, играя, занесло
Домишко ветхий. Над водою
Остался он, как черный куст,
Его прошедшею весною
Свезли на барке. Был он пуст
И весь разрушен. У порога
Нашли безумца моего,
И тут же хладный труп его
Похоронили ради Бога.

Sunday, will visit the desolate island. Not even a blade of grass has ever grown there. The flood in its play had driven a ramshackle little house there. Above the water it had remained like a black bush. It was taken away last spring on a wooden barge. It was empty and all in ruins. By the threshold my madman was found, and on that very spot his cold corpse was buried, out of charity.

INDEX OF RUSSIAN TITLES AND FIRST LINES

INDEX OF RUSSIAN TITLES AND FIRST LINES

INDEX OF RUSSIAN TITLES AND FIRST LINES

INDEX OF ENGLISH TITLES AND
FIRST LINES